The Two Horizons New Testament Commentary

Joel B. Green, *General Editor*

Two features distinguish The Two Horizons New Testament Commentary series: theological exegesis and theological reflection.

Exegesis since the Reformation era and especially in the past two hundred years emphasized careful attention to philology, grammar, syntax, and concerns of a historical nature. More recently, commentary has expanded to include social-scientific, political, or canonical questions and more.

Without slighting the significance of those sorts of questions, scholars in The Two Horizons New Testament Commentary locate their primary interests on theological readings of texts, past and present. The result is a paragraph-by-paragraph engagement with the text that is deliberately theological in focus.

Theological reflection in The Two Horizons New Testament Commentary takes many forms, including locating each New Testament book in relation to the whole of Scripture—asking what the biblical book contributes to biblical theology—and in conversation with constructive theology of today. How commentators engage in the work of theological reflection will differ from book to book, depending on their particular theological tradition and how they perceive the work of biblical theology and theological hermeneutics. This heterogeneity derives as well from the relative infancy of the project of theological interpretation of Scripture in modern times and from the challenge of grappling with a book's message in Greco-Roman antiquity, in the canon of Scripture and history of interpretation, and for life in the admittedly diverse Western world at the beginning of the twenty-first century.

The Two Horizons New Testament Commentary is written primarily for students, pastors, and other Christian leaders seeking to engage in theological interpretation of Scripture.

1–3 John

Thomas Andrew Bennett

William B. Eerdmans Publishing Company
Grand Rapids, Michigan

Wm. B. Eerdmans Publishing Co.
4035 Park East Court SE, Grand Rapids, Michigan 49546
www.eerdmans.com

Published 2021
Printed in the United States of America

27 26 25 24 23 22 21 2 3 4 5 6 7

ISBN 978-0-8028-7577-8

Library of Congress Cataloging-in-Publication Data

Names: Bennett, Thomas Andrew, 1981– author.
Title: 1-3 John / Thomas Andrew Bennett.
Description: Grand Rapids, Michigan : William B. Eerdmans Publishing Company, 2021. | Series: The two horizons New Testament commentary |Includes bibliographical references and index. | Summary: "An exegetical commentary on 1-3 John with special attention to theological concerns"—Provided by publisher.
Identifiers: LCCN 2020040440 | ISBN 9780802875778 (paperback)
Subjects: LCSH: Bible. Epistles of John—Commentaries.
Classification: LCC BS2805.53 .B46 2021 | DDC 227/.94077—dc23
LC record available at https://lccn.loc.gov/2020040440

Contents

Acknowledgments ix

Abbreviations xi

Introduction: The Two Horizons of the Letters of John 1

John's Horizons and Ours 1

Genre 3

Authorship 4

Historical Contexts 7

"John's" Purpose 8

Conclusions 11

Interpretation: Theological Interpretation of 1–3 John 13

1 John 1:1–4 13

1 John 1:5–2:2 18

1 John 2:3–6 23

1 John 2:7–11 28

1 John 2:12–14 37

1 John 2:15–17 41

1 John 2:18–23 47

1 John 2:24–27 51

1 John 2:28–3:3 53

1 John 3:4–10 58

1 John 3:11–18 64
1 John 3:19–24 67
1 John 4:1–6 71
1 John 4:7–10 75
1 John 4:11–16 79
1 John 4:17–18 84
1 John 4:19–5:1 87
1 John 5:2–4a 90
1 John 5:4b–12 93
1 John 5:13–21 100
2 John 1–3 109
2 John 4–6 112
2 John 7–11 114
2 John 12–13 118
3 John 1–2 119
3 John 3–4 120
3 John 5–8 121
3 John 9–10 124
3 John 11–12 126
3 John 13–15 127

Theological Horizons of 1–3 John 128
The Trinity 128
Theological Epistemology: Knowing God 128
Trinitarianism in 1–3 John: Ambiguity in Speech about the Persons of the Godhead 132
From God Is Love to Nicaea: Incipient Trinitarianism in 1 John 134
Christology 135
Christ the Co-priest: The Fulfillment of the Temple 135
Soteriology in 1–3 John: In Jesus's Name 139
In the Flesh: Incarnation and Christology in 1–3 John 141
Novel but Never New: Orthodox Theology in 1–3 John 144

God and Creation 147

A Redeemable Creation 147

Time in 1–3 John 149

The Unseen World: Spirit and Spirits in 1–3 John 150

On the Importance of the Physical in 1–3 John 153

God's Character 155

God Beyond, God In: Transcendence and Immanence in 1 John 155

Divine Pathos in 1–3 John: God's Joy 158

Theological Aesthetics in 1–3 John 159

The Love of God and the Death of God 166

God Listens: Divine Passibility in 1–3 John 168

Election and Eschatology 170

Transformation: Soteriology and Purgatory in 1–3 John 170

Eternal Security and Purgatory in 1–3 John 174

Eternity and Election: The Economy of Election in 1–3 John 178

Being Rewarded: Eschatology and Divine and Human Economics in 1–3 John 181

Scripture 184

Apostolic Authority and Truth 184

Theological Epistemology: Community and Discernment 186

What a Canon! The Theological Import of 2–3 John 188

The Church 190

The Spirit of Anointing: Church as Spirit-Temple in 1–3 John 190

Ecclesiology in 1–3 John: The Family of God 192

Gender and Leadership: The Role of Women in 1–3 John 196

Intolerance and the Power of Speech in 1–3 John 198

True Church and Excommunication in 2–3 John 200

Ethics 202

Ethics in 1–3 John: In Him 202

Open and Closed Doors: Christian Hospitality in 1–3 John 205

Money in 1–3 John 206

Power and Authority in 1–3 John 207

Bibliography 211

Index of Authors 217

Index of Subjects 219

Index of Scripture and Other Ancient Writings 221

Acknowledgments

Christians should be well-accustomed to unpayable debts; the matchless self-giving of God in the incarnation, life, death, and resurrection of the Son who "loved me and gave himself for me" ought to instruct us in grace first, now, and always. For me personally, there is a certain joy in owing so many so much that this book might exist because I believe that the opportunities and sacrifices that were made were done so in *imitatio Christi* and are thereby an extension of his love and, as this commentary argues extensively, proofs of the divine union I share with the Father and the Son and so many brothers and sisters.

In all things academic, my greatest debt will always be to Joel B. Green. The "B" stands for Bennett, by the way, and was the subject of our first teacher-student interaction thirteen years ago. First teacher, then mentor, and now friend, Joel has nudged—and maybe sometimes kicked—open every door of opportunity. Not many New Testament commentaries are given to theologians; I hope and pray I have honored his faith and faithfulness in the writing of this one.

Many other friends and colleagues at or from Fuller Theological Seminary have extended credit to this work in one way or another. My debts to Marianne Meye and John Thompson are probably mostly unknown to them but nevertheless quite deep and wide. John Goldingay has so fundamentally shaped how I think Israel that most any echoes and resonances I find in the Old Testament intimate at his influence. Seth Heringer, Heidi Riley, Renee Dutter Miller, Michael and Darlene Bischof, David Hunsicker, Ben Lappenga, Tim Reardon, and YouLim Hahn Kim, I have loved working, sharing, and conversing with you all over the years!

Many thanks to Trevor Thompson at Eerdmans for his endless patience and quiet prodding. What clarity and accuracy the text possesses is owed entirely to Craig Noll. Without his attention to original languages this theologian would have embarrassed himself in multiple instances. Also, nobody would know what any of the thousands of sentences beginning with "This" were referencing. So Craig, cheers to your professionalism and expertise. And though she did not edit this book, I relearned much of the joie de vivre of writing while working with Jordan Rowan Fannin on *Labor of God*, and I hope some of that has spilled over into the present work.

One of the great joys of my life has been to do life with the people of Coast Bible Church. Their generosity to me and to my family is boundless: I know no other small church pastors who are encouraged to teach grad students and produce scholarship. I am endlessly humbled by their Christian love and deep commitment to unearthing the hidden things of God. I am especially grateful to Rachel Coblentz, John Mitchell, Jon Varela, Scott Eichler, and Marilyn Diebold for their curiosity and willingness to peer into the academic side of my life.

Of all the unpayable debts, the greatest is owed to Erin Christine, my wife and love and friend. She is as tolerant as she is committed; I have no idea where I would be without her. And Alice, Olivia, and Soren—maybe one day you will read this and find out what "fake doctors" like me actually do.

Abbreviations

AYBC	Anchor Yale Bible Commentary
b.	Babylonian Talmud
BDAG	Bauer, Danker, Arndt, and Gingrich, *Greek-English Lexicon of the New Testament and Other Early Christian Literature*
CD	Karl Barth, *Church Dogmatics*
CEB	Common English Bible
JATS	*Journal of the Adventist Theological Society*
JBL	*Journal of Biblical Literature*
JSNT	*Journal for the Study of the New Testament*
JTI	*Journal of Theological Interpretation*
LXX	Septuagint
m.	Mishnah
$NA^{27/28}$	Nestle-Aland *Novum Testamentum Graece*, 27th or 28th ed.
NASB	New American Standard Bible
Neot	*Neotestamentica*
NICNT	New International Commentary on the New Testament
NIV	New International Version
NKJV	New King James Version
NLT	New Living Translation
NRSV	New Revised Standard Version
PG	Patrologia Graeca. Edited by J.-P. Migne. 162 vols. Paris, 1857–86. http://patristica.net/graeca/
PL	Patrologia Latina. Edited by J.-P. Migne. 217 vols. Paris, 1844–64. http://patristica.net/latina/
PNTC	Pillar New Testament Commentary
Princ.	*First Principles* (Origen)
Sacrifices	*On the Sacrifices of Cain and Abel* (Philo)

Sanh.	Sanhedrin
THNTC	Two Horizons New Testament Commentary
TNIV	Today's New International Version
WBC	Word Biblical Commentary

Introduction: The Two Horizons of the Letters of John

The Letters of John have been, especially since the advent of critical scholarship, the subject of numerous pointed historical questions: What circumstances occasioned their writing? Who is writing to whom? What literary or historical relationship holds between the letters and the Fourth Gospel and Revelation? How can we know?

John's Horizons and Ours

Before we remark on these questions, it is worth remembering that our historical knowledge is limited, and whatever suggestions we may ultimately endorse, the only answers that will be reliable will address these questions in only the broadest way. Furthermore, such answers will have to be extracted from intimations and whispers found only in the texts of 1–3 John, since no other writings pertaining to them exist. Such pessimism about our knowledge of the exact historical circumstances would once have been a counsel of despair, for if we do not know beyond doubt the authors, the dates, the exact state of the church at each writing, and so forth, then how can we say that we understand what the letters say? It must be that the impenetrable mists obscuring the past damage our ability to understand these letters clearly. Or perhaps not. To begin, it must be said that one surely hopes this is not the case, for if critical scholarship is to be believed, we will never know the authors and dates and editors and circumstances of a great many biblical texts with any certainty at all, and yet Christians continue to read them week in and week out with confidence that through them the Spirit of God continues to sew flesh onto dry bones. Indeed, our lack of certainty concerning the times and reasons behind 1–3 John should not render them inscrutable artifacts of a bygone age. Nor should we be dispirited concerning their ability to speak life into the communities of Christian faith as they exist globally in the twenty-first century. The reason for this counsel is not, as some suggest, that the texts are self-contained units of meaning from which we can extract theological ideas and principles. Rather, the reason that the Johannine Letters speak to the church today is that the church today is the same church, the self-same community, that received these writings in the late first century. To make this claim is to base the authority and relevance of these texts on a theological conviction about ecclesiology rather than whatever confidence (or lack thereof) we have in historical reconstructions of internecine warfare between Christian and heretical factions in the Ephesian churches.

But what can we mean by "same church"? Surely the intervening millennia drive a cultural and sociological and historical and, yes, theological ditch between "us" and "them." In the beginning of his systematic theology, James McClendon Jr. explains that Christians interpret Scripture from a "shared awareness of the present Christian community as the primitive community and the eschatological community." This continuity of identity means that "the church now is the primitive church and the church on judgment day."[1] They are we. We are they. These writings are to us and for us, just as the apostle Peter found the prophetic words of Joel to be "now" on the day of Pentecost. With this theological and (really we should add) interpretive principle in mind, we might find as we read John's letters nothing surprising in communities of faith apparently splintering and losing members long ago, but much-needed pastoral counsel in light of the splintering and breaking up of churches today. We might find our own notions of "church," "community," and—yes—"love" and "truth" called into question. We might even find that all John's admonitions and insights are grounded in a coherent vision of the God of Israel freshly revealed as Father, Son, and Spirit.

Our goal, then, is not merely to explain what the texts of 1–3 John mean, nor is it only to describe John's "theological vision," if such a thing can be said to be grasped. Of course we will attend assiduously to these topics, but we ultimately seek to offer fresh theological proposals *with* John, to *respond in theological creativity* to what he has to say to us. Thus, close attention to John's linguistic horizon will set the terms of a conversation with the horizons of the church in the twenty-first century as it actually is in the twenty-first century, living amid voices from, particularly, the academic disciplines and the attendant concerns of a culture informed by them. To wit, Christians in and around Ephesus in approximately 90 CE and Christians today in North America and indeed around the world each face aberrant or suspect teachings, permeable and impermeable communal barriers, and related concerns about how to confront betrayal and treat those

1. James W. McClendon Jr., *Ethics*, vol. 1 of *Systematic Theology*, rev. ed. (Nashville: Abingdon Press, 2002), 31.

who, though once family, are now black sheep. We remain confused about what is true, whether the truth can be known, and the right way or ways to go about seeking it. We continue to be surprised and dismayed that even though God is revealed to live in the eternal communion of the Trinity, we appear doomed to chase after true communion only to see it fractured by falsehoods and pride. We still wonder about what it means to trust, and how and to what extent our trust in God and others should issue in particular actions and practices.

Encountering these sorts of questions with John can and should push us to consider theological implications. What is "salvation" and who has it, or can it even be had? What real relations exist between human persons and God if we are to be called God's children? Can these relations change? If so, how? What of the relations holding between one's grasp of the truth and one's ethical conduct? At the metalevel, engagement with John might push us to think more clearly about modes of discourse. What does it mean that John so pervasively uses metaphors to describe reality? What is "light"? What does it mean to be a "child"? What or who constitutes the "world"? What implications might our answers to those questions have for language that—traditionally, at least—has not been taken to be metaphoric at all? "Sin?" "Righteousness?" "Fellowship?" In 1–3 John, moreover, we meet much of the material that compelled the early church to articulate and flesh out the doctrine of the Trinity. One supposes that if that is no accident, then 1–3 John will continue to offer readers opportunities to consider God's triune nature and how that "triunity" relates to human persons, the corporate church, and the world.

These are our ultimate concerns; whatever we say of the historical circumstances lurking behind the text, its date and author, genre and composition, all must be aimed at clearing the way for theological engagement that nourishes Christians. The assumption of this theological commentary, therefore, is that John and the contemporary church are not that far from one another; any notion to the contrary must be overturned. Moreover, a proper hearing of John's language and the conversation it inspires with contemporary academic voices and concerns will, when contextualized within the living tradition of Spirit-driven inquiry that is the church, speak boldly and truthfully in the here and now. The Johannine Letters and Christian theology are thus two horizons that are—God willing—here revealed as one.

Genre

There is little in the way of academic consensus regarding typical historical considerations such as authorship, context, and even genre for the Johannine writings. In fact, we say "writings" rather than "letters" because 1 John defies simple categorization, while 2 and 3 John are paradigm examples of ancient epistolary. Despite John's being self-referential in a number of places about the fact that he—singular—is "writing" to a plural "you" (e.g., 2:1, 12, 14; 5:13), this alone does not an epistle make, for surely Luke 1:3–4—decidedly not an "epistle"—features something of the same convention. Letters in the Greco-Roman world feature an address to a specific audience, a greeting, and an identifiable closing.[2] As we have noted, a paradigm example of this format is 3 John, where the author self-identifies ("the elder"), names the recipient (Gaius), and ends with a blessing ("Peace to you"). Since 1 John features nothing comparable, it must be categorized differently. Suggestions abound, with it being deemed a "tract" or "a written sermon or pastoral address"[3] or "an attempt to expound [the Gospel of John's] ideas";[4] perhaps it is a "circular letter," an epistle meant for multiple similar audiences.[5]

The trouble, it seems, for those seeking to categorize 1 John's genre is the widespread assumption that 1 John was written in order to counter some particular set of heretical beliefs. This view is itself a belief influenced powerfully by the notion that 1 John is an occasional letter written to a specific community headed by someone called John, or by close associates of such a person. Thus the Gospel of John and the rest of the Johannine writings are thought to be meant for this group of Christians—with all their theological idiosyncrasies—over and against other early churches.

Authorship

Despite the confusion over 1 John's genre, scholarship does display macrolevel agreement on a few things. To begin with, the author or authors of 1–3 John are, if not the same person, at least closely related, and some will refer to a "Johannine school." Moreover, whoever authored these writings is almost certainly closely

2. Rudolf Bultmann (*The Johannine Epistles* [Philadelphia: Fortress Press, 1973], 83–84) suggests that "I write these things" in 5:13 "naturally refers back to the whole Epistle" and therefore functions as a closing. He therefore treats the remaining verses (14–17 and 18–21) as two appendixes. Raymond E. Brown (*The Epistles of John*, AYBC [New York: Doubleday, 1982], 86) rightly points out that "I have written these things" alludes to John 20:31 and is not a sign of epistolary format.

3. I. Howard Marshall, *The Epistles of John*, NICNT (Grand Rapids: Eerdmans, 1978), 14.

4. Brown, *Epistles*, 90. Stephen S. Smalley (*1, 2, and 3 John*, rev. ed., WBC [Grand Rapids: Zondervan, 2008], xxxiii) largely agrees, suggesting that 1 John corrects misinterpretation of the Gospel.

5. Colin G. Kruse, *The Letters of John*, PNTC (Grand Rapids: Eerdmans, 2000), 28.

related to the author of the Gospel of John and probably Revelation as well. Even those who posit separate authorship of, say, the Gospel and 1 John, will admit that the authors must have been a part of the same community. Most will also agree that the writer or writers bore some relatively close relationship to a known disciple of Jesus, and may have even been John, "the son of Zebedee," or perhaps an anonymous disciple who was mightily impacted by Jesus's ministry.

Questions concerning authorship have animated academic discussion of the Johannine writings and, concomitantly, Gospel of John and Revelation scholarship since the work of Dionysius of Alexandria in the third century.[6] Does 1 John come from the same author (or authors) as the Gospel? What of 2 and 3 John—were they written by the same person? And if so, was that the same person who wrote 1 John and, possibly, the Gospel and Revelation? Finally, we have traditions from Polycarp and, possibly, Papias—both writing near the turn of the second century—attributing the Gospel, Revelation, and the Johannine writings to John, "the beloved disciple." Are these traditions reputable? Is it indeed the case that 1–3 John were written by one of the apostles?

Raymond E. Brown outlines the classic strategy for determining authorship. First, comparisons are made between 2 John and 3 John in order to determine whether they share an author. Since 3 John has very little in common linguistically either with 1 John or the Gospel but much in common with 2 John, the logic goes that if we determine common authorship between 3 John and 2 John, a chain of identity could connect the author of 3 John with 1 John and, potentially, the Gospel.[7] The salient questions are, then, do 2 and 3 John share an author, do 1 John and 2 John share an author, and do the Gospel of John and 1 John share an author? No one denies the clear similarity in thought and language between the Gospel, 1 John, and 2 John.[8] There is, therefore, a strong prima facie case to be made for a single author. This position has nevertheless been challenged.

As has been noted, we cannot do much more than make an educated guess, but some striking analyses may nudge us in one direction rather than another.[9]

6. It is worth noting that some, such as Marshall (*The Epistles of John*), Kruse (*Letters of John*), Robert W. Yarbrough (*1–3 John* [Grand Rapids: Baker, 2008]), and Smalley (*1, 2, and 3 John*), do not even bother with the critical linguistic questions, presumably because the similarities are so great.

7. Brown, *Epistles*, 14–15.

8. Karen H. Jobes (*1, 2, and 3 John* [Grand Rapids: Zondervan, 2014], 25–27) provides an in-text grid showing literary similarities across the writings. Brown (*Epistles*, 755–59) offers three charts, showing similarities between 2 and 3 John, 1 and 2 John, and John's Gospel and 1 John.

9. The following section is based on the charts supplied by Brown (*Epistles*, 755–59) and Jobes (*1, 2, and 3 John*, 25–27)

For example, 86 percent of the significant vocabulary in 2 John and 70 percent of that of 3 John is found also either in the Gospel of John or in 1 John. What is most compelling, however, is not only that significant vocabulary is largely held in common but that it is similarly deployed. Take, for example, what we might call the Johannine use of "truth." In 3 John 3 the elder says, "I was overjoyed, brothers and sisters, coming and confirming your faithfulness, how you're walking in the truth." Here, truth is something that one "walks in," that is, does, and not primarily something that one thinks. Note similar wording in 2 John 4, where the elder notes that some of the lady's children are "walking in truth." Likewise, 1 John 1:6 warns that those who claim fellowship with God but are "walking in darkness" actually "lie and so are not doing the truth." Finally, in the Gospel of John, Jesus teaches Nicodemus that the ones "who do the truth, come to the light." The Johannine literature uses "truth" as a verb and does so consistently. We can make a similar comparison about how the Johannine literature tightly relates love and truth; note the beginning of the letters (2 and 3 John), where John mentions that he loves the recipients "in truth." Similarly, in 1 John 3:18 it is important to love not just with words "but in action and truth." The same relation holds in the Gospel, where those who do not love Jesus or the Father are devil-born and do not "stand in the truth" (John 8:42–44). Also, those who love Jesus have "the Spirit of Truth" (John 14:15–17). Not only is truth itself an action, it is the mark of genuine love. It is perhaps significant that 1 John and the Gospel both use the word "devil," but it is notable that both characterize people as having the devil as a father (John 8:44; 1 John 3:10). Vocabulary and use both give us good reason to think that the Gospel and 1–3 John are composed by the same person. Arguments to the contrary rely on perceived theological differences between, primarily, the Gospel and 1 John, but these are really perceived only out of "a critical analysis of the development of ideas within the Johannine tradition."[10] Since we have already suggested that reconstructions of this sort are problematic—and will shortly demonstrate why this is so—it is best to assume that the Gospel and the writings are all the work of the same person. The final question, whether the John who wrote the Gospel and 1–3 John is "John the son of Zebedee," is impossible to answer, though it is, I think, quite likely that the writer knew and followed Jesus.[11]

10. Brown, *Epistles*, 25.

11. We are again relying here on arguments made by Richard Bauckham (*Jesus and the Eyewitness: The Gospels as Eyewitness Testimony*, 2nd ed. [Grand Rapids: Eerdmans, 2017], chs. 14–17).

Historical Contexts

With respect to the historical contexts out of which the Johannine writings came, commentators tend to agree that the communities of faith that produced them had experienced schism to one degree or another, such that people who had once named each other as brothers and sisters were now torn apart. The community or communities had also certainly been exposed to various teachings that were deemed to be untrue, with many suggesting that the core of these teachings involved Christology, that is, the nature of Jesus as both divine and yet fully "in human flesh." It is worth reviewing why views of this sort cropped up.

With respect to 1 John, it is noteworthy that much of John's language involves an almost Manichaean dichotomy between, for example, those in the dark and those in the light (2:8–11), those who love the world and those who have the Father's love (2:15–16), the devil-born versus the God-born (3:8–10). Moreover, the enigmatic reference that "they departed from us" (2:19) perhaps suggests that John's church has undergone schism and that references to darkness, love of the world, and being devil-born are all meant to identify a specific group of docetic heretics and distinguish "them" from "us," that is, the faithful believers who have remained in John's orthodox church. For those who posit docetism in the background, it is significant that John emphatically rejects any "spirit" that denies that "Messiah Jesus came as a human being" (1 John 4:2–3).

Some will suggest that the Johannine writings come from a specific, even sectarian version of Christianity. Reconstructions of this sort point out how the Fourth Gospel's portrayal of Jesus's life and ministry is very different from that of the Synoptics, exhibiting what some call a "theology of glory" rather than a "theology of the cross." Given that the Johannine writings are therefore strongly related internally and apparently odd with respect to the other writings of the New Testament, it is not hard to imagine how scholars in search of a plausible history behind the texts might have supplied such a backstory.

The problem, of course, is that nowhere does 1 John actually specify any particular heresy beyond simple denials of the Son (e.g., 2:22; 5:12–13), nor is the writing itself addressed to a discernible, concrete group of Christians. Moreover, beyond the basic affirmations that "Jesus is the Messiah" and that only those who reckon the Son likewise reckon the Father (2:22–23; 4:2, 15; 5:1, 20), it is difficult to identify the actual content of "right belief" that might aid church members as they strive to maintain "Johannine faith," if we can suppose that such a thing existed and can be accurately characterized. In point of fact, one begins to wonder whether the very idea of a "Johannine sect" or "community of churches" is anything more than scholarly whimsy, for nothing of our actual evidence from early church writings—whether canonical or otherwise—attests to anything of the sort. To wit, our earliest references to "John" in Papias (ca. 130 CE) and Polycrates (ca. 190 CE) come in the midst of lists of trustworthy witnesses to Jesus. Though Papias writes in the early second century, he is writing about what he did to collect words and traditions about Jesus in the late first century (ca. 80 CE).[12] Since that time frame makes him active roughly contemporary to the writing of the Gospel and the Johannine literature, it is worth noting that those active in the Ephesian churches are treated as no different from any other Christian community. There is no suggestion whatsoever that the church or churches in and around Ephesus were strange or peculiar in any way. They are, rather, considered what we might call "mainstream." And since that is the case, we must wonder what sense it makes to posit "John's audience" as a kind of subset of Christians easily distinguishable from "Pauline" or "Petrine" believers. Nothing presented here obviously counts as a knockdown argument against any particular historical reconstruction, but these considerations should raise the specter of doubt. And so long as we pursue this line of thinking, we must be careful to think through the implications of doing so.

Thus far, the logical corollary of abandoning the various historical reconstructions has not been adequately considered, even as scholars have begun self-consciously distancing themselves from such views about what is or is not behind the text. Once we have done away with the notion of a "Johannine community," we have radically democratized the audience of the Johannine writings. The Gospel and 1 John are now written for Christians qua Christians, and perhaps for nonbelievers as well. The pronouns "we" and "you" as they appear in 1 John cast much wider nets than was once thought. Thinking along the same lines, if John is not writing to a specific group in an attempt to shore up faith in the midst of psychically catastrophic schism, then what, we must ask, is 1 John accomplishing? This returns us to the question of 1 John's genre. Since it is not, like 2 and 3 John, a letter, we must ask what it is.

"John's" Purpose

Recent advances made in Gospel of John studies and studies in the relations between orality, literacy, and aurality in 1 John fruitfully point the way forward. With respect to the Gospel of John, recent scholarship has convincingly resuscitated the once-common view that the Gospel of John itself was the eyewitness testimony of "the beloved disciple"—who may or may not have been "John the son of Zebedee"—and that it was meant to convince both Jews and gentiles in

12. Bauckham, *Jesus and the Eyewitnesses*, 14.

the furthest reaches of the empire to believe in Jesus as the Messiah and the Son of God in order to have life in his name (John 20:31).[13] We may piggyback on these insights. For if the Gospel of John really is "written that you may believe," then it might likewise be the case that 1 John really is written "that you might have union with us," having joy that is "made complete," and "that you can know that you have eternal life" (1 John 1:3–4; 5:13). More important, however, it might be the case that this is a message meant for all.

This remains the case whether we can know that the author of the Fourth Gospel is the same person as the author of 1 John. The reasoning for this assertion is as follows: as we have already seen, even those who are skeptical about the author of 1 John being the same person as the writer of the Gospel admit the strong theological and probably historical relationship between the two. The similarities in theme, language, and theological concerns between the Gospel of John and 1 John are so strong that some have suggested that 1 John is something like a commentary on the Gospel or a clarification of some of its teaching. While we disagree with that analysis, the common linguistic patterns and theological insights cannot be ignored. So whatever we say about the genre and purpose of the Gospel may very well have implications for 1 John as well.

Richard Bauckham has argued that the Gospel of John is best understood as historiography and would have been received in that way—as a trustworthy biography of an important person. Furthermore, of particular importance is the self-identification of the beloved disciple in John 21:24 as the one offering eyewitness testimony.[14] One of Bauckham's critical points is that eyewitness testimony is important because it confers authority to speak on a subject before an audience that may not yet view an author as credible. That is, the Gospel of John is—at least partly—written to those who do not believe. Rather than being composed as a church's autobiography theologically projected onto Jesus, it is more in keeping with the language and structure of the Gospel of John to take it at face value, as, well, "good news" to those who have not yet believed in Jesus as the Son of God and as a life-changing testimony to those who have. It is critical to note that 1 John begins with a parallel—a claim of an eyewitness account, a privileged insight—that confers the authority to speak about "the word of life" (1 John 1:1). If 1 John, like the Gospel, is making claims about credibility, then we are compelled to conclude that it is not—or at least not only—a sermon preached to the choir, as it were. Hearers of this message are not all expected to be "Johannine Christians" or members of a "Johannine community."

Instead, John's audience is expected to include those who are communityless,

13. Bauckham, *Jesus and the Eyewitnesses*, 358–411.
14. Bauckham, *Jesus and the Eyewitnesses*, 368–73.

joyless, and eternal lifeless. It also comprises Christians who live in a pluralistic empire, who have seen once-beloved "brothers and sisters" give up the name of Jesus, who know the power of sin and temptation, and who wonder if they really do have access to truth and light. And so we may finally decide what kind of literature we are dealing with: 1 John is an early sermon, meant to be read aloud to believers and nonbelievers alike, wherever they may be found. For believers, 1 John therefore functions as what the ancients called epideictic rhetoric, in this case pastoral encouragement meant to confirm the wavering to maintain their faith and have it strengthened. This kind of exhortation is for any Christian congregation that has experienced what every Christian congregation eventually experiences when living in the midst of a pagan culture: self-doubt, members who have lost faith, confusion about the truth, difficult ethical questions, and concerns about right fellowship with God and one another. For nonbelievers, 1 John functions as what the ancients might have deemed deliberative rhetoric, an attempt to convince or persuade an outsider to become an insider.[15] In particular, 1 John seeks to convert by asserting what could be the case as what is already the case; throughout 1 John the inclusive "we" offers every hearer the opportunity to self-identify—right here and right now—as part of the community so addressed.

We can assert this kind of exhortation with confidence, thanks in large part to rhetorical analyses of the structure and verbiage of the text. In particular, John uses persuasive techniques cataloged in Greco-Roman texts on the art of rhetoric.[16] For now, what matters most is that these techniques are designed for orators, that is, they are the kinds of rhetorical practices that good speakers—and here we should add good preachers—use, often without being terribly self-conscious about doing so. That is, great preachers do not often obsess over how they will convince and persuade; they just, thanks to a time-honed skill set, do it. Then, those who study rhetoric are able to pore over speeches to identify different methods or tactics that aid preachers in winning over an audience.

15. Sociorhetorical scholars might balk at categorizing 1 John as functioning as two kinds of rhetoric, but 1 John is a sermon and not a self-conscious attempt to write the quintessential piece of Greco-Roman rhetoric. As such, it does what sermons do, deploying rhetorical tools in the service of a sermon's ends. In "Reconciling Rhetorical Criticism with Its Oral Roots" (*Neot* 35 [2001]: 95–110), J. A. Loubser excoriates rhetorical commentators for dubiously supposing that the gospel writers or Paul or John is writing with copies of Quintilian's *On the Education of the Orator* (92 CE) open on the desk. The relationship between orality and literacy is much more fluid in the first century: preachers write the way they preach, which is influenced by their experiences of preaching and hearing sermons.

16. Duane F. Watson, "Amplification Techniques in 1 John: The Interaction of Rhetorical Style and Invention," *JSNT* 51 (1993): 99–123.

In 1 John especially, the language is that of a preacher who has something to convey to an audience. Recent scholarship shows how even the repetition of particular sounds causes particular phrases to pop up and stand out in the ears of hearers in 1 John 1:1–4.[17] Repetition and sounds and ideas convince hearers of the text that they are "us" and not "them" and persuade them to do, say, and think whatever is needed to ensure their status as "us" and not "them." As a sermon, 1 John is fundamentally about identity-making, or, borrowing from a venerable evangelical patois, conversion. By listening and identifying with John's "we," 1 John converts you from one who does not know whether or not you have eternal life—or indeed who you are at all—to a child of God and member of the community of faith and possessor of all that that status entails.

Conclusions

If this is indeed the case, then it may be right to suggest that 1–3 John were written in the 80s or 90s CE in and around Ephesus, where John is said to have lived. If this all sounds a bit thin, it is because we have very little aside from the actual texts of the Gospel, 1–3 John, and possibly Revelation on which to draw.

Moreover, it is worth wondering why it is exactly that these identifications matter in the first place. If the issue of authorship is said to matter because we must know that these books are trustworthy for faith and practice, then we must reply that because the Johannine writings have been received into the Christian canon, the church assumes their authority and their keeping with apostolic faith, regardless of who wrote them.[18] Or if it is suggested that the writings must share an author in order that we might draw on, say, the Gospel of John in order to understand something in 2 John, then we reply that the very fact that the Gospel of John and the second letter of the elder are taken by the church as two parts of the very same book—namely, the Christian Bible—theologically requires that

17. Jeffrey E. Brickle, *Aural Design and Coherence in the Prologue of First John* (New York: Bloomsbury T&T Clark, 2012).

18. While we do not practice Robert W. Wall's canonical interpretation of texts, we can recommend reading 1–3 John as part of the broader "Johannine literature"—which includes John's Gospel and Revelation—in part because the church canonized these texts as having come from John. That is, whoever wrote them, they were received into the canon on the strength of their shared progenitor: John the apostle of Christ. So there is a historical warrant for reading 1–3 John as "written by the apostle" and treating the Johannine writings as a corpus, even though we may not be certain about the identity of their author(s). See the introductory matters in Robert W. Wall with Richard Steele, *1 and 2 Timothy and Titus*, THNTC (Grand Rapids: Eerdmans, 2012) for an analogous discussion on treating so-called deutero-Pauline or pastoral letters as Scripture and as part of the Pauline corpus.

they illumine one another. Some might say that if we do not know the circumstances that led to the production of 1–3 John, then we will not know how to read them properly. One hopes that this is not the case, since we can unqualifiedly claim this kind of knowledge about next to nothing found in the Scriptures. Moreover, whatever we surmise about the history behind the text will necessarily come from a deep study of the text itself because we have very little in terms of external witnesses.

With these considerations in mind, we will refer to the author as "John" throughout and assume that even if one person did not write all of the Johannine literature, for practical purposes we might as well act as if someone did. Interpretation of 1–3 John, then, will inevitably prioritize linguistic, thematic, and theological relationships with the Fourth Gospel and Revelation. This is not to say that 2 John will have nothing to do with Isaiah or Matthew, only that the resonances will be stronger with literature that, again, for all practical purposes, shares an author. We might draw an allusion here to how interpretation of the disputed Pauline letters features more intercanonical interaction with 1 Corinthians and Romans than, again, Isaiah or Matthew. The language and themes are more clearly related, which gives the interpreter firm theological purchase. And given the location of the Fourth Gospel, 1–3 John, and Revelation within the Christian canon, we will further assume that we should find deep thematic and theological resonances between all these works, even if they might be in tension here or there. We will not attempt any historical reconstructions not strictly demanded by the text; the text and only the text will have the last word—though we will try to listen to the tradition and historical contexts to see what they might help reveal. Last and most important, 1–3 John are Scripture, and as Scripture they are for us and to us today as we share in and interpret in light of the same Spirit that all Christians—John included—have received across the millennia. What follows is a fresh translation and commentary on 1–3 John. May it be a word from the Spirit and a blessing to our Lord's church.

Interpretation: Theological Interpretation of 1–3 John

1 John 1:1–4

[1] We are announcing to you what was from the beginning, what we have heard, what our eyes have seen, what we have gazed upon, and what our hands have touched concerning the word of life. [2] This life was made visible, and we saw and witnessed it and now announce to you the eternal life that was with the Father and has been revealed to us. [3] We are announcing what we have seen and heard to you so that you might have union with us; for indeed our union is with the Father and his Son, Jesus Christ. [4] So we write these things that our joy be made complete.

Ancient letter writing was conventional and formulaic: the author self-identifies, names the intended recipient(s), and offers a greeting. John does no such thing. It might be argued that the beginning of chapter 2 features something resembling a classic greeting, and certainly 1:4—along with 2:1, 12–14 and 5:13—explain reasons for writing, but the "first letter" of John just does not follow the form of an ancient letter. 2 and 3 John plainly do, suggesting that 1 John ought to be read as something else.

If John's opening cannot be said to be the introduction to a letter, it certainly can be said to introduce a piece of ancient rhetoric. The verbs μαρτυροῦμεν and ἀπαγγέλλομεν (*martyroumen*, "we witnessed," and *apangellomen*, "we announce") seek to persuade hearers about what is the case. They demand a response. The response is predicated on what is being said and by whom. Rather than self-identify—as in epistolary literature—John indicates that he and those who are with him are known to the hearers, but what is important about them is not a name or a position. Rather, what is important is what they have seen and announce. 1 John 1:1–4 is nothing less than an invitation to receive or rereceive the good news about God and his Son Jesus and in so doing join or rejoin or reaffirm one's joining with John, his compatriots, God, and Jesus Christ. This approach causes problems for those wishing to classify 1 John as either deliberative rhetoric (speech intended to make people take action) or epideictic rhetoric (speech intended to reaffirm values already held in the present).[1] As 1 John unfolds, it becomes clear that the text does both.

As with many of Paul's letters, 1 John is written—at least in part—by committee. As for John himself, there is no straightforward identification offered, but it does seem that John and his coauthors claim to have had some direct, physical contact with Jesus. It is difficult to know what exactly that contact looked like, given the enigmatic character of the way it is communicated, but it certainly sounds as if 1 John is written by people who claim to have known the risen Lord. The repeated references to the divine, eternal life indicate that the kind of life they encountered was not regular human life but a special kind of experience that—at least in the Gospel of John—is witnessed by the disciples after the resurrection.

The Greek of 1 John 1:1–4—obscured a bit in the translation here—begins with a succession of neuter relative pronouns, ὅ (*ho*, "what"), that is, "*what* was from the beginning," "*what* we have heard," and so forth. English translations tend to give the impression that these "whats" refer, perhaps, to the "word of life" at the end of the verse or the "eternal life" of the second verse or even the "union" of the third. These are misleading but helpful impressions, because, as we will see, life and community are indeed some of John's primary concerns throughout the sermon. Nevertheless, the "whats" do not actually refer to any particular noun that we can find in 1 John, since they are grammatically neuter, and the salient possibilities for referents (e.g., "son," "life," or "union") are either masculine or feminine. Thus, John's use of the relative pronouns is likely analogous to the English sentence "What you said was very good."[2] In such a sentence the referent of the pronoun is "everything" or "the whole content of your statement." The pronoun generalizes so as to capture the sum or the whole of what was said. That John writes in this way indicates that a summary statement itself may have some trouble encapsulating the enormity of the thing that "was from the beginning . . . heard . . . seen," and so on. Some have tried to suggest that John is referring to the

1. See, for example, Kruse, *Letters of John*, 29–30, where a recitation of classical arguments leads to a somewhat tortured defense of epideictic rhetoric. One senses that were the option given (as it is here), Kruse and others would leap at the chance to avoid unitary classification. There is no reason to suppose a priori that John or the cowriters endeavor to follow the classical rules of rhetoric and, in fact, every reason to suppose they do not. The very ambiguity about the epistolary nature of the literature indicates that whatever 1 John is, it is not concerned about fitting in with this or that genre of literature or rhetoric.

2. Jobes, *1, 2, and 3 John*, 44.

"good news" of salvation or perhaps to Jesus's whole career and ministry, even God's wisdom, but these explanations fall short of grappling with John's actual language. Consider: the whats refer to something that is "from the beginning," an echo both of "In the beginning God created" from Genesis 1:1 and "In the beginning was the Word" from John 1:1. Moreover the whats have been seen by eyes and handled by hands and concern the "word of life," which is itself "eternal life." John speaks here about more than the good news of salvation, since salvation is, for us, recent, and "the beginning" quite assuredly is not. He moreover speaks about more than Jesus's life and ministry and death and resurrection on earth. True, these events were all seen by the disciples, and Jesus was indeed touched by them, but whatever significance we attach to such happenings, they can hardly be deemed "from the beginning" or "eternal" in any straightforward manner.[3] Indeed, "what was from the beginning" is something altogether more cosmic.

Clement of Alexandria comments, "So when he writes 'from the beginning,' the Elder is explaining that the 'beginning [origination]' of generation is not separated from the 'beginning [origination]' of the Creator. For when he says, 'What was from the beginning' he touches on the generation-without-beginning [origination] of the Son, who is co-existent with the Father. Therefore, the word 'was' signifies eternity, a 'not-having-had-a-beginning,' just as the Word himself, that is, the Son of God, who is one with the Father in equality of substance, is eternal and unmade." Clement's suggestion is no doubt startling, for he would have us think of the "whats" of verses 1 and 3 as referring not just to Jesus or his life but to the "without-beginningness" and uncreatedness of the Second Person of the Trinity. John's announcement pushes on the bounds of language, Clement thinks, because he is telling the story of people who have seen, heard, and handled a being who is eternal and uncreated.

Though Clement wrote in Greek in the late second century CE, we have this fragment only from a Latin translation by Cassiodorus in the sixth century. Cassiodorus is probably translating γένεσις (*genesis*), which, interestingly, is the word for "origin" or "birth" used in Matthew 1:1, which gives us an account of the "generation" or "ancestors" of "Jesus the Messiah, the son of David, the son of Abraham." If Matthew gives us Jesus's earthly generation, it is counterpointed, Clement supposes, by his heavenly generation, which is eternal, that is, temporally unoriginated and uncreated (Wis 6:22; 7:5).

As we have noted, eternal heavenly generation does not prevent the Word from being seen, heard, and handled by human beings on earth, and in the case

3. Similarly, Smalley notes that "'life' expresses one aspect of his being and activity" (*1, 2, and 3 John*, 9), though he suggests that perhaps it also encompasses the preaching about Jesus. The use of "life" rather than "Jesus" or "Son" is significant.

of Thomas's touching in John 20:24–29, being the cause of belief in the Son as "my Lord and my God!" John's language thus gives trinitarian content to the person of Jesus Christ, namely, that he is the Son of the Father and yet still Lord and God.[4] Moreover, while the Son shares the Father's "from the beginning" eternal nature, the Son is nevertheless distinguishable from the eternal and invisible Father in that he has been seen, heard, and handled. John continues to complicate the picture: though the Father and the Son share an eternal nature, and though they are distinguishable as unseen and seen, the encounter with the latter that John is announcing leads to "fellowship" or "union" or "communion" with the former. This extension of communion with the divine may be why St. Augustine points to the story of Thomas in his homilies on 1 John—what seeing and touching accomplishes for Thomas comes as a blessing (John 20:29) for those who believe when seers and touchers like Thomas bear witness to them. In any case, it is clear that the revelation by the Father of the Son has had a particular effect, namely, that certain persons—John among them—now share union, that is, share life intimately with the Father and the Son.

Most translations suggest that Christians are to "have fellowship" (κοινωνίαν ἔχητε, *koinōnian echēte*), an interpretation that loses some of the emphasis of the Greek, where fellowship is something had or possessed rather than something done, that is "have union" rather than "come into union with us," and thus requiring the verb form of the root. Likewise emphatic is the Greek behind "indeed" (καὶ . . . δέ, *kai . . . de*) and "our" (ἡμετέρα, *hēmetera*).[5] Given the strength of the language, we gloss in English as "union" to indicate ontology rather than simply interpersonal relations such as might be suggested by "close associations" or "warm affections" or "fellowship." John's repetition of "this *life*" and the "eternal *life* that . . . has been revealed to us" is relevant here. Those who have witnessed in the flesh the eternal, uncreated Word of God are not only "on good terms" with the Father and the Son, as it were; rather, they are actually participating or

4. One suspects that hard-nosed historians will balk at the term "trinitarian" here. Larry Hurtado, *Lord Jesus Christ: Devotion to Jesus in Earliest Christianity* (Grand Rapids: Eerdmans, 2003), 151–54, for example, treats Pauline language about Christ as "binitarian worship," that is, a form of devotion to Jesus that acknowledges some real attribute of divinity. Our concern here is logical. Since it is impossible to know what John or his coauthors were thinking, we can only attend to the text. And the text proposes both Jesus's uncreatedness and Jesus's Sonship. This is at least "binitarian" and probably incipiently trinitarian, since Jesus is eternal like the Father but exists as Son-to-the-Father. If this is not hierarchical, then some other relationship must be supplied to explain the conflict. Ultimately, the church resolves the issue with trinitarian theology (see Robert W. Jenson, *Canon and Creed* [Louisville: Westminster John Knox, 2010], esp. part 1, on the formation of the canon and the Apostles' Creed with respect to the *regula fidei* and apostolic witness).

5. See Smalley, *1, 2, and 3 John*, 12–13.

experiencing divine life itself because they are bound up in the family of God. Sharing God's DNA (see comment on 3:9 below) is an ontological reality that, however strange it might sound in twenty-first-century ears, gives believers a kind of access to God's life as such. John and the other witnesses have natural access to God's life that—mirroring the relations holding between the Father and the Son—is best characterized here as familial. The metaphor of children in God's household has currency here, with "union" or "fellowship" indicating sharing in the divine character.[6]

And whether we live in the first generation after Jesus's life and ministry or the present day, this notion that we truly share God's character should strike us as utterly scandalous, for the relations holding between the Father and Son are endlessly mutual. The Father loves and lavishes glory on the Son, who obeys and returns glory to the Father, and because we are sharing in the union and mutual life experienced triunely, we are able to live here and now as one (see John 17:20–24). While this mutuality and sharing do suggest present experience of future consummation of total union, they do not suggest a thorough overcoming of difference.[7] The Father and the Son remain infinitely differentiated, even as they are one. That is, the Father is never the Son but always remains the Father of the Son, and vice-versa. This is, of course, the doctrine of perichoresis (Greek), or circuminsession (Latin), in which we confess the eternal coinherence of the persons of the Trinity without allowing for their dissolution as persons.

Note also that this understanding assumes that our fellowship with Father and Son is "eschatological," meaning that it is to be fully consummated at the end of days. There is no copula in the Greek here, meaning that we have to supply the "is" of "our union *is* with . . . ," but this fact does not detract from the present-tenseness—if we may put it that way—of John's language. John announces what he has seen and heard in order to explain the present state of things and to invite others to join in. This wording does not mean that there is not an aspect of our union with the Father and the Son that will not be fully realized until the eschaton, but it does mean that whatever that is, it is not the aspect of union on which John wishes to focus. This understanding may help to explain the stark differences we will encounter between light and dark, truth and lies, and so forth:

6. See comment on the family of God below (1 John 2:7–11).

7. Georg Strecker (*The Johannine Letters*, trans. Linda M. Maloney [Minneapolis: Augsburg Fortress, 1996]) notes that this fellowship "allows [us] to participate in the eschatological 'fellowship' with God the Father and the Son, Jesus Christ." Moreover, such a union "bridges the undeniable differences between God and humanity as well as those between one human being and another" (20). While he happily at least notices the ontological import of union with the Father and the Son, Strecker may be in danger of overplaying a bit the overcoming of difference, as it were.

the eternal life to which we are united is holiness untainted and unacquainted with sin, the purest purity. It is enough to mention this point now, as John will return to it in detail below.

We may therefore say that John's sermon is an invitation to "taste and see that the Lord is good" (Ps 34:8), as it were, an announcement to all that the divine life itself is freely available to any who wish to share in it. Acceptance of this invitation will result in a full, complete joy for John and those who make the announcement with him. Fellowship with Father and Son is meant to be expanded and shared with all, not kept to a particular group or tribe. Indeed, the Father has shown this attitude in the revelation of the Son. Rather than keep the mysterious divine life hidden, the Father sends the Son to be seen, heard, gazed on, and touched. It is therefore in keeping with God's nature to share and reveal the divine life as communal.

At the same time, communality is not meant to eradicate difference. The Father reveals the Son but is differentiated from the Son. By analogy, Christian union transcends differences of race, class, and gender but does not make them disappear. Rather, the unity that transpires in and through these formerly divisive traits constitutes mature Christian joy. Many of our existing manuscripts read "your joy" rather than "our joy" in verse 4. The oldest and best manuscripts read "our joy," however, which is almost certainly what John actually wrote.

1 John 1:5–2:2

5 This is the message we have heard from him and are announcing to you: "God is
light, and there is no darkness in him." 6 If we say, "We have union with him" while
we are walking in darkness, we lie and so are not doing the truth. 7 But if we are
walking in the light as he himself is in the light, we have union with one another,
and so the blood of Jesus his Son cleans us from all sin. 8 If we say, "We have no sin,"
we deceive ourselves, and so the truth is not in us. 9 If we confess our sins, the one
who is faithful and just will forgive us our sins and so cleans up all our disorder. 10 If
we say, "We have never sinned," we make him a liar, and so his word is not in us.
2:1 My little children, I write these things to you so that you do not sin anymore. But
if anyone does sin, we have a co-priest before the Father, Jesus Christ, the one who
is truly righteous. 2 He is the atonement sacrifice for our sins, and not ours only but
also the sins of the entire cosmos.

In verse 5 John announces the fundamental character of God as revealed to those who have experienced the resurrected Son firsthand. The ἀγγελία (*angelia*, "message") may carry the connotation of news, that this message is fresh and surprising.[8] This is how it is used in Proverbs 25:25 LXX and explains the use of ἀναγγέλλω (*anangellō*, "announce," "report") later in the verse. The surprise is surely not that God is light and that there is no darkness in him. What is a surprise is that human beings, who are surely a mix of both light and dark, can be in union with God. Verse 5 thus generates an unspoken question. If God is light unbedarkened and we are not, how is this union possible?

John answers this unspoken question in verses 6–10, where he mentions three ways that we—and perhaps others he and his companions have known—might wrongly try to square this circle. The first false explanation (v. 6) comes from those who say they have union with God but walk in darkness. This is the heresy of antinomianism, the belief that wrong ways of acting have no effect on our union or fellowship with God. Interestingly, John suggests that anyone who espouses such a view is lying, that is, intentionally being deceptive. John seems to think that no one who espouses this view really believes it, that such a one is simply trying to turn others astray. Furthermore, such a person οὐ ποιοῦμεν τὴν ἀλήθειαν (*ou poioumen tēn alētheian*, "does not do the truth"). Another possible explanation comes in verse 8, where we might claim to be sin-free; a third explanation might be that we have never sinned at all (v. 10). For the first two false claims, John includes a clarification of sorts (vv. 7, 9), a way to discern whether his hearers are those who are wrong in their accounting of their standing before or with God. The third claim, "We have never sinned," needs no sustained counterclaim, presumably because it is self-evidently ludicrous to anyone who, like John, has truly encountered the light. If any sincerely claim never to have sinned, they are to be dismissed out of hand.

In the first of these claims and counterclaims in verses 6–10, John notes that it is better to check for union with one's fellows than simply declare union with God. God is invisible; other believers are not. John's counterclaim, therefore, is that any evaluation of a person's claim of union with God or walking in the light begins with an examination of that person's relations with other children of God. As we will see in our discussions below on blood, Israel's sacrificial cult, with its attendant splattering of blood, was meant to set in order what was disordered. Thus, sin-cleansing and rightly ordered relations with God's people go hand in hand. Rabid sectarianism, lone-wolf religion, divisiveness—none of these is compatible with walking in the light. To think in terms of the visible and invisible, right living in community is the physical, tangible, visible expression of our ongoing cleansing by the blood.

John's second counterclaim involves confession, forgiveness, and further cleansing from sin's disordering effects. It logically mirrors the first. Of course

8. So Smalley, *1, 2, and 3 John*, 19.

sin's disordering is at work in our lives; the key is to identify it, confess it, and be rid of it. As with ritual contamination in Israelite religion, sin gloms on to us; hypervigilance is required. Our continual self-examination and confession and subsequent forgiveness are the visible, here-and-now instantiations of the ongoing sin-scrubbing of Jesus's blood.

There is no need for a sustained counter to the claim of never having sinned, because to make such a claim is to have fundamentally misunderstood Israel's God and his Son Jesus. The long story of Israel is of a saving God righting, carrying, and forgiving the wrongs of his people. These actions are brought to a culmination in the incarnation of the Son, whose eternal life stands in stark contrast to the life human beings regularly live. To claim sinlessness is to make God a liar, for why would the light need to come to us unless we were hopelessly darkened?

Rhetorically, the claims and counterclaims function as warnings. In the twenty-first century, the postmodern West encounters secularized (and sometimes "Christian"!) variations on such beliefs. Once the very notion of sin has been dispensed with, however desultorily, it is the corollary move to announce, as Nietzsche's Zarathustra rather infamously did, that one is quite sinless and walking in the light of one's own lamp. In 2:1–2 John explains why such warnings are necessary: the disordering of the whole world is a powerful, possibly inescapable, phenomenon. John brings the warnings about what some convince themselves of in order to help us avoid falling into the same traps. That said, he reassures us that when the shadows get the best of us, all is not lost. The light, the right-ordering of the universe himself, Jesus Christ, jointly ministers with us before God the Father. He illumines and sets right not just our lives but the universe itself. Everything is, or perhaps we should say will be, bathed in the glorious beauty of God's intention and embrace; and the very one through whom this future is known and in whom it is accomplished, Jesus, is working at our side, ministering for us and cleansing us in God's sight. In 2:1–2 John explains how this works.

It is quite common for Christians to think of Jesus's blood as something like soap. Sin—traditionally understood as, say, any violation of God's law—results in moral stain, and Jesus's blood can wash the stain out. The imagery arises from Israel's sacrificial cult, where sprinkling the blood of an animal functions to purge impurities from people and holy places, especially the temple (so, e.g., Lev 16:15–19). The logic works this way: as people intentionally and unintentionally depart from God's ordering of the world, they become polluted; it is suggested that they carry about them an "aerial miasma" that infects the person and rubs off wherever he or she may go. When this infection happens at the temple, God's house becomes an unsuitable abode for God's being.[9] The blood of the goat,

9. Jacob Milgrom, *Leviticus 1–16*, AYBC (New York: Doubleday, 1991), 255–61.

when sprinkled in accordance with the proper ritual, purifies the person or the place, that is, cleans everything up (see Heb 10:22). There is something mysterious about blood; it suggests life, vitality, and power, and it should not be surprising that God uses it as a purgative.[10]

Purgation is not a verdict of "not guilty," however. Sacrificial blood does not address a violation of an abstract moral code. It aims, rather, at expunging the real results of wrongdoing in the world. And it is perhaps instructive to note that pollution occurs not only in an event of intentional wrongdoing but also in inadvertent—and, as is with the case of some genital discharges, unavoidable (Lev 15:1–13)—impurities as well. God freely forgives sin—and John notes that this happens whenever we recognize our wrongdoing and confess—but the real effects of wrongdoing continue to be a pollutant. Put another way, sin not only puts us at odds with God, it also distorts and disorders the world God created. In fact, it is probably helpful here to think of sin just as distortion or disorder of God's right-putting of the world. For this reason the translation renders ἀδικίας (*adikias*) as "disorder" rather than "unrighteousness." Jesus's blood functions like the blood of the goat in the priestly ritual, applied, however, not to the furniture of God's house but to the whole person of the Christian. But if we take seriously John's use of temple and priestly language to describe both the Christian community of faith and Jesus who co-ministers God's worship with it, then perhaps the distance between the two notions is not so far as we might have thought. Regardless, we are pollutants bringing disorder to the world. The blood of the Son purifies us so that we no longer act as infectious agents. This purgation makes us ready, like the high priest Aaron, to properly worship the Father "in Spirit and truth," as we read in John 4:23–24.

Prerequisite to our purification, however, is our walking in the light. In verse 7 the present-tense form of the verb καθαρίζω (*katharizō*, "cleanse") indicates that a process of purification is ongoing. In keeping with the light/darkness motif, we have noted that even those who walk in the light sometimes sin, that is, shift back into an old mode of seeing the world according to the shadows, which requires corrective action: identification of our failure to see rightly and confession to God. Cleansing, however, is something God does for us through the blood of Jesus, his Son. We again see how John eschews any strong division between being and act.

Thus, the person who "walks in the light" is continually sprinkled with the cleansing blood of the Son. In this way John sees Jesus's once-for-all sacrifice

10. Yarbrough (*1–3 John*, 57) is dismissive of "magical blood" and points to the Kippur rituals in Leviticus 16 but fails to explain why blood is used for purification while sins are placed on a live goat and sent away without any spilling of blood.

as in keeping with Israel's cult, but in a fresh and definitive way. That is, just as the priests and people of Israel needed to regularly practice purification—and therefore regularly engage in rituals of sacrifice—so we need to regularly receive the metaphoric sprinkling of Jesus's purifying blood. The metaphoric nature of John's language is crucial: John does not envision an "aerial miasma" of ritual impurity so much as he, having encountered the living God in the flesh, recognizes how deeply subject human beings are to life in the shadows. Relentless self-examination, a life-pattern of vigilance, is needed in order to remain conformed to God's beautiful ordering of the universe. Remember that John's warning is directed against three kinds of benighted thinking. In the first, we think we are in the light but are very much wrong, as evidenced by disunion with others. In the second, we think that we have attained a state of sinlessness, that is, perfect union with God. This presumption fails to apprehend God's true, glorious nature of eternal, gracious, self-giving overflow. The third sort is as audacious as it is absurd, wherein a person supposes that he or she has never sinned, that is, has always been in perfect union with God. To John, who truly knows both Father and Son, this idea would be laughable, were it not so offensive to the God who actually does desire union with us. The Christian who desires never to fall into any of these three kinds of thinking must carefully control and examine thought and action in order that the former be illumined and shaped by God's revealing Word, and the latter evidence the Word's loving, life-filled inner nature.

We have translated 1 John 2:2 to emphasize the cosmic nature of the atoning sacrifice that is Jesus himself. In Greco-Roman literature ἱλασμός (*hilasmos*, "atoning sacrifice") could mean "a way to appease," or "expiation." But as we have seen, John's language draws deeply on Old Testament themes in which blood is almost like a cleaning agent, and we have also seen that God is interested in a complete reordering of the universe, one that puts God "at one" with the cosmos. Thus, rather than the abstract "expiation" or the highly personal "appeasement," it is better to leave ἱλασμός as "atoning sacrifice." This wording is in keeping with the Old Testament logic of sacrifice. But there might be something a bit troubling about the fact that despite two thousand years of Christian faith, the world often appears as malformed today as when Jesus died.[11] But this is where it is important to recognize the co-priestly nature of Jesus's ministry. Yes, Jesus's blood is sufficient to clean everything up, but his blood still leaves room for the willing ministrations of believers who seek to worship God rightly. Reverting to the light metaphor, we might think that wherever there are trusting, obedient hearts, God is setting up zones of light, spots of illumination, places—that is, churches—that run counter to the darkness of the world. In these places the light

11. See comments on 1 John 2:7–11 below.

takes hold, and lives and relationships—even if only for a time—take a form that is in keeping with God's own divine nature.

1 John 2:3–6

3 In this we know that we have come to know him: if we obey his commands. 4 So
anyone who says, "I have come to know him," while disobeying his commands is
a liar, and the truth is not in such a one. 5 But the one who obeys his word, truly
in such a person the love of God has reached its goal. By this we know that we are
in him. 6 The one who says, "I am still in him," ought to walk just as he walked.

This section begins with the peculiar use of ἐν τούτῳ (*en toutō*, "in this"). In general, it is best to read this phrase as pointing forward, which is why our translation typically ends these phrases with the English colon. This is because John's arguments are moving forward, and he is making a definitive connection between two states, events, and so forth.[12] Here, ἐν τούτῳ prepares the reader to understand what it means to "know him." Who, we might wonder, is "him"? Jesus? the Father? John has been privileged to see and handle the one who was from the beginning, but many he worships with and preaches to have not been so privileged, and so the question of knowing the Son and, by extension, knowing the Father is a real one. Many claim to know God; John, because of his authoritative position as one who has actually—in the flesh!—known the Son who shares union with the Father, has special insight into what knowing God entails. It is probably useless to make a sharp distinction between "knowing God" and "knowing the Son" in this section because, as we have already seen, John confesses a tight unity between the two. Union with one is union with both. So

12. The phrase ἐν τούτῳ (*en toutō*, "in this") appears seven times in 1 John—meaning "in this" five times and "in this person" twice. Because the syntax of the sentences where these uses appear are often quite awkward, scholars have taken to pained exegesis at each instance, usually trying to divine whether the phrase is pointing backward to an antecedent or forward to what comes next. Mostly following Raymond Brown, I read these as a sort of Johannine verbal tic that functions as a marker that what comes next is definitive and important—thus treating it as a colon. Whenever John uses ἐν τούτῳ to mean "in this," he is preparing the hearer to equate, relate, or subordinate two states or events or meanings that follow. See Brown, *Epistles*, 248–49, for an extended treatment. Brown disagrees with "sweeping statements in many commentaries about the direction in which ἐν τούτῳ 'always' points (usually forward)" (249). This conclusion strikes me as a bit pedantic; in no place do we simply ignore what has gone before as though John is beginning a new thought ex nihilo with every ἐν τούτῳ, but John's tone always seems to be moving forward, and it makes good sense that he brandishes a go-to phrase to indicate that this is what is happening.

the phrase "I know him" likely does not have a strongly fixed referent (i.e., either Father or Son) because the two share a nature. Nevertheless, John is keen to emphasize the special result of knowing God, and here he begins to share it. The bottom line, of course, is obedience to God's commands issued through the Son. But this assumption about knowing and doing should strike us as a bit strange because it is not quite normal for us to make the association that is so natural for John: knowledge issues in obedience. John is nevertheless quite clear. Anyone who claims to know the Son (or perhaps the Father through the Son) while not doing what God has commanded or, as in verse 6, walking or living day-to-day with the same life patterns the Son himself demonstrated, such a one is lying to others and, quite possibly, to himself or herself.

There is a question about just what, exactly, God's commands are. John uses ἐντολή (*entolē*, "command") fourteen times in the sermon. For English speakers deeply conversant with the Bible, it might be tempting to hear an echo of the Ten Commandments in "his commands," but this conclusion would be misleading, though not because John has simply moved past the Old Testament.[13] If he has, it is argued, then John cannot be referring in any substantive way to the Ten Commandments or really the Torah at all because, it is thought, the logic of Old Testament law-keeping is precisely the opposite of what John is after. But this is to misconstrue the logic of Old Testament law-keeping, something that John himself has not done. John has already referred to Christian life as metaphoric temple worship—surely the sine qua non of "Old Testament law-keeping"—and has indicated a strong rootedness in Jewish religious devotion. What Christians often misunderstand but John does not is that obedience to particular laws in the Torah is not so much an expression of "knowing God" as a response to God's gracious, saving initiative. Broadly, the law contains the guidelines for a flourishing communion between God and God's people. The Israelites are called to follow Torah as an expression of trust in the God who liberated them from slavery in Egypt. In short, what John is proposing is not somehow a different ethical logic from what we find in the Old Testament.

When John preaches that one's intimate knowing of God is fleshed out in obedience to God's commands, he suggests that the Christian community is very much the same as any faithful Jewish community was in the ages before the coming of the Son to the world: devotion to God's way of life and worship is paramount, enthusiastically pursued and jealously guarded. As God spoke through Hosea, "I desire faithful commitment [חסד, *ḥesed*], not sacrifice" (Hos 6:6). The

13. Judith Lieu (*1, 2, and 3 John: A Commentary* [Louisville: Westminster John Knox, 2008], 69) notes that "it is not a particular set of instructions about behavior that proves knowledge of God; what comes first is an acceptance that to be brought into . . . a relationship with God is to recognize and to respond to whatever God requires, simply because it is what God requires."

point of Torah was never to create a great deal of sacrifices but to supply an avenue for the expression of a great deal of commitment from God's people. Thus, it is unhelpful to hear the Ten Commandments lurking in John's language of his commands unless we first understand that the Ten Commandments are themselves an opportunity to demonstrate devotion to a saving God rather than a foolproof plan that guarantees God's favor. If, however, we have a right understanding of Torah, then it is helpful to hear something of Old Testament law-language in John's language here.

In some ways this discussion is prolegomena: John will be quite explicit about the meaning of "his commands" in the next chapter (3:23) where he spells it out as to "believe in the name of his Son" and "love each other." We will have more to say there. For now, let us merely suggest that the Torah—and perhaps even the Ten Commandments specifically—is strongly implicated in this apparent double command.

Thanks to John's ambiguous syntax, it is difficult to say whether "his commands" in verse 3 refers to commands given by the Father or to those given by the Son. For now, it is worth being reminded again of the Fourth Gospel, where Jesus claims, "Those who love me will keep my word, and my Father will love them, and we will come to them and make our home with them. Whoever does not love me does not keep my words; and the word that you hear is not mine but is from the Father who sent me" (John 14:23–24). Words from the Son are the Father's, and words from the Father come through the Son. Any strict distinction is to misapprehend the revelation of "what was from the beginning" to those who handled, heard, and touched it. And this is an important point from the perspective of trinitarian confession.

Another interesting feature of John's teaching is that a life characterized by living in accordance with God's words is the end goal of God's gracious outpouring of love. Though the Greek genitive is ambiguous, with "God's love" meaning either "the love God has for us" or "the love we have for God," John brings up the same theme in 4:12 and 4:17, and in both cases he uses the former meaning. This interpretation of the genitive matters because John expects the love that God has for his people to change them in quite radical ways. Some translations read the verb τελειόω (*teleioō*) as "made perfect." But really this understanding does not quite capture its meaning in English because we tend to associate "perfect" with "flawless." John has already claimed that flawlessness is not something anyone should claim to have achieved. One wonders whether it might not even be something worth aspiring to. Instead of thinking about perfection, John is thinking about trajectories, that is, starting from here and getting to there. God's love is vectored, it is aimed at accomplishing a goal. And that goal, John tells us, is knowledge of the Son, fleshed out in obedience.

This section should echo for us some of Jesus's farewell prayer in the Gospel of John, especially 17:1–3, where he says, "Father, the hour has come; glorify your Son so that the Son may glorify you, [2] since you have given him authority over all people, to give eternal life to all whom you have given him. [3] And this is eternal life, that they may know you, the only true God, and Jesus Christ whom you have sent." The gospel suggests that "life eternal"—in verse 3 the usual order, "eternal" followed by "life," has been switched—is not, or at least not only, living forever, but that it is also the state of knowing God the Father and Jesus his Son. Marianne Meye Thompson notes, "John does not write that knowing God leads to eternal life, as if it were the reward for faith, but that knowing God, to be in communion with God, *is* life."[14] So knowing God is life itself, and the one who has this life does what the Son commands, and this knowing and doing is the ultimate goal of God's loving gift of the Son to the world.

In verse 6 the Greek ἐκεῖνος (*ekeinos*, "that one")—usually translated "he"—is closer to "that man." That is, a particular person is being picked out as having walked, and it would be hard to conclude that that could be anyone other than Jesus. The NIV and TNIV even go so far as to simply translate it as Jesus. John's "walking" language is closely tied to language about light and darkness. Of course this connection makes good sense, especially to those in any culture who, having no access to abundant electric light, are keenly aware of how difficult and dangerous it is to walk about on a cloudy night. Walking suggests journeying, movement.

It might be tempting to treat περιπατέω (*peripateō*, "walk") as a cipher for "live," but this would be to ignore the premium John places on Jesus's physicality, the actual mode in which he lived and ministered. To put it bluntly, Jesus *walked*. His *missio Dei* was predicated on having been sent by the Father (e.g., John 5:23; 8:29) to come and walk among and before those given to him (John 10:27–29) and those who would eventually walk away from him (e.g., John 6:66).[15] Near the end of the Fourth Gospel, Jesus remarks to Peter that as a young man he, Peter, was free to "walk about" as he wished, but that in his later ministry he would be led to martyrdom (John 21:15–19). The episode ends with Jesus calling

14. Marianne Meye Thompson, *John: A Commentary* (Louisville: Westminster John Knox, 2015), 349.

15. Andreas J. Köstenberger (*The Missions of Jesus and the Disciples according to the Fourth Gospel* [Grand Rapids: Eerdmans, 1998], esp. 45–140) helpfully summarizes the classical treatments of Jesus's "modes of movement" and concludes that movement in the Fourth Gospel is intimately related to mission. While Köstenberger does not entertain περιπατέω as a "mode of movement," an examination of its use in John indicates that it too is connected to Jesus's divine purposes. It is strongly associated with those who follow (ἀκολουθέω, *akoloutheō*, John 8:12; 21:18), as well as those who emphatically do not (John 6:66; 7:1; 11:54).

Peter to follow him in continuation of his mission. In a homily on John 16, the Venerable Bede comments briefly on 1 John 2:6, drawing strong attention to the kind of walking Jesus did. "Let us eagerly pursue [*sectemur*]—by the best efforts of the whole mind—his footsteps [*vestigia*] [to Heaven]. And so, let us seriously consider by what steps of action [*actionum gressibus*] he proceeded [*incesserit*] while on earth so that, upon arrival, we may be worthy to enter [*intrare*] the door of the kingdom."[16] The Latin is almost martial, mentioning feet, steps, marching, pursuit. Of course Bede subverts any literal soldierly expectations, reminding his hearers in the next line that Jesus's steps of action led to suffering and death. Perhaps Bede hears an echo of Peter's walking in John 21:15–19, after which Jesus's repeated command to Peter "Feed my sheep" is followed by a prediction that doing so will end in Peter's martyrdom. If so, "walk just as he walked" is less about achieving some pinnacle of holiness and more about the response that one's walking ought to generate in a culture utterly hostile to the light.

Verses 5 and 6 introduce a refrain of sorts in 1 John, "in him," which occurs some fourteen times in the sermon. As we have noted, the referent is ambiguous, sometimes seeming to indicate God and other times indicating Christ. As metaphor, the meaning is likewise a bit obscure. There are many things we can think of metaphorically "being in," such as love or a cloud of confusion, but note that these are abstracts; persons are not usually included. It is not uncommon to suggest that being "in him" is to be acting and believing in the right way.[17] One wonders whether such a view is not properly circumscribed however by John's aesthetic bent. That is, such an ethical interpretation of being "in him" could quite easily be reduced to the observance of some set of rules or even attitudes that do not appear to be present in John's sermon. It is probably not a coincidence that 1 John does not feature either recitations or subversions of, say, Greco-Roman household codes (as does Paul) or revivified accounts of com-

16. Bede, *Homiliae*, 2, 6.

17. So Yarbrough (*1–3 John*, 87) deems it "to be in the positive domain marked out by the pistic, ethical, and agapic trajectories sketched [in verse 2:1]." Yarbrough appears to mean by "pistic, ethical, and agapic" that it is a state of believing rightly, acting rightly, and loving rightly. And Yarbrough appears to take the location part of the metaphor as literally as possible, with some abstract faithful-ethical-loving space that we can inhabit, and when we are correctly doing these things, we can claim to be "in him." It is worth noting that our departure from Yarbrough here is likely the interpretive fallout of rejecting historical speculation about the circumstances (or even existence) of an identifiable "Johannine community" as the basis of meaning in 1 John. That is, if we follow the broad consensus that 1 John is addressed to a group of Christians that have survived recent schism with some protognostic group, then it makes sense to graft in certain content to "being in him" that just does not exist in John's actual language. By giving the text interpretive priority—rather than imagined historical circumstances—1 John speaks as a sermon to all rather than an obscure letter to some.

mands in the Torah (as featured in, e.g., the Sermon on the Mount in Matthew). To do so would be to give unnecessary concretization to what is ultimately better understood as an aesthetic mode of being.

This understanding would be much more in keeping with a notion of being "in him" that avoids acultural ethical norms in favor of an ethical elasticity that refigures the *imitatio Christi* when and wherever the gospel lands. Walking in Jesus's footsteps is therefore not something that can be defined timelessly. Moreover, it is partially constituted by the reaction of the darkness to those who claim to be in the light. Where the dark cheerfully accepts the light, we might think that the "light" is not light at all. Those who are "in him" must be an offense, an unsettling presence that has the effect of chasing shadows away and, in many cases, provoking them. It would be too much to say that every example of walking as he walked ends in a martyr's death, but it would be too little to say that those who so walk can expect a tranquil, uneventful coexistence with a darkness that, we must remember, hates the light (e.g., John 3:20; 1 John 3:12–13). If a Christian is not ruffling the world's feathers, then such a one cannot claim to be "in him" because that one certainly does not "walk just as he walked."

1 John 2:7–11

7 Dear friends, I am not writing a new command to you, but an old command, one
you have had from the beginning. The old command is the word that you heard.
8 But in a way, I am writing to you a new command, something made real in him
and in you – that the darkness is fading away and the true light is already shining.
9 The one who says, "I am in the light," while hating a Christian brother or sister is
still in the dark. 10 The one who loves his brother or sister continues to live in the
light and does not lure them away. 11 But the one who hates a brother or sister is in
the dark and wanders about the darkness. Such a one does not know where to go
because the darkness has blinded their eyes.

This section begins with John's first invocation of ἀγαπητοί (*agapētoi*, "beloved," "dear friends"). The plural form appears six times in 1 John and, in the singular, four times in 3 John. It is a common way to address believers in the New Testament—especially in epistolary literature—but in 1 John it takes on a decidedly familial cast. That is, in the Johannine literature, "beloved" is almost always closely conjoined to ἀδελφός (*adelphos*, "a brother or sister") or τεκνίον (*teknion*, "little one"). So in 1 John 2:7–14 "dear friends" is followed by "brothers and sisters," "little children," "parents," "young people." 3 John 1–5 features a similar medley of co-texts as does 1 John 3:2–12.

The family metaphor is also prominent in the Fourth Gospel, though to a lesser degree, as the new divine family does not really expand until the spiritual birth that takes place through the labor of God on the cross.[18] After the resurrection, Jesus tells Mary to announce the good news to "my brothers and sisters" and tells her, "I am going up to my Father and your Father." The familial language is striking because this is the first time in the Gospel of John that the Father is known as Father to anyone but Jesus, and also the first time that Jesus's "brothers and sisters" are his spiritual siblings rather than siblings by earthly parentage (as in, e.g., John 2:12; 7:3–10).[19]

The importance of the divine family becomes apparent when John brings up the issue of hate. While it is tempting to think of hate as an affect directed at internecine, say, political or martial opponents, John understands hate as the deep bitterness that can grow up between those to whom we are closest—members of our own family. Far from the sentimentality that permeates popular discourse about close relations, families are the locus of the most hostile, vicious, and interminable modes of being. Those to whom we are closest have the power to wound us most gravely.

To put this another way, John uses the family metaphor to describe the church not because it is cute or poetic but because it best describes what has happened in and through the union revealed in the Son and brought by the Spirit to believers. The believing community has become a community of people whose commitment to each other rivals and often supersedes the kind of commitment one would normally expect from close family members. As one's blood family can nurture the deepest love and affection or inflict the sharpest hurt and isolation, so is the family of God susceptible to the same union and division.

There is, to put it simply, great danger in entering into union with strangers. This is something God has long known: from the very outset of God's relations with humanity, human beings have viscerally and then consistently rebelled. To say nothing of humanity at large, even God's chosen covenantal people rejected the strictures of faithfulness. In an egregious act of self-giving, the Godhead nevertheless invites all into union through Christ and initiates a divine family on earth—despite all the historical evidence suggesting that this plan would end in disaster.

When John opens with a term of endearment ("dear friends"), he is speaking to those with whom he has union, fellow believers, with whom he expects to wield authority. Of course his authority derives from his connection to Jesus, and

18. See comments below on 1 John 3:9.

19. J. Ramsey Michaels, *The Gospel of John*, NICNT (Grand Rapids: Eerdmans, 2010), 1001–2.

Jesus's authority comes from the Father. But since John shares union with the Son and thereby the Father as well, he is a trustworthy conveyer of divine commands. In this case, the command is to love, and specifically to love fellow Christians, brothers and sisters in the family of God. As before, the Christian community is "in the light," that is, operating in basic accord with the right-ordering of the universe as God created it and now freshly revealed in the incarnate love of the Son. Those who express love in and for the community demonstrate that they do in fact remain true to the nature of the light as this is most naturally revealed in the community mirroring the union that holds between Father, Son, and Spirit.

If there is one thing that someone who is in the light simply cannot do, it is to fracture this union. The community of faith cannot mirror the union holding in God's being when hate erupts between believers. In fact, hate "lures" those in the light into the darkness as it spreads and furnishes schism. Hatred sows division; it is a trap that pulls a brother or sister out of the light and into the dark. Thus, a wooden rendering of verse 10 might be, "The one who loves his brother or sister continues to live in the light and in such a one is no trap." The given reading glosses this a bit in order to explain what, exactly, those in the light do not do, namely, lure others into the dark.

John's extreme language here is not to be ignored: hatred that fractures the church betrays the very essence of God's being and shows those who engage in it to be completely outside God's ordering of the cosmos. In effect, a believer who allows hatred and schism to take root has abandoned the very core of the Son's command and is as blind and anathema to the purposes of God as one who has never known the light revealed in the Son at all. Whatever beauty, whatever perfection, whatever rightness holds in the divine ordering of all things, it has been utterly lost in the heart of any person who hates another believer. This is a severe teaching, especially when we recognize that hate is much more common—and indeed much more enticing—than we might like to admit. And if the history intervening between John's writing and the contemporary church is any indication, the church has not been very successful in recognizing and excising hatred before it inexorably leads to division and schism; the work of ecumenism is surely of the highest priority in the twenty-first century.

We should notice that John assumes the right to give orders, but this right is not somehow special to him. In fact, whatever commands he delivers must not be from him at all, but from someone else. A few interesting textual cues. First, John again uses the phrase ἀπ' ἀρχῆς (*ap' archēs*, "from the beginning"), just as he did in 1 John 1:1. This phrase signals the Word's preexistence and union and shared nature with God. In a temporal sense, what has been heard "from the start" is likely the good news of divine, eternal life, but this life is itself eternal and now has been made incarnate and present in the person of the Son of the Father.

Moreover, the command is both new and old. We have translated πάλιν (*palin*, "again") at the beginning of verse 8 as "But in a way" to capture the contrastive nature of the term without lapsing into contradiction. Some translations provide something like, "Yet I am writing you a new command" (NRSV). This wording is contrastive, but it is also a contradiction. John sounds as if he is saying that he is *not* writing a new command, and that he *is* writing a new command. This impression needs to be corrected because what John has on offer is absolutely in keeping with an older command, but it is also fresh, given that it comes in a new time and circumstance in which "the darkness is fading away." When the old command was given, the darkness had not yet been dealt a decisive blow; it was still in power, reigning. Now, as it recedes, the old command has space to speak anew.

While we do not know the exact literary and historical relationship between 1 John and the Gospel, the linguistic and thematic similarities are too obvious to ignore. One of these similarities is the use of ἐντολή (*entolē*, "command"). It is a striking choice because in the Fourth Gospel Jesus presents himself as receiving or delivering or passing on a command or commands from the Father. Consider a few examples. In John 12:49 Jesus claims not to have "spoken by myself," but rather, "the Father who sent me gave me a command [ἐντολή] about what to say and speak." In the following verse, Jesus expands on the command: "And I know that his command [ἐντολή] is eternal life; whatever I speak, therefore, I speak just as the Father said to me." It is ambiguous here whether the Father is commanding eternal life or whether the Father's command leads to eternal life, though we will address that question below in comments on 1 John 3:19–24. Nevertheless, Jesus's words have authority because they are the Father's words. And as we learn in John 10:30 and again at the beginning of 1 John, Jesus has special access to the Father's words because the Son is in union with the Father.

It would not be entirely correct to say that Jesus's authority is derivative of the Father's because the two share the divine life. But neither would it be correct to say that Jesus's commands stand on the Son's authority alone, for the Father and the Son share in their triunity. Economically, the Father wills or commands, and the Son executes the Father's command, but the Father's command is always "Son-shaped" or "cruciform"[20] or "Christly" and is accomplished only in the Spirit's power. While the command is not given by the Son, it does have its origin in the Son's graciously self-giving divine nature.

20. I borrow the term from Michael J. Gorman (*Cruciformity: Paul's Narrative Spirituality of the Cross* [Grand Rapids: Eerdmans, 2001]), who uses it to describe Pauline Christology. A Johannine *teologia crucis* leans less into Christ's suffering and more into the language of being "lifted up" (John 3:14–15) or "glorified" (John 12:23). However we characterize the Son, he shares the Father's nature and shape.

We can see this dynamic in John's language. The command "is made real in him and in you" (ἐστιν ἀληθὲς ἐν αὐτῷ καὶ ἐν ὑμῖν, *estin alēthes en autō kai en hymin*). More wooden translations read "is true in him and in you," though this wording obscures rather than highlights the meaning of "true" in John's usage. What is "true" is that which is fully in keeping with God's right ordering of the cosmos according the beauty and perfection of the divine being. The point John makes here is that that "truth" is seen and known in the Son and in the church.

What follows from this observation is that John's authority, his right of command, as it were, comes not from, for example, a recitation of the Son's words while on earth or a "faithful transmission of the gospel," but rather from the union he shares with the Father and the Son. Since John's authority issues from union with the divine, that authority can faithfully pass from generation to generation of Christians. We noted above the gloss of ἐστιν ἀληθὲς ἐν αὐτῷ καὶ ἐν ὑμῖν as "made real in him and in you." The translation is difficult because the preceding neuter relative pronoun does not agree grammatically with the feminine antecedent ἐντολήν (*entolēn*, "command"). We have supplied "something" to capture the ambiguity, but it does little to help us know what John means. Since the grammar disallows the neuter pronoun to refer to "command," modern commentators tend to suggest that it refers to "the newness (the new quality) of the law of love."[21] A better solution, however, takes into account the previous verse's use of "from the beginning," an allusion to 1 John 1:1. Remember that John began his sermon with five neuter relative pronouns describing "what was from the beginning, what we have heard, what our eyes have seen, what we have gazed upon, and what our hands have touched concerning the word of life." It is striking that the same grammatical problem—the use of a neuter relative pronoun with no obvious referent—confronts us here as it did at the beginning of the text. In the previous case, we suggested that the best solution was the ancient solution: reading 1 John 1:1–4 as acknowledging the incomprehensible collision between the eternal, preexistent Word and the present experience of that Word in human life. The "whats" of 1 John 1:1–4 are necessary because John's message treads perilously close to the unutterable. The Word is unoriginated, beyond history, and yet it is the means through which history comes into being, finally entering that history to be heard, seen, and touched, offering union into the life of the Godhead.

Union is the key to understanding John's message. John knows (and will tell us in ch. 4 below) that God is love, and God's endless love spills out in creation through the Word. That love is revealed and commanded in Torah, distilled in

21. Smalley, *1, 2, and 3 John*, 56.

the life, teaching, death, and resurrection of Jesus, and now enlivened by the Spirit in the church. When Christians experience union with God and each other, the very love that precedes, sources, and invades creation in the Son is re-incarnated; it is instantiated in what Paul called the "body of Christ."

All of this is to suggest that if John is using the neuter relative pronoun here in a way similar to his use in 1 John 1:1–2, it would be something like "unorigination" or "uncreated being" or "the eternal divine life." It would mean that the same substance or being or existence that was "made real in him," that is, incarnated in Jesus of Nazareth, is also "made real in you," that is, the church, when the love of God (see comment below on 1 John 4:7–10) unites the brothers and sisters of the family of God. Likewise, that divine life is absent when the family of God is divided by hate.

In terms of John's thought, then, the unoriginated being of the Godhead, in which union-in-love reigns from eternity, has been given as a command "from the beginning," that is, in the created order itself, in the election of Israel, in the giving of the Torah, in the teaching of the prophets, in the exile and the return. The same message has been on display for any with eyes to see and ears to hear, but human beings have a stunning capacity to look but not see and to listen but not hear. Nevertheless, God renews the command in the giving of the Son, revealing in human life and flesh the true being that undergirds the universe. Then, through the Spirit, God renews the command yet again, enfleshing it in the body of Christ, the church. Like the right of command that John enjoys, the same Spirit animating John and the Ephesian church enlivens and renews every generation of Christians, making the command of divine love-in-union fresh again and again as it is revealed in different ways in the church's mutual love in every age.

It should be clear, then, that when we hear that "the darkness is fading away and the true light is already shining," the "true light" is not, as some have suggested,[22] Jesus, but the ongoing reordering of the world according to the very being and nature of God that has settled first in Jesus of Nazareth and now the Spirit-empowered church.[23] This interpretation all hangs on how we read ὅτι (*hoti*, "that," "because," "since") in verse 8. John's use of ὅτι in 1 John very often corresponds to a colon in English (see, e.g., 1:5, 6, 8, 10; 2:4, 5; 3:2, 11; 4:9). It is a stylistic feature of the sermon that "that" is often used to signify a moment when John—much as in Hebrew poetry—will reemphasize or further explain a point

22. So Jobes, *1, 2, and 3 John*, 95–96; Smalley, *1, 2, and 3 John*, 58. Yarbrough (*1–3 John*), following Schnackenburg, is closer to the mark.

23. For more concerning the Holy Spirit, see especially comments below on 1 John 4:1–13 and 5:6–8.

he has just made. We have already noted that verse 8 is grammatically strange, with John using a neuter relative pronoun where it would not normally make sense to do so. We should not be surprised if what follows it is also a bit odd. We propose to read ὅτι much like an English colon here, a further explanation of "something made real in him and in you" rather than as an explanatory "because" or "since." Woodenly, English replacements of the Greek words would sound something like this: "Yet, I am writing to you a new command, what is true in him and in you, *that* the darkness is fading away and the true light has already started shining." The problem with this reading is that it sounds in English as if "that" is referring to "a new command," such that the "new command" just is "the darkness is fading away and the true light is already shining." To our ears, it sounds as if the relative pronoun is referring to "command"—this is a feature of English syntax that Greek simply does not share. Since the relative pronoun is neuter and has no antecedent, the Greek is jarring, disruptive in a way that is difficult to capture. There is no reason—other than a certain syntactic inelegance—that ὅτι should not be read as fleshing out what it means that the uncreated divine life is real in Christ and now, increasingly, in the church.

John is very specific about the present age: it is not merely a period in which the church waits for the promised return of its Lord; it is instead a time when the reordering of the world according to God's perfection and beauty is already taking place. That is, "the darkness is fading away and the true light is already shining." The image John conjures for the present age could bring to our minds something like the predawn or the dawning of a new day. The arrival of the Son and the completion of his mission have ushered in a new historical moment. Before Jesus's arrival, it was the dead of night; the world was deprived of the proper ordering of the divine life. The incarnation, life, death, and resurrection of the Son change all that, bringing the eternal life of God into the world and inaugurating an age in which the church—united to the Father and the Son—will spread the divine light and life. It will, presumably, grow and continue growing.

One might be forgiven for noticing that if this has been taking place since John's writing, it has done so slowly and with a tremendous amount of backtracking. It would bedim the light of history to egregiously claim that the triumphant church has—always and everywhere—brought the flourishing of divine life to the world. Whatever we may want to say about the eschaton, any "realized eschatology" has come in fits and starts and reversals, three steps forward and two steps back and sometimes more. It would seem, then, that John is wrong—the dawn is not leading straightforwardly to the day.

There is, however, another way to read this image. Rather than simply chalking up John's notion of the burgeoning light to naïveté, it might be better to set this use of light and darkness in the context of John 8:12, which is itself set in the context of one of the rituals associated with the Feast of Tabernacles.[24] In John 8:12 Jesus says, "I am the light of the world. The one who follows me will not walk about in darkness but will have the light of life." The immediate context has been the Festival of Booths, or Tabernacles (John 7:2). According to the Mishnah, a part of the water-drawing ritual that took place on the evening of the first day of the festival involved the lighting of four massive golden candelabra in the Court of Women in the temple. When lit, "there was not a court in Jerusalem that was not illuminated by the lights of the water-drawing" (m. Sukkah 5:2). Rather than the dawning of a new day, it might be better to know the church as the reinstantiation of Christ-as-Temple.

Jesus's claim to be the light of the world in the midst of Tabernacles is a symbolically concomitant claim to fulfilling the theological purpose of the temple. Just as the temple literally and figuratively shone light into the world, so does Jesus as the truest enfleshment of the divine ordering of God. As we noted above in commenting on 1 John 2:1, John assumes that now the church takes up the fulfillment of the temple, with the "light of the world" indeed "made real in him and in you."

If so, then John's claim that the darkness is fading away and the true light is already shining might be fashioning an image of the church as little temples of God's light, popping up wherever the gospel goes forth and true union takes place. As with the Jerusalem temple, however, these oases of light may be extinguished. Division in the church or among churches, mutual hatred, denial of the truth about the Son, rampant corruption from sin—these real events have caused, and continue to cause, the light of the church to flicker and even go out. The implication is clear: just as Jesus came as the light of the world, so now the church has been so commissioned; this is a task that cannot be taken lightly.

In verses 9–11 John spells out a defining feature of what it is for the darkness to be receding and for the true light to be already shining: mutual love in the divine family. Verse 9 features John's first of five uses of μισέω (*miseō*, "hate"; also in 2:11; 3:13, 15; 4:20). It would be tempting to read "hate" here as "dismiss[ing] as silly, wrong, or dangerous," thus giving the word a "softer yet insidious sense."[25] On such a reading, one Christian "hates" another by rejecting another's ideas and perhaps ignoring that one. The advantage to such a reading is that it seems to have more relevance for current contexts, for surely few hearers of John's words will immediately indict themselves as "haters"!

Such a reading does not take into account that John is explicitly talking about the Christian family. He speaks of one's "brother or sister" as opposed to one's

24. Thompson, *John*, 183.
25. Yarbrough, *1–3 John*, 104.

neighbor or a stranger. But the family is the locus of one's most visceral emotions—the love and hate one feels for family easily rivals and often exceeds the sort of jingoistic hate a soldier might feel toward his enemy. In the former case, family members know each other intimately; the hurts and harms they receive and inflict are not faceless, nor are they assigned to an unknown other as in the latter. Idealizing family life by softening John's notion of "hate" risks ignoring the abundance of biblical narratives that feature the rejection, alienation, and often violence between close family members. Cain murders Abel, Jacob defrauds Esau, Absalom rebels against David, relations between Judah and Tamar are fraught and incestuous, and Joseph's brothers first conspire to murder him and then relent and sell him into slavery. It would be an egregious handling of the evidence to suggest that the Bible takes a rosy view of familial relations.

So it is that John's use of "hate" is quite serious and quite literal. The world is said to "hate" Jesus in the Fourth Gospel (John 3:20; 7:7; 15:18–25). The world is not "dismissive" of Jesus, considering him "silly"; the world tortures him to death because of the threat he poses. The world possesses deep animus against Jesus because he exposes it as evil (John 3:20; 7:7), and such an affront simply cannot be tolerated.

We may not wish to think that members of the Christian family do in fact hate each other, but this is what John says, and a modicum of reflective introspection demonstrates that he is quite right. Verse 10 tells us that mutual love is a feature of one who "continues to live in the light and does not lure them away" (ἐν τῷ φωτὶ μένει, καὶ σκάνδαλον ἐν αὐτῷ οὐκ ἔστιν, *en tō phōti menei, kai skandalon en autō ouk estin*). As noted above, a wooden translation might read the second clause as "and in him is no cause for stumbling." The dative pronoun could be neuter and refer to the light ("and in the light there is no cause for stumbling"), but the force of John's teaching here focuses on the dangers of brothers and sisters living in darkness and succumbing to hate.

It is worth noting that the New Testament writers often use σκάνδαλον (*skandalon*, "stumbling block") in this way: to refer to one party luring or enticing another. Within the Johannine corpus, we might note the use of σκάνδαλον when the author of Revelation cautions the church of Pergamum in Revelation 2:12–16. In verse 14 (NRSV), the author warns, "But I have a few things against you: you have some there who hold to the teaching of Balaam, who taught Balak to put a stumbling block [σκάνδαλον] before the people of Israel, so that they would eat food sacrificed to idols and practice fornication." This verse references Numbers 25:1, where the Israelites begin to engage sexually with Moabite women; we learn in 31:16 that Balak accomplished this treachery according to Baalam's schemes.[26]

26. See the discussion of Revelation 2:14 in Robert H. Mounce, *The Book of Revelation*, rev. ed., NICNT (Grand Rapids: Eerdmans, 1998), 80–81. See the rabbinic discussion in the

If John has something like this in mind, the picture becomes a bit clearer. Christians living in the dark first seek to lure those who remain in the light to join them. Once rebuffed, these darkened family members begin hating those who will not join them in once again living according to the world's reckoning. Simply by retaining fidelity to seeing and ordering according to God's design, the children of light sow the seeds that will blossom into hate in the children of the dark. And as mentioned above, this sequence repeats a pattern enacted by blood-family members in the Old Testament: Cain, jealous of Abel, kindles hate in his heart. Simply because Christians have been given an entrée into the reordering of the cosmos according to the divine light does not mean that they will consistently choose to live in it. And when they do not, they risk being overcome by a particularly vicious kind of hate, one directed against those they once considered closer than blood relatives.

What these considerations suggest is that the church's first and most powerful apologetic to a hateful world is Christian union in love, or in the parlance of our day, ecumenism. The natural state of human families is one of division and hate; precisely because this is a real temptation for the church, it can only be in the power derived from the divine life that real individuals and communities, with real, substantive differences, might live in mutual, self-giving union. Such graciousness itself testifies to the reality of the one seen, heard, and touched by John and his associates. But John understands—and he will be explicit below in verses 19–25—that such union can take place only within an orthodox confession about Jesus. This is the key to the light, and it is what separates the light from the darkness. God's right ordering of the world cannot be seen rightly apart from the incarnate manifestation of that ordering, which is Jesus.

1 John 2:12–14

12 I write to you, little ones, because your sins are forgiven through Jesus's name.
13 I write to you, parents, because you have come to know the one who has existed
from the beginning. I write to you, young adults, because you have defeated the evil
one. 14 Let me say it again: I write to you children, because you have come to know
the Father. I write to you, parents, because you have come to know the one who has
existed from the beginning. I write to you, young adults, because you are powerful
and the word of God remains in you and you have defeated the evil one.

Talmud (b. Sanh. 106a), where Balaam devises the plan with Balak to lure Israelite men into prostitution and idolatry with their Moabite neighbors. After selling linens at a low price, the Moabite prostitute plies the Israelite man with wine and "[brings] forth an idol from her bosom," entreating him to worship and deny Torah.

It is helpful to think of John's sermon as being composed of little vignettes that demand a response. Notice that he often begins with a direct address (e.g., "my little children" in 2:1, "dear friends" in 2:7), gives instruction or direct comments, and then generalizes or abstracts, creating rhetorical space for hearers to self-identify within the world of the sermon.[27] So, for example, in 2:7 he addresses all hearers as "dear friends" and subsequently explains the oldness and newness of the commands he passes on and the way that the newness of the command is instantiated in the community. Then he generalizes, speaking now not directly to the congregation but to "the one" who claims to be in the light. This style alternates between telling the cosmic truth about the hearers and the current state of affairs and then offering a chance for reflection, one that demands a response.[28]

1 John 2:12–14 has been the locus of considerable scholarly argument because it is difficult to know who the "children," "young adults," and "parents" are. Our translation obscures the issue by introducing gender-inclusive nouns, but this is, of course, John's point. His vocatives *always refer to the entire family of God.*[29] They function, in fact, to push every listener to define himself or herself with respect to it. Am I a child in this family? A young adult? A parent? Am I a part of this family at all? The sermon forces these questions on every hearer. Moreover, John is concerned with his hearers' spiritual condition vis-à-vis union with him and with the divine, eternal life that has been revealed in the Son of the Father. Is this family in union? Am I advancing or retarding the union that God has ordained and desires? In what way or ways? These are the responses John's rhetoric elicits. A good reading of the text therefore identifies "young adults" and "parents" as spiritual categories rather than a comment on the actual ages or biological sexes

27. The best "structure" for the sermon involves using John's vocatives as boundary or section markers. Kruse's analysis (*Letters of John*, 32) "does not seek to trace any developing argument through the letter because there isn't one," which is the right move. Instead, John's "vignettes," as we are calling them, are marked off by the use of the vocative and end after a generalizing statement that functions as a speech act, encouraging hearers to self-identify either as a faithful, orthodox member of the family or as an outsider, schismatic, and so forth.

28. As discussed in the introduction, 1 John's rhetoric is—according to classical schema—epideictic, meaning that it is concerned primarily with confirming and strengthening values and attitudes already held by hearers. John is exhorting believers to "keep the faith," as it were. See the extended argument in Watson, "Amplification Techniques in 1 John." Moreover, there has been considerable debate over how to translate the six occurrences of ὅτι (*hoti*, "that," "because," "since") in this section. Here we have used "because" rather than "that" because we are reading 1 John as rhetoric inviting self-reflection. John had to write because this group of people have done *x*. This approach causes all hearers to decide whether they should be included in the group.

29. Thus this reading is closest to those favored by C. H. Dodd (*Johannine Epistles* [New York: Harper & Brothers, 1946], 37–39) and Marshall (*Epistles*, 138), though for different reasons.

of hearers.[30] All hearers are (or are potentially) "children"; John consistently uses this semantic field to identify believers (τέκνον [*teknon*, "child"] in 3:1, 2, 10; 5:2; τεκνίον [*teknion*, "little child"] in 2:1, 12, 28; 3:7, 18; 4:4; 5:21; παιδίον [*paidion*, "infant," "child"] in 2:14, 18). What is novel here is his use of "fathers" or "parents" (πατέρες, *pateres*) and "young men" or "young adults" (νεανίσκοι, *neaniskoi*).[31]

Reading in this manner frees us up to recognize the theological import of this section. We should note first that John is emphatic. Where our translation uses the gloss "Let me say it again," the Greek switches verb tenses. John uses the present tense in verses 12 and 13 ("I am writing to you") and then deploys the aorist in verse 14 ("I wrote to you").[32] This is, as Yarbrough memorably puts it, "the literary equivalent of hitting a mule between the eyes with a two-by-four."[33] We have left the translation in the present tense to smooth the English, but this choice has the disadvantage of blunting John's emphasis. The language is memorable precisely because the three themes John brings up are memorable.[34] First, all the children of God have been forgiven of sin in the name of Jesus and have come to know the true nature of their true Father (vv. 12, 14). The family has been made right before God in and through the actions of Jesus the Messiah. Moreover, by recognizing the incarnation as the ultimate manifestation of God's eternal life in the cosmos, all children of God have come to know the nature of

30. Commentaries that lean heavily on historical reconstruction of the "Johannine Community" (e.g., Brown) tend to fall into this trap, assuming that John is referring to, say, offices in the church. The problem is that there is just no evidence to confirm or disconfirm such readings.

31. At this juncture, few will disagree that, however translated, πατέρες (*pateres*, "fathers") and νεανίσκοι (*neaniskoi*, "young men") refer at least metaphorically to both men and women. In defense of the gender-inclusive translation, it is worth noting that the LXX does use νεανίσκοι inclusively (contra Jobes, *1, 2, and 3 John*, 104) in, for example, Exodus 10:9, where σὺν τοῖς νεανίσκοις καὶ πρεσβυτέροις (*syn tois neaniskois kai presbyterois*, "with our young and old") contrasts the "young people" and the "old." Presumably, Moses is not commanding only young and older men to participate in the feast. Given that he follows this by specifically addressing "sons and daughters" (υἱοῖς καὶ θυγατράσιν, *huiois kai thygatrasin*), we can be quite certain that both young men and young women are included in σὺν τοῖς νεανίσκοις (see also Josh 6:21 for a similar usage).

32. For an extensive treatment of the form and structure, as well as alternate explanations of the tense change, see Smalley, *1, 2, and 3 John*, 76–79. None of the explanations is terribly convincing (see C. F. D. Moule, *An Idiom-Book of New Testament Greek*, 2nd ed. [Cambridge: Cambridge University Press, 1994], 12), and one is tempted to simply note that what is important is the repetition of the content of what John has been writing.

33. Yarbrough, *1–3 John*, 116.

34. Brown rightly references the last vignette in which John reminds us that his commandment is old and new: "The alternation is a stylistic stratagem to give emphasis that what he is saying is nothing new" (*Epistles*, 317).

the Father. The Father is obscenely gracious. His love is as outrageous as it is extensive. The invitation to live the very life of this God is nigh incomprehensible. What is available and present to all children of God issues in two requirements that John applies to spiritual "young adults" and "parents." As we will see below, John more or less sums up the nature of a Christian's complete union as what the tradition has come to call orthodoxy ("come to know the one who has existed from the beginning") and orthopraxy ("defeated the evil one").

Following his teaching on all the children of God, John next addresses spiritual parents, those who "have come to know the one who has existed from the beginning." As before, John's use of ἀπ' ἀρχῆς (*ap' archēs*, "from the beginning") alerts hearers to the eternal existence of the Son. Indeed, this is what makes spiritual adults, adults: they have "come to know" (ἐγνώκατε, *egnōkate*, perfect active of γινώσκω, *ginōskō*) the nature and character of the one God, who is known as Father and revealed in human life as the Son. Truly, this is the kind of comprehension available only to those who have plumbed the theological depths, scoured the Scriptures, and found the person of Jesus to share the same life and existence as the one known to Israel from time immemorial as YHWH.

Such spiritual adults are not swayed by incipient Marcionism (the heretical belief that the God of the Old Testament is not the same as the Father of Jesus Christ in the New), for Jesus shares from eternity the life of the Father. Nor do they lapse into insouciant docetism (the heretical belief that Christ only appeared to be an actual human being) because they remember that Jesus came in the flesh (1 John 4:2). The one they have come to know is not new or secret; indeed, this one's interactions with humanity in general and Israel in particular have been chronicled in the Hebrew Scriptures, and his character—forged in uncompromising, committed love (חסד, *ḥesed*)—has been praised at the temple, and so they will not succumb to seductive gnostic intimations. Spiritual parents guard the church's orthodoxy. They have received and protected the testimony and teaching of John and his associates who knew Jesus in the flesh.

It is worth emphasizing, however, that John uses a term that indicates knowledge that comes from experience. He does not call these people "teachers" or "disciples." Rather, they are "parents," meaning that their authority derives from having raised children, having worked through the challenges and vicissitudes of navigating faith and truth in the midst of various heterodoxies. The unseen world and the nature of the divine are particularly attractive targets for those who would speculate wildly and thereby gain power in a following. Parents are those who have endured such rebellions and weathered them and remained stable.

After the parents, John highlights the church's young adults. Wars are primarily fought by the young. In some ways this is a sad truth because it is the young who are less likely to understand life's fragility, who are more likely to dream of glory and slurp up the romantic tales of battle told by those who have never suffered it. Yet the young are also hot, bold, and strong—or as John has it, "powerful," maybe even "violent" (ἰσχυρός, *ischyros*). Surprisingly, even the fact that the "word of God remains" in them might have martial overtones. Consider Revelation 19:11–21, where the warring, conquering Christ is wearing a "robe dyed in blood, and his name is called 'the Word of God'" as he executes the wrath of God.

Like it or not, the church is at war with the darkness and its minions. John hails the spiritual young adults who have "defeated the evil one." The language of defeating or overcoming is common in the Johannine literature, used once in the Gospel, five times in 1 John, and fifteen times in Revelation. In the vast majority of uses, either spiritual forces (as here) or those caught up in darkness deceive, tempt, or harass and even kill (see Rev 2:10) the children of God. Against these powers the church needs soldiers whose jealousy for the light and the life of God and passion for holiness lead them into direct conflict and, ultimately, victory. Of course biological age is not really a factor here; a spiritual young adult simply possesses the will and ability to stick to the truth, avoid catastrophic moral failure, and endure persecution.

1 John 2:15–17

15 Do not love the world or the things in the world. If someone loves the world,
love for the Father is not in that person. 16 Because everything in the world –
the things the body craves, the things eyes long to see, and our overconfidence
in what we have – has its origin not in the Father but in the world. 17 Look, the
world is fading away and its cravings with it, but the one who practices God's will
is living forever.

Having established the church as children of God who have been forgiven, and then having encouraged the spiritual adults and young adults who guard orthodoxy (true, apostolic faith) and commit to orthopraxy (true Christian action), John generalizes his teaching to give hearers an opportunity to self-identify and respond. In verses 12–14 John addresses his readers as those who have already identified as spiritual adults (i.e., those committed to orthodox faith) and spiritual young adults (i.e., those whose right practice has resisted and defeated the wiles of the enemy). In order to maintain this posture, however, the children of God must be on guard.

Interestingly, John chooses to focus on threats not to orthodoxy but to orthopraxy: in this section he highlights three common categories of enticements that can lead Christians astray, and we will attend to each in turn. The switch from the indicative in verses 12–14 to the imperative in 15–17, however, should alert us to an important implication, namely, that the most important threat to orthodoxy is the failure to maintain orthopraxy. John begins, "Do not love the world." Note that this wording sounds a critical Johannine theme: believers do not have their origins in the cosmos; they are rooted in union with the Godhead. Moreover, the call is not to escape the world but to live in it without loving it "or the things in the world." The key language in verse 15 is, "If someone loves the world, love for the Father is not in that person." John consistently teaches that a right understanding of the Father—to say nothing of one's love for him—depends on a right understanding of the Son (e.g., 1 John 2:22–24). By implication, then, love for the world disrupts or distorts one's understanding and/or love for the Son and therefore one's understanding and/or love for the Father. The corollary should not be surprising. After all, John has spent considerable time reminding us that the light and the dark are incompatible. Those who know the Fourth Gospel will remember that Jesus, the true light, came into the world, but the world did not recognize him (John 1:9–10). John's suggestion is striking: right belief follows from right practice, not vice-versa. Where Christians are not living in the light, they will not be able to know the light because the darkness will have blinded their eyes. And indeed, this is precisely what we saw above in 1 John 2:10–11.

St. Anselm of Canterbury famously wrote, "The one who believes does not seek to understand in order to believe, but believes in order to understand: indeed, unless one has already believed, one will not understand." (*Homo fidelis non quaerit intelligere ut credat; sed credit, ut intelligat: quia, nisi crediderit, non intelliget.*)[35] So begins Anselm's ontological proof for the existence of God. The mechanics of the argument have been the subject of endless debate; what is interesting for us is what Anselm subsequently recommends if one is to know God. Consider:

> Come now, insignificant man, fly for a moment from your affairs, escape for a little while from the tumult of your thoughts. Put aside now your weighty cares and leave your wearisome toils. Abandon yourself for a little to God and rest for a little in Him. Enter into the inner chamber of your soul, shut out everything save God and what can be of help in your quest for Him and having locked the door seek Him out [Matt 6:6]. Speak now, my whole heart, speak now to God: "I seek Your countenance, O Lord, Your countenance I seek" [Ps 26:8 Vulg./27:8 Eng.].[36]

35. Anselm, *Proslogion*, 1.1.

36. Anselm, *Proslogion*, in Brian Davies, ed., *Anselm: The Major Works*, trans. M. J. Charlesworth (Clarendon: Oxford University Press, 1998), 84.

Perhaps taking a cue from Augustine's *Confessions*, Anselm begins the task of knowing God by entreating the reader (and, by implication, himself) not to carefully reason but to *pray*, going so far as to allude to Jesus's teaching about righteous prayer in the Gospel of Matthew and using the language of the psalmist to begin. Notice too the assumptions Anselm makes about prayer: the place of prayer is quiet, away from distractions and enticements; it is a focused, meditative labor. This is hardly the kind of environment in which one might be distracted by—returning again to John's sermon—"the things the body craves, the things eyes long to see, and our overconfidence in what we have." Whatever the philosophers may say about the quality of Anselm's argumentation, we must insist that any personal assessment qualitatively fails if it does not first reckon with Anselm's presupposition that knowledge of God is predicated on a regular practice of right action. Anselm just assumes that no one will succeed in understanding the infinite without first entering into silence, Christian prayer, and Scripture.

Likewise, the unstated assumption that John draws in this text is that one's spiritual adulthood is predicated first on one's prior spiritual young adulthood. Without first defeating the wiles of the enemy, one cannot grow into the adult who has come to know the one who has existed from the beginning. Verses 15–17 address first things—holy living liberated from the fetters brought on by addiction to one's various bodily appetites.

This is, of course, quite backward from a post-Enlightenment perspective where we assume, in general, that right action follows right belief. In most Protestant and certainly most evangelical traditions, "evangelism" is an attempt to convince someone to believe a certain thing or things. But John's (and Anselm's) logic would see this approach as putting the cart before the horse. First, pray in and with the Scriptures. Then, under the work of the Spirit through divine providence, you might begin to know God.

John interweaves all this teaching with "love." If you love the world, you cannot love the Father. We will treat love with greater depth in chapter 4 below, but here it is worth at least mentioning that for John, love is where action and knowledge unite in the divine, eternal life that has been enfleshed in the Son and is now available to all who believe.

Some would try to make a conundrum out of John's use of the word "world" (κόσμος, *kosmos*).[37] It is frequently noted that in some cases "the world" seems to be a good thing that God is interested in saving (1 John 2:2; 4:9, 14, 17), but in the majority of the twenty-three appearances of this word in 1 John, "world"

37. So, for example, the extensive treatment of the Johannine use of the term in Brown, *Epistles* (222–24).

is the domain of the enemy's power (besides the six occurrences in 2:15–17, see esp. 5:19). It is probably best to judge that 1 John holds both to be true, since this is what the text clearly states.[38]

In verse 16 John cautions that πᾶν τὸ ἐν τῷ κόσμῳ (*pan to en tō kosmō*, "everything in the world") . . . οὐκ ἔστιν ἐκ τοῦ πατρὸς ἀλλ' ἐκ τοῦ κόσμου ἐστίν (*ouk estin ek tou patros all' ek tou kosmou estin*, "has its origin not in the Father but in the world"). We have glossed the latter phrase as "has its origin not in the Father . . ." because Johannine "of" language ("is not of the Father but is of the world") consistently denotes the root or the source of the thing in question.[39] This wording is close to tautology, since presumably everything in the world must have its origin in, well, the world, but this is not quite the case. The Fourth Gospel suggests that everything that came into being (i.e., "the cosmos") did so through the Word, the eternal Second Person of the Trinity, and did so at the command of the Father (John 1:1–4).[40] But there is one element that comes into the world that is neither the uncreated Word nor something created through him: the divine, eternal life. Eternal life is not coterminous with either the Father or the Son; it is, however, an aspect of the divine substance shared between them. As the Gospel of John's prologue makes clear, the divine life is "in him" and comes to be shared with the created order. It is perhaps the spiritual analogue to the energy that animates physical life. This is important for our purposes because it helps to explain John's meaning when he says that "everything in the world . . .

38. Admittedly the stakes are raised for those interpreting the Fourth Gospel, where there appears to be much more overlap (e.g., John 8:12 juxtaposed with 8:23). But, happily, we are not.

39. So, for example, John 15:19, where Jesus is explicit about this relationship.

40. John 1:3–4 is difficult to translate because it is hard to judge where one sentence ends and the next begins. The CEB follows the example of the ancient commentators, reading, "3 Everything came into being through the Word, and without the Word nothing came into being. What came into being 4 through the Word was life, and the life was the light for all people." The NIV follows the tradition of the Vulgate and early English translations, beginning the second sentence with "in him": "3 Through him all things were made; without him nothing was made that has been made. 4 In him was life, and that life was the light of all mankind." Ancient commentators' facility with Greek indicates that the NRSV is probably a more natural reading to classical readers, but the Gospel of John frequently begins sentences with "in" (e.g., 1:10; 7:37), so however stilted it might have sounded to ancient readers, the author has no compunctions about writing in that manner. As Michaels points out in his extended treatment (*The Gospel of John*), the issue is ultimately theological: was the "life" of verse 4 created or not? Thinking canonically, perhaps 1 John 1:1–4 can help here. At the beginning of 1 John the text makes it clear in verse 2 that what is "from the beginning" is the eternal, divine, *uncreated* life of the Trinity ("2 This life was made visible and we saw and witnessed it and now announce to you the *eternal* life that was with the Father and has been revealed to us"). Since the Gospel's prologue goes on to indicate that the life that is "in him" is in fact eternal life (as opposed to, say, the life that animates physical beings), Johannine theology favors the latter reading rather than the former.

has its origin not in the Father but in the world." By this, John indicates not that God did not create through the Son but that when the things in the world are deprived of connection to the eternal, divine life, they become unrooted from their proper origins. John's statement here is not tautology; it is a pronouncement on the corruption that takes place when the disordering effects of sin sever the created order from divine life: what is in the world *but* of the Father becomes in the world *and* of the world.

Our translation of verse 16 admittedly lacks the poetry of the classic English "lust of the flesh, lust of the eyes, and the pride of life" (NKJV), but it does so for good reason. In the context of the larger thought unit, John is concerned about those who have overcome or would overcome the enticements and deceits of the evil one. This overcoming matters because, as we have just argued, orthopraxy is the first and best guard of orthodoxy. So in this section his teaching is generalized: If you would be a spiritual young adult, one who defeats the evil one, be on the lookout for these things! And what he mentions are the things that are good but can ensnare when they are not properly animated by eternal life. This bears repeating. The world is not inherently evil; it is subjugated. The things in it currently fail to have their origins with the Father, but they can regain origination with the Father when appropriated in the context of shared divine, eternal life. The goal of the enemy, therefore, is quite simple: tempt or deceive Christians to approach the world as captives to it rather than the bearers of the light who see it and interact with it properly.

We therefore render ἡ ἐπιθυμία τῆς σαρκός (*hē epithymia tēs sarkos*) as "the things the body craves" to draw out the potential for good, bodily things—such as food, drink, shelter, sex, also music and poetry and art—to reassert mastery over those who might otherwise walk freely in the light. The key word is "crave" or "craving." It is quite likely that every human being has experienced something far beyond the good, natural delight afforded by the prospect of satisfying this or that appetite. But consider: if a person becomes addicted or ruled by an appetite, the next step is to find a way to justify that addiction as a part of one's being in the light. We know that this downfall has happened because in the first chapter John specifically mentioned people mired in sin who claim to be freed from it (1 John 1:6–10). In that section John seems to recognize how common sin is and suggests an alternative to justifying one's behavior or brazenly claiming it to be good: confess it.

Likewise, "the things eyes long to see" (ἡ ἐπιθυμία τῶν ὀφθαλμῶν, *hē epithymia tōn ophthalmōn*) captures the same notion of craving. Again, John probably does not have in mind feasting the eyes on something inherently corrupt so much as letting one's desire for novelty run amok. It is true that the Scriptures consistently portray the sin that besets the eyes as being connected to illicit sexual activity. Proverbs 6:25 LXX even uses a similar construction with ἐπιθυμία (*epithymia*, "lust," "craving") and a genitive as well as a form of νικάω (*nikaō*, "conquer," "defeat"): "Neither let craving for beauty defeat you, nor be trapped by your eyes; and don't be caught by her eyelashes." But it would be too narrow to restrict John's language here to referring to the male gaze, since there are other concerns that the eyes can bring. Proverbs 17:24 LXX contrasts the eyes of the fool with the face of a wise person: the fool's eyes "[look] to the ends of the earth," while the wise one's face exudes "good sense." This is a more expansive view of the danger of unharnessed eyes: they are constantly looking for the next thing. In the case of sexual lust, they are never satisfied with this image or that body; in the case of fashion, it is the next lineup or newest designer; in the case of books, it is the next de rigueur idea. It is not hard to see how this heteropraxy (illicit practice) can quickly lead to heterodoxy (heretical belief), since the search for novelty is itself antithetical to the preservation of stable, historic faith. One's beliefs simply must accommodate this or that fresh wind of couture; failing to do so might leave one behind the times.

We have rendered ἡ ἀλαζονεία τοῦ βίου (*hē alazoneia tou biou*) as "overconfidence in what we have," thereby explicitly thinking about τοῦ βίου (*tou biou*, "of life") as referring to materiality, goods, stuff, and ἡ ἀλαζονεία (*hē alazoneia*, "arrogance") as boastfulness or swagger or overconfidence. Since the latter term is used almost exclusively in the apocryphal literature to connote boasting (e.g., Wis 5:8; 17:7; 2 Macc 15:6; 4 Macc 1:26; 2:15), the translation seeks to make sense of what it would be to have "the boasting of life." Given John's relentless focus on the material world divorced from the divine life, it follows thematically to render τοῦ βίου as "stuff we have" or "subsistence goods," as in Mark 12:44. And again, it is not hard to see how arrogance springing from abundance can push the mind and heart to heterodoxy. Like the cravings of the body and the desire for novelty, the process is insidious—and quite likely beneath the notice of the one so caught up—but the subtle shift of one's faith in God for provision, joy, and so on to what one has heaped up in this realm leads to an unnecessary dualism between the spiritual and the physical. God, Christ, church: these realities animate piety in the spiritual realm but have little to do with money, provisions, or status, for which we alone are responsible.

Such a dualism has been hardened in the wake of modern philosophy, but it shows signs of cracking up as theology presses toward a holistic approach that, interestingly, is quite comfortable with the importance of being embodied, physical human beings rather than immaterial souls. That is, as we increasingly recognize that the spiritual is always instantiated in physical systems, persons, and networks, it becomes increasingly incoherent to hold the physical and the spiritual apart. As we will see below, John consistently collapses the practical distinctions between the spiritual realm and physical, relational manifestations of it, while holding them conceptually distinct. This is good practice we would do well to emulate. We can speak of the demonic while always locating its power and influence in specific people, communities, corporations, and governments. John's basic point must not be missed: overconfidence in what we have is not just a sin; it is a slippery slope that ends in heresy.

If we think of "the world" as an enemy territory whose defining characteristic is disconnection from the eternal life of the Godhead, the condition of its "fading away" is clearly not that it is disappearing or ending. Rather, it is in the process of being redeemed. Where it has been bathed in darkness, the light of eternal life is dawning.

John's rhetorical move here is simple: he asks, "Are you caught up in heteropraxy?" If so, heterodoxy is not far behind, and you are not a part of the light. If, however, you are someone who makes a practice of doing the will of God, you are already living in the next age, enjoying the life of the light and eschewing the darkness. We have translated μένει εἰς τὸν αἰῶνα (*menei eis ton aiōna*) as "is living forever," though that translation obscures the use of the prepositional phrase. John pictures us as living at the intersection of two ages: that of the rule of darkness and that of the rule of light. To revert to the martial metaphor, the evil empire still holds sway, but the light has begun its invasion and is rapidly taking ground. Those who live according to God's way will continue living exactly as they are living as the first age bleeds into the second, or as the empire of darkness is swallowed up by the liberating rule of the light. These doers of God's will—not distracted by what the body craves, what the eyes long to see, or overconfidence in possessions—will experience no change; the eternal life they are already living is the life that the whole cosmos will know once everything has been fully and finally redeemed.

1 John 2:18–23

18 Children, it is the last hour! And as you have heard, Antichrist is coming, and so
many antichrists have already come. This is how we know it is the last hour. 19 They
departed from us, but they were not rooted in us. For if they had been rooted in us,
they would have stayed with us. But by leaving they made it obvious that not one
of them is really ours. 20 But you possess an anointing from the Holy Spirit, and you
all are in the know. 21 I'm not writing to you because you don't know the truth, but
because you do know it, and because you know that no lie is rooted in the truth.
22 Who lies if not the one who denies that Jesus is the Messiah? This person is the
Antichrist, the one who denies the Father and the Son. 23 No one who denies the
Son has the Father; everyone who confesses the Son has the Father too.

John has consistently marked the present as an inflection point in between times. The sermon must go out so that many can join in fellowship with the Father, the Son, and the church (1:3–4); the expectation of God for humanity is unchanged but also newly instantiated in the coming of the Son and the gathering of the church (2:7–8); the darkness is fading away, and the true light of eternal life is shining (2:8); spiritual adults have come to know the Father, and spiritual young adults have successfully defeated demonic forces (2:12–14); ultimately, the old world order is coming to an end, and eternal life is usurping its reign (2:17). In this context, John's claim that it is "the last hour" is a proclamation that the ages are turning, that our "now" is the eleventh hour of the regime of darkness, so to speak, and that the first moments of the regime of light are already at hand. Furthermore, life in the regime of light is "eternal life," or "living forever," or "union with the divine life." Theology tends to speak of this coming age as the eschaton, the end of days. This wording is appropriate because this is not just the last hour of one regime and the beginning of another, as in the succession of kings or presidents. Instead, this final hour marks the end of the cruel and inexorable tyranny of time entirely.[41]

Biblical and apocalyptic language resembling "the last hour" that John uses here is abundant. Although this particular phrase appears nowhere else in the Bible, it overlaps semantically with the words of Jesus in the Synoptic Gospels (e.g., Mark 13:7, 32–33), Peter's evangelism in Acts 2 (2:17; see also 2 Tim 3:1; Jas 5:3), and the apocalyptic-sounding exhortations in Jude and the Petrine letters (Jude 18; 2 Pet 3:3). It is impossible to divine the precise nature of eschatological expectation in these texts. Modern scholarship tends to assume that early Christians were waiting on a parousia that was believed to be imminent.[42] This assumption about early Christian expectation may or may not be the case, but it is somewhat beside the point, at least as John sees it.

The problem with the turning of the ages is, again, a martial concern, for when a dying empire is gasping its last, it is at its most dangerous. John reminds his hearers that they have heard that Antichrist is coming—and this is indeed so. The identity of "Antichrist" will likely always remain mysterious; it may be that Paul, in 2 Thessalonians 2:3, refers to the same person or being when he speaks of "the lawless one" (ὁ ἄνθρωπος τῆς ἀνομίας, *ho anthrōpos tēs anomias*). It could also be that this figure is to be identified with the beast of Revelation 13:1 and 19:19. But John is quick to point out that whether Antichrist comes tomorrow or the next day or the next, Christians are better off dealing with the problem at hand, which is that "many antichrists have already come." The use of the perfect

41. In the second part of this book, see "Time in 1–3 John."

42. For example, Brown, *Epistles*, 330–38.

tense of γίνομαι (*ginomai*, "become," "be") indicates that these antichrists have arrived and were probably identified as being what they are. Because the regime of darkness has now been dealt a decisive blow, its minions are attacking in force. Even if the last, final, ultimate Antichrist has not yet been revealed, plenty of antichrists have been sent to wreak havoc in the church.

We should make neither too much nor too little of the appellation "Antichrist." To say too much would be to try to pinpoint a person in history or current events or future history such as Caesar Nero or a contemporary politico or a mysterious future bringer of blasphemy. If John had wished to make such a person's identity clear, he would have. To say too little would be to ignore the etymology of the designation entirely: "anti-Christ"—the one or ones vehemently opposed to the church's risen Lord. The church has real enemies that are not likely to be won over by love; in point of fact, these enemies seek to infiltrate the church and devour it from within. When John notes that "this is how we know it is the last hour," he refers to the nature of enemy action. In addition to overt hostilities, here in the eleventh hour, the forces of darkness are launching insidious attacks—enemy agents are already in our midst.

Our translation glosses John's genitives "out of us" or "from us" (ἐξ ἡμῶν, *ex hēmōn*) with "rooted in us" to capture again the Johannine sense of origins. The true church has its origin or source or rootedness in God and the divine life. There are many antichrists, who initially appear to possess the same origins, to be a part of the same family, but this appearance is shown to be a farce because such enemy agents always end up leaving. As John notes, any who are really rooted in the divine life will not want or need to leave it: we have glossed ἀλλ' ἵνα φανερωθῶσιν ὅτι οὐκ εἰσὶν πάντες ἐξ ἡμῶν (*all' hina phanerōthōsin hoti ouk eisin pantes ex hēmōn*) as "But by leaving they made it obvious that not one of them is really ours," thereby supplying the implied verb "leaving" and rendering the passive third-person plural of φανερόω (*phaneroō*, "reveal," "make manifest") with the more colloquial "they made it obvious."

These infiltrators never possessed the divine life; they were never rooted in it. This is, remember, enemy action, a flailing, fading empire of darkness lashing out in desperation to hold on to power in the face of the inevitable. They were never rooted in union with John and his associates. They were wolves in sheep's clothing the whole time. If we are to compare them to anyone, perhaps they mimic the character of Mr. Wickham from *Pride and Prejudice*. They appear winsome and committed, but this persona camouflages selfish ambition and a desire to drag down and destroy the good and the beautiful.

We should not miss the logical connection between staying with John and the church and confessing the truth. In verse 20 John reminds the readers that they are the fulfillment of temple worship and co-priests with Christ: they have a special anointing and, as a result, are "in the know" (οἴδατε πάντες, *oidate pantes*). Many surviving manuscripts read "you know all things" (οἴδατε πάντα, *oidate panta*), which is probably an attempt to make sense of awkward Greek phrasing and to help reconcile verse 20 with verse 27, where John does indicate an anointing that "teaches you about everything." Perhaps the wording in verse 20 is an awkward way of emphasizing that everything of import has been revealed to the hearers of the sermon. But this conclusion is plainly false! Had his audience known everything, John's sermon would itself be a clumsy redundancy: his warnings unneeded, and his persuasive rhetoric preached, as it were, to the choir. Rather, it is more likely that John is reminding us that we who have been made co-priests have been ordained into a way of conceiving the world that is fundamentally at odds with the prevailing zeitgeist.[43] The very idea that there are "antichrists" is predicated on the notion that the world is in fact experiencing a turn of epochs and that the old order sees a crucified Nazarene peasant as a threat. The absurdity of this idea is likely obscured by the intervening two thousand years, during which Christians, so it is claimed, begat Christendom, and the histories have—perhaps wrongly—suggested that "Christianity" seized imperial and world power. From such a perspective, John's sense of time and place ought to be delusional; nevertheless, he claims that the ages are turning: the Holy Spirit, who has been sent by God, inducted believers into a spiritual priesthood and furnished them with access to true worship and holiness.

The term χρῖσμα (*chrisma*, "anointing") is critical to understanding the spiritual breadth of what John professes. This word is unique to 1 John in the New Testament and is also rare in the Septuagint, where it is notably used to render the Hebrew משׁח (*mšḥ*, "anointing," "consecration"; Exod 40:15) and שׁמן משׁח (*šmn mšḥ*, "oil of anointing," "consecrating oil"; Exod 29:7; 30:25; 40:9). These sections outline the Hebrew rituals for priestly ordination. The oil is applied to Aaron, and he becomes a priest, suited for priestly duties that are inaccessible and perhaps quite mysterious to the uninitiated. The teaching in Exodus indicates that these rituals and their meanings are to be held and passed down in perpetuity, thus creating a class of individuals who have special insight into the nature of God, holiness, and proper relations between God and humanity. In point of fact, this special class is privy to a special way of seeing the world, one that is sanctuary- or temple-centered and especially cognizant of how spiritual realities are manifested in material ways. The anointing encompasses both a way of living according to statutes and commands and forms of worship/liturgy and a way of seeing how the world actually is, since the latter affords meaning and

43. So Jobes, *1, 2, and 3 John*, 127.

purpose to the former. This insight is of course precisely what John claims to have has happened to those who have believed: their ministerial work is coordinated with Christ and informed by a recognition that they are the true priests, whose worship takes place at the fulcrum of history.

It is interesting that John borrows his language from the priestly ordination teachings of Exodus. In the narrative, Moses receives instructions from YHWH at Mount Sinai and relates them to the people. And this event is, narratively, taking place in a *liminal space*. Israel has been rescued from slavery in Egypt and is poised to enter the promised land, but they must journey there, and as it turns out, that journey will be extensive. God gives the people the necessary commands for right living, worship, and worldview—to borrow a postmodern term—and then makes it their responsibility to live this out *before* they actually even enter the land of promise. The anointing of Aaron takes place in between times—neither in the time of slavery nor in the time of fulfillment. It is perhaps not coincidence that John has witnessed antichrists and expects more to come. Like Israel journeying from Egypt to Canaan, beset by Amorites and Hittites (e.g., Num 21:31–35), the enemy will send antichrists to slow or derail those who have come to know union with the Father and the Son.

This, then, is the truth that John reminds us that we do, in fact, know (vv. 20–21). Then, as is his custom, he generalizes, offering hearers a chance to self-identify, to decide to confess or to continue to confess some nonnegotiable christological and trinitarian convictions (vv. 22–23). The emphasis on knowing Jesus as Messiah carves out the kind of world John's hearers live in. There are those who recognize the import of the coming of the Son, the turning of the ages, and the cosmic war that is taking place, and there are those who do not. Some have been ordained, initiated, and inducted into the fullness of the divine priesthood, and some have not. And one's understanding of who Jesus is determines which camp one occupies and the age in which one lives.

1 John 2:24–27

24 As for you, what you have heard from the beginning must remain in you. If what
you have heard from the beginning does remain in you, you will continue in union
with the Son and the Father. 25 This is the promise he promised to us: the eter-
nal life. 26 I have been writing these things to you about those who are trying to
deceive you. 27 But you, the anointing you received from him remains with you,
and you do not need anyone to teach you. Since his anointing teaches you about
everything – and the anointing is true and not fake – just as it has taught you, stay
in union with him.

This section veers from deliberative rhetoric to epideictic rhetoric. In verses 18–23 readers are warned about the state of the world and given the opportunity to respond. Do we confess Jesus as Israel's Messiah or not? Do we recognize that we are at the turn of the ages or not? In verses 24–27 John assumes that we have agreed with him and join him in confessing Jesus as Christ. The section begins with an emphatic use of ὑμεῖς (*hymeis*, "you all") to make the tonal shift explicit and features a second "you all" in the final clause. Interestingly, the neuter relative pronoun ὅ (*ho*, "who," "which") is used again here (just as in 1:1–3) to describe "what" we have heard "from the beginning." From a rhetorical perspective, the text ascribes to readers the confession of the unoriginated Word and commands them to continue or remain in that confession. Then it explains the benefit: if hearers continue acknowledging Jesus, they will remain in union with Son and Father. The Greek text does not add "union" here. It reads ὑμεῖς ἐν τῷ υἱῷ καὶ ἐν τῷ πατρὶ μενεῖτε (*hymeis en tō huiō kai en tō patri meneite*, "you will remain in the Son and the Father"). But John has already explained what it is to "remain in the Son and the Father" in 1:1–3 and repeats it here: it is divine union, the experience here and now of "the eternal life."

Verse 25 is apposite to verse 24; union with Father and Son is eternal life, or the life of the age to come. Verse 25 has "promise" as both a noun and a verb: literally, "this is the promise that he promised us," with focus on the content, not the action. This explains the abrupt accusative phrase "the life the eternal" (τὴν ζωὴν τὴν αἰώνιον, *tēn zōēn tēn aiōnion*), since John has set the hearer up to expect what that promise was. The question remains open who "he" is, and the question will remain open throughout the entire section. The Father? The Son? As before, it is better to endorse incipient "binitarianism," a sort of prototrinitarian theology that acknowledges the divinity of the Father and the Son. John is intentionally vague because the unoriginated Son shares ontological union with the Father. Finally, there is no reason to suppose that "the promise he promised to us" is relegated to an eschatological future. Instead, soteriology, the experience of divine, eternal life, is a promise fulfilled in the present for all who embrace John's Gospel.

Verse 26 begins with another instance of the first-person singular aorist of γράφω (*graphō*, "I have written"). This is a quick shift from the first-person plural in verse 25 ("us"). This is rhetoric; John is reminding his hearers that he has gone out of his way to put pen to paper, as it were, in order to emphasize the gravity of the situation. And as above, the situation is grave, so John must write "about those who are trying to deceive you." We have glossed the plural present participle of πλανάω (*planaō*) as "trying to deceive" rather than "deceiving," since the context makes it clear that the act of deception has not (so far!) worked. This is especially clear in light of the emphatic "But you" that begins verse 27.

In verses 26–27 John continues the rhetorical push: the antichrists want to derail orthodox confession of Christ, to remove all from divine union and the experience of eternal life, but simple reflection on who his hearers are and have been should be sufficient to see these deceivers for what they really are. Again, John uses the language of anointing, but in verse 27 he does so in a provocative echo of the Fourth Gospel.

In John 14:26 Jesus tells the disciples that the Holy Spirit "will teach you everything and remind you of everything I said to you." Given that it is the "anointing" that does exactly the same thing here in 2:27, it sounds as if John is associating Christian anointing with the Holy Spirit. If the church constitutes a renewed temple, the Holy Spirit acts as a seal on the renewed priesthood—that is, Christian believers—giving them a special initiation into the mysteries of God. In Exodus 40:15 such a priestly initiation is irrevocable and passes down from one generation to the next. Similarly, John sees the confession that his readers had "from the beginning" as continuing to be effective, guaranteed, as it were, by the Spirit's seal. John's logic is therefore a bit strange. On the one hand, he forces his readers to respond in either affirmation or rejection of his message. On the other hand, he assumes that they will inevitably respond affirmatively because they possess an irrevocable seal from God's Spirit. If that is really the case, then why make the persuasive case to begin with?

Perhaps an affirmative response to John's message is a kind of continuing attestation to the ongoing seal of the Spirit. Those who embrace the message of Jesus's messiahship and uncreatedness are those who have been truly anointed and have their origins in God, and those who reject that message show that they were never anointed or originated from God at all. It is a sort of litmus test for having access to divine union and the eternal life: many will claim union with God or experience of the life of the age to come, but only those who hold fast their confession about Jesus are trustworthy.

A final point. It is interesting that in John 14 Jesus calls the Holy Spirit παράκλητος (*paraklētos*, "companion," "advocate")—which we rendered "co-priest" when speaking of Jesus himself in 1 John 2:1. It should be clear that when predicated of the Holy Spirit, the Johannine corpus uses the term to mean "helper," as in, one who helps the believer know, recognize, and remember the truth (John 14:16–17; 15:26; 16:13; 1 John 2:27). When used of Jesus, the meaning shifts more toward advocacy and help with various ministrations, namely, the ongoing atonement of the believer to and with the Father.

1 John 2:28–3:3

[28] And now, little children, continue in union with him so that when he appears you
have confidence and are not ashamed in front of him at his arrival. [29] If you know
that he is righteous, you know that everyone who practices righteousness has been

born from him. 3:1 Now just look at what kind of love the Father has given to us, that
we have been called God's children – and we really are! This is why the world does
not know us: it did not know him. 2 Dear friends, right now we are God's children,
and what we will be hasn't been revealed yet. We do know that when he appears,
we will be like him, because we will see him as he really is. 3 And all who have this
hope about him purify themselves just as he is pure.

John begins this section in verse 28 just as he did the section before last, with "and now." The transition gestures to what has gone before, so we may expect to hear some of the implications of the previous section. The diminutive τεκνία (*teknia*, "little children") speaks to John's genuine affection. This tone likely explains why a few manuscripts added "my" to make the affection even more apparent. As above, our translation glosses μένετε ἐν αὐτῷ (*menete en autō*) as "continue in union with him" for previously stated reasons. John's reminder is important because Jesus is going to appear at some point. The Greek here, ἵνα ἐάν (*hina ean*, "that if," "in order that when"), indicates not uncertainty about whether Jesus will appear but rather uncertainty about when. English shares this usage of the conditional; "have my will ready *so that if* I die, everything will be in order." No one would think that I am not certain about my death, only the when and possibly the how of it.

Hearers of the sermon know that "the true light is already shining" (2:8) and that the domain of darkness has been put on notice. Now John brings up Jesus's arrival, or parousia—the expected future moment when Jesus returns and the kingdom of darkness is wholly subsumed by the God who is light and in whom there is no darkness at all (1:5). Some suggest that the referent here is the Father rather than the Son, with John imagining something like an Old Testament theophany.[44] But the Johannine literature does seem to expect a return of Jesus. John 21:22–23 gives this impression, as does Revelation 22:7. Moreover, disparate authors in the New Testament share a common understanding that Jesus is coming back and that when he does, this age (αἰών, *aiōn*) will come to an end (Matt 24:3). It is no coincidence that John so often calls divine life "eternal" life, that is, the life of the "ages" (αἰῶνες, *aiōnes*). Paul expects that the arrival will feature the resurrection of believers and the end of every authority and power of

44. For example, Brown, *Epistles*, 394–95. Brown's argument turns on—of all things—John's use of ἐκεῖνος (*ekeinos*, "that [one, man]") in verse 3:3, suggesting, "In the next verse, where Christ is meant, the author uses *ekeinos* to identify him; this pronoun is hard to explain if Christ has already been discussed in this verse." This explanation strikes me as thin gruel, given that the same tic appears in 2:6. Better instead to take the pronoun as emphatic, drawing attention to Jesus's human personhood and reckoning this section as referring to the return of Christ.

earthly origin (1 Cor 15:23–24). James counsels patient expectance, presumably because, like a farmer awaiting a crop, what has been sown in the ground does not much resemble what grows up from it (Jas 5:7–8). 2 Peter mocks those who laugh at the possibility of the arrival and expects it to coincide with an ending of this world order and possibly even the very stuff of which the present world is composed (2 Pet 3:3–10).

John's understanding of Jesus's arrival is therefore predicated on his reckoning that faith in Christ makes us God's children. The emphatic appendage καὶ ἐσμέν (*kai esmen*, "and we really are!"), the observation that "we have been called God's children," draws attention to the idea that being a "child of God" is not just a metaphor indicating some close relationship. It is much more. In fact, later in this chapter John will suggest that Christians possess God's DNA (3:9), which is appropriate, since in this section John acknowledges that they have "been born from him." The heavy reliance on familial imagery throughout the sermon should not be taken lightly, because clearly union with the divine life has consequences here and now: something of the character and nature of God has been inherited by those who have believed! Just as biological children exhibit physical characteristics, mannerisms, and behaviors of their parents, so do God's children exhibit something of the eternal life of God in the here and now. The correlation is often vague and inexact. This daughter talks like her father, has her mother's eyes, and we just do not know where her interest in biology came from. That son is the spitting image of his father at the same age, and he takes after his father's interest in sport and other forms of competition; perhaps a resemblance to his mother will blossom later. Family similarities abound and can be so pronounced that a particular clan might become synonymous with this or that characteristic.

For Christians, the family resemblance is righteousness and holiness (2:29; 3:3). In verse 29 the verb γινώσκετε (*ginōskete*, "you know" or "know!") could be either indicative or imperative. If it is imperative, John would be commanding his hearers to realize that everyone who "practices righteousness" is God-born. While grammatically possible, John has emphasized before (in 2:27) that much of the material in his sermon is already known. The close relationship between knowing Jesus's practices and the practices of his followers would probably be intuited by the community made up of Jesus's followers. Those born from Jesus practice the things that make the world right according to the ordering of light. And they want to be found doing so when he comes back so that the family reunion is a happy one. The God-born ought to be godlike when the Son comes home; otherwise they will experience shame (αἰσχύνω, *aischynō*, 2:28). Conceptually, much of what John preaches here echoes gospel parables dealing with Jesus's return, such as those in Matthew 25. Staying alert, being about the master's business—these are the hallmarks of wise virgins (vv. 1–13) and celebrated servants (vv. 14–30).

Of course, one question that 2:29 might raise is, What about those who confess Jesus as Christ but do not "practice righteousness"? The problem with this question is that it misunderstands (or has ignored) what the sermon has taught about confessing Jesus's messiahship. To confess Christ is just to recognize that the world is not what the world thinks it is. It is to be reordered according to the light, to see things differently. To come to terms with the Son as the uncreated revelation of divine life is to concomitantly de-center the order of darkness. Once you have seen the light, it will illuminate your path. It would be impossible to have the light shining and to continue walking desultorily, as though the paths had not been exposed. Thus "practicing righteousness" is probably best understood as "living life in light of the way things actually are" rather than doing *x*, *y*, or *z* or refraining from *a*, *b*, or *c*.

Using the emphatic "Now just look at," John draws special attention to the quality of God's love to make believers his children. As with union and sharing in the divine life, the notion that God would make human beings his family is as shocking as it is egregious. But the story does not end with our sharing in God's family. Whatever union we now have and whatever characteristics of God we have inherited by becoming children, these somehow pale in comparison to what we will become when the arrival happens, when "we will see him as he really is" (ὀψόμεθα αὐτόν, καθώς ἐστιν, *opsometha auton, kathōs estin*). In light of the possibility of being ashamed when he arrives, John recommends that believers purify themselves—that is, make themselves holy—in the same way that Jesus is holy. The logic seems to be this: the transformation process in which we move from being children of God to whatever we will ultimately become might be an uncomfortable or even painful one.

How can seeing something or someone transform us? The question arises because of some of John's syntactic awkwardness. Near the end of 3:2 John uses two ὅτι (*hoti*, "that," "because," "since") clauses in succession. Translating the first as "that" and the second as "because" smooths things in English but is not really an argument in its favor. The text could just as easily read, "that we will be like him, [indeed] that we will see him as he really is." Both clauses could be declarative. The judgment is ultimately theological rather than exegetical. The question is whether 1 John testifies to human transformation and on what basis that transformation comes about.

In the Greco-Roman world it was common to assume that genuine knowledge of a thing brought about conformity to it. Indeed, this is the assumption of Plato's allegory of the cave in the *Republic*. The challenge—also addressed in the cave allegory—is that of gaining genuine knowledge. John is simply adapting a common ancient belief about the transformative effect of a genuine encounter with Being to the second coming of the Lord. Moreover, John's insistence from the beginning has been that Christ is the primary actor in human transformation. The reception of the gospel in 1:1–3 has the effect of creating union with God. Jesus is the ongoing atoning sacrifice that cleans us in 2:1–2. In 2:23–25 the eternal life is promised not on account of our desire but on account of God's act. Later in this chapter believers are deemed the God-born, and it would be certainly strange to suggest that we somehow bore ourselves! The theological freight of the text as a whole pushes us to read the second clause as explanatory.

The metaphysics of the idea must necessarily elude us, but the logic is quite familiar to human experience. Bearing witness to great beauty or great ugliness has transformative impact. We are not surprised when those who witness violence and degradation on a regular basis become themselves violent and likely to degrade. Likewise, it is not uncommon for those who witness positive, good behaviors to take them on as their own. While the correlation is imperfect, there is a sense that human beings become like their surroundings—what we see is what we become. During the Sermon on the Mount in the Gospel of Matthew, Jesus teaches that "the eye is the lamp of the body" and that healthy eyes lead to an illuminated body (Matt 6:22). John imagines that this principle will apply in toto when we are confronted by the unvarnished beauty of Christ at his arrival. Seeing him "as he really is" indicates that up until that time, human eyes will not really have apprehended the full beauty and divinity of eternal life and that when they do, the sight will overwhelm and change them.

Thus, the wise move is to do all that one can to ensure that the transformation is as minimal as possible—to purify oneself inasmuch as is possible to be pure like Christ. Again, the logic is not hard to grasp. For human beings change is difficult; the greater the change we face, the more difficult is the transformation. Consider what it would be like to emigrate to a foreign country with absolutely no knowledge of the language or customs. The isolation and culture shock will be enormous. Now, consider the same move after several years of learning the language and studying the culture. The move will still be difficult—all change is—but it will be considerably less so. The rhetoric is clear: if believers wish to transition seamlessly into the next age, then they ought to think, live, and act as if that age is already upon us. And to some extent it is! Conformity to what the light has illuminated issues in present union with Father and Son and a joyful transition into the eschaton.[45]

45. See "Transformation: Soteriology and Purgatory in 1–3 John" in the Biblical Theology section for some consideration about what a painful/shameful transition might look like. See

1 John 3:4–10

4 Every person who practices sin also commits rebellion, because sin is rebellion.
5 You know that the Father incarnated him to carry sins away; also sin is not in
him. 6 No one in union with him sins; those who sin have never seen or known
him. 7 Little children, don't let anyone tell you otherwise. Everyone who practices
righteousness is righteous, in the same way that Christ is righteous. 8 Anyone who
practices sin originates from the devil, since the devil sins from the very beginning.
The Son of God was incarnated for this reason: to destroy the devil's works. 9 Those
born from God don't practice sin, because they have God's DNA in them. They can't
sin because they are God-born. 10 This is how the children of God and the children
of the devil are revealed: the one who does not practice righteousness is not from
God, including the one who does not love his brother or sister.

1 John 3:4–10 has confounded interpreters because it appears to be in contradiction with much of what John has already said in the sermon. For example, in verse 6 there is the statement that no one in union with Christ sins, and those who do sin "have never seen or known him." Doubling down, John implores his readers to ignore any statement to the contrary in the following verse. But if this is the case, then hearers certainly should be ignoring John because in verses 8 and 9 of chapter 1, he declares, "If we say, 'We have no sin,'" then we lie and are self-deceived. Unless John is hopelessly confused, it is difficult to know what to make of this conundrum.

In chapters 2 and 3 John has reminded his readers of the epoch in which they live—the transition between times, with the arrival of Jesus on the horizon. As the kingdom of darkness is steadily swallowed up in light, enemy forces have begun lashing out, with antichrists infiltrating the light, subverting it as precursors to a final or perhaps penultimate anti-Messiah (2:18). It is therefore no coincidence that John introduces the term ἀνομία (*anomia*, "lawlessness") here in the sermon. While it can be a simple term denoting something beyond or outside the law, ἀνομία was also used in apocalyptic literature to describe a sort of ultimate eschatological rebellion against God. A few examples. In the pseudepigraphic Testament of Dan, the patriarch associates the "last days" (ἐσχάταις ἡμέραις, *eschatais hēmerais*; 5:4) with the "time of rebellion" (καιρῷ ἀνομίας, *kairō anomias*; 6:6). The Testaments of the Twelve Patriarchs may have been Jewish texts altered by Christians or Christian texts with no previous Jewish versions, but the versions we have are roughly contemporaneous to 1 John. In pseudepigraphic

also Jerry Walls, *Purgatory: The Logic of Total Transformation* (Oxford: Oxford University Press, 2011), for a contemporary Protestant account of the theology of purgatory.

texts such as the Coptic Apocalypse of Elijah there are repeated references to an antichristic person called "the son of lawlessness" or "the man of lawlessness." In the Pauline corpus, 2 Thessalonians 2 introduces ὁ ἄνομος (*ho anomos*, "the rebel," "the lawless one"), presumably an antichrist or the Antichrist, since we are told that "the Lord Jesus will kill" him. In context, the author is assuring the Thessalonian church that the arrival, the "day of the Lord"; 2 Thess 2:2), will not have occurred until the Rebel has come and deceived many on Satan's behalf (2 Thess 2:8–12). In the Gospel of Matthew, Jesus associates the end of the age with "the expansion of rebellion" (24:12). It may be that John 8:34, where Jesus teaches that anyone who "sins is a slave to sin," apocalypticizes more traditional sin language. For again, it seems that everyone sins, but not all are "sin-slaves."[46]

John is speaking about the end of days, the time right before Jesus's arrival. In one way, this time is always upon Christians as they anticipate the swift return of the Lord. But just as believers may live in the light right now—though the full consummation of the light has not yet arrived—people may also participate in the rebellion, the complete and final rejection of Jesus as the unoriginated Messiah, the eternal Son of the Father. Remembering that "practicing sin" is just another way of saying "living as though the light has not come and illuminated the eternal life," John can say that there is a sense in which the antichrists of the present day are committing rebellion—the categorical rejection of the revelation of Jesus the Messiah.[47]

To put it bluntly, there is a difference between sin and apocalyptic sin, between sinning and living completely without the light. The sad fact of the matter is that there will come a day when a final decision will be made, when some—many?—will embrace rebellion and join the Rebel, come what may. And Christians can see the prefigurations of that day here and now, in the actions of antichristic forces and peoples.

Verse 4 features the now-familiar phrase ὁ ποιῶν τὴν ἁμαρτίαν (*ho poiōn tēn hamartian*, "the one who practices sin"). Critical to the exegesis of this section is the use of the present participle of ποιέω (*poieō*, "do," "make"), which suggests a continuous practice, as opposed to using an aorist or perfect of the verb ἁμαρτάνω (*hamartanō*, "sin") to indicate a single, specific action done in the past (such as in, e.g., 1 John 1:10 or 2:1). Given the apocalyptic context, we have good reason to expect that the sort of person involved in this ongoing rejection is the same sort of person amenable to the eschatological ἀνομία (*anomia*), or as we

46. So Lieu, *1, 2, and 3 John*, 129.

47. So Kruse, *Letters of John*, 128–29: "When the author of 1 John says that 'sin is lawlessness' he does not mean that sin is the violation of the Mosaic law, but rather that sin constitutes opposition to and rebellion against God, like the opposition and rebellion of Satan."

have translated it, "rebellion." Since John has already conceived the "final hour" in martial terms, it makes sense to render lawlessness as rebellion, since those who are fundamentally opposed to God's right ordering of the cosmos are, by practicing lawlessness, in a kind of doomed revolt against the light.

In verse 5 John uses the pronoun "that" (i.e., "that [man or person]") to emphasize the personhood of Christ and follows it with the divine passive aorist ἐφανερώθη (*ephanerōthē*, "was manifested," "was revealed") to describe the first coming or manifestation or arrival of Christ. Given John's use of "that man" to emphasize Jesus's humanity (see 1 John 2:6 above),[48] and given John's comfort with describing tight ontological union between the Father and the Son, it makes sense to gloss ἐφανερώθη as "the Father incarnated him," thereby making the divine passive explicit and identifying what exactly the Father's act entails. Such a rendering makes a clear connection with the coming of Christ on a mission from the Father to "carry sins away." John's use here of αἴρω (*airō*, "take up," "carry away") echoes the confession of John the Baptizer in John 1:29, who identifies Jesus's mission as being the lamb of God "who carries away the sin of the world." The Johannine image of the lamb of God is probably a pastiche of Old Testament imagery that includes the Passover lamb (Exod 12:3–8), the scapegoat that carries away Israel's sin (Lev 16:8–10), the suffering servant of Isaiah 53:7, and perhaps the regular temple sacrifice of lambs (Lev 9:3–13).[49] Here we have elected "carry away" to highlight the Levitical scapegoat, though all of these images bear some sense of removing sin, guilt, and impurity. This reading best makes sense of the appendage "also sin is not in him." Just as the scapegoat is not itself sin or sinful (how could an animal be sinful?), so Jesus is innocent, even as he is the one on whom the sin of the world is laid to be carried away.

A wooden translation of 3:6a is awkward in English because of the use of the negatives in Greek: "Everyone in union with him is not sinning," but the wooden rendering helps to explain the meaning. As noted above, commentators have puzzled over how to harmonize this sentence with 1:8–9, where John indicates that no one is sinless. The key to understanding here is to again remember the apocalyptic context: John is talking about the last hour and ultimate rebellion, not about telling a lie or having too much pride. In verse 4 he has noted that sin—the state of being terminally opposed to the light and delighting in the dark—is participating in or perhaps foreshadowing the final antichristic rebellion. This is what the present active verb refers to: persistent, obstinate rootedness in the

48. The Greek of verse 7 is ἐκεῖνος (*ekeinos*, "that one," "that man"). The given translation glosses this pronoun as "Christ," since John is obviously referring to Jesus, as in 1 John 2:6 above.

49. See Thompson, *John*, 47, for an extended treatment of *agnus Dei* in the Fourth Gospel.

devil, not the daily work of resisting this or that temptation to commit this or that sin. There is a distinction here between "sin" and "apocalyptic sin," between sin that we commit, even sin that besets, and the ongoing practices of those committed to rebellion. "Rebellion" is the ongoing intentional state of fundamental opposition to the light; "apocalyptic sinning" or "practicing sin" is the kind of life pattern one expects of rebels. As such, those who have recognized the turning of the ages and given themselves to union with the one in whom there is no sin (3:5) cannot possibly be "sinning," that is, in rebellion. Likewise, in verse 6b the corollary is also true: "those who sin have never seen or known him." Truly seeing or truly knowing the one who is himself the Light is transformative and brings the true seer or knower into the light. That sort of person is rooted in the Godhead, living in the light, and thoroughly unacquainted with rebellion.

Verse 7 is notable for the way it parallels verse 4. In verse 4 John tells us that those who practice sin also commit rebellion. This term describes the life practices and intentional state of those rooted in the darkness. In verse 7 we read, "Everyone who practices righteousness is righteous." We have heretofore spent little time on the language of righteousness in 1 John and the Johannine corpus in general. Given the prevalence of forms of δικαιοσύνη (*dikaiosynē*, "righteousness") and δίκαιος (*dikaios*, "righteous," "just") in the New Testament as a whole, it is surprising how sparing its use is in the Johannine literature.[50] In John's Gospel we find a high correlation between *dikaio*-language and co-texts concerning the κόσμος (*kosmos*, "world," "universe") or the right-ordering of life in it (e.g., John 16:8–10; 17:5). Revelation features a similar confluence (Rev 16:5–7; 19:2, 11). The same pattern holds in 1 John, where Jesus Christ, "the one who is truly righteous" (2:1), is the atoning sacrifice for the whole cosmos (2:2). Similarly in 2:29–3:1 the world does not know the righteous God-born. John's use of *dikaio*-language consistently describes the reordering of the world according to the light and the resistance of the world to that reordering. At the end of Jesus's prayer in John 17:25, Jesus uses "righteous" to describe the Father ("O righteous Father"). This usage is interesting because of, according to Thompson, the prayer's "orientation of the mission of God to the world," for "this is the world that God made, that God loves, and into which God sent the Son. Into this same world Jesus now sends his disciples."[51] This wording accords with the conceptual world of 1 John, where the light is invading the darkness and where the last hour will feature a final confrontation between the two. Given the parallelism between "rebellion" in verse 4 and "righteous" here in verse 7, and given the consistent use in the Johannine literature to correlate *dikaio*-language with the reordering of

50. See Michaels, *The Gospel of John*, 535.
51. Thompson, *John*, 357.

the world according to the Father's will, I think it appropriate to treat "righteous" here as the apocalyptic counterregime to the rebellion of verse 4.

Reading in this way helps to make sense of what otherwise might seem like an abrupt turn to the origin/birth and devil/God language in verses 8–10. In 8b the devil is the one who "sins from the very beginning." The present tense ἁμαρτάνει (*hamartanei*, "sins," "is sinning") is striking here and uncomfortable in English when conjoined with the familiar, and necessarily past, qualifier, "from the beginning." We have elected not to gloss as most translations do by pushing "sins" into the past tense because, as we have been at pains to argue, John is thinking about sin here as a fundamental opposition to the light and eternal life, rather than some set of concrete actions that abrogate an atemporal moral law. If we were to gloss along these lines, the whole verse would read, "Anyone who practices sin originates from the devil, since the devil has been rebelling from the very beginning." Compare this reading to John 8:44, where Jesus, condemning the Pharisees, tells them that their father is the devil and that the devil has been a "murderer from the beginning." This understanding coincides with that of 1 John 3:15 below, where anyone who hates a spiritual sibling is also deemed "murderer," thus having origins with the first murderer, the devil.

Verse 8a parallels verses 4 and 7b, using the same logic: "The one who practices *x* is *y*." In this case, John correlates those participating in rebellion (v. 4) with those who have their rootedness in the devil ("Anyone who practices sin originates from the devil"). In the final clause in 8c, John parallels 5a, where we have translated, "the Father incarnated him to carry sins away." Just as the righteous will oppose the rebellion (vv. 7 and 4, respectively), so was Jesus sent to "carry sins away" and, in so doing, "destroy the devil's works" (vv. 5a and 8c, respectively). It is difficult to say exactly what such works might be, but at the abstract level they should be understood to be any institutions, actions, or peoples that advance the rebellion against the righteous. This is the ultimate battle, a spiritual war instantiated in a fractured world, and it should be so conceived over and against paltry actions such as jealousy or this or that vice. Of course, the sins of individual Christians can be compounded and appropriated by minions of the rebellion, but this detail is not John's purview, and reading this section so parochially inevitably misses the scope of John's conceptual world and leads to confusion about the possibility—or inevitability or impossibility or frequency or habituation—of Christian sin.

Such considerations have been the focus of classic Wesleyan interpretations of this section that preserve strong notions of "sinless perfectionism."[52] As we have noted, 1 John 1:8–9 indicates the reality of sinning, but here in 3:4–10 there

52. Kruse, *Letters of John*, 126–32, offers a helpful history of interpretation.

appears to be a kind of life that is completely sin-free. To square the circle, it is suggested that chapter 1 addresses occasional sins, while chapter 3, deploying the present-tense verbs for sin, refers to habitual sinning. Such a view would picture the Christian life as a sort of ascent, where over time the believer comes to arrive at a state in which he or she no longer commits the same sins repeatedly. Such a view is internally consistent—and certainly admitted by the text—but might suffer from a lack of contextualization according to genre. That is, we have shown that the language of 1 John 3 is *apocalyptic* in a way that the language of 1 John 1:8–9 is not. In chapter 3 John adopts the antichristic language of chapter 2, as well as language about ultimate beginnings and endings and about the devil. Such a reading is advantageous because it is firmly textual, ameliorates the tensions between chapters 1 and 3, and does not egregiously invoke any dualism to do so.[53]

We have argued that 1:8–9 and 3:4–10 have entirely different conceptions of sin and rebellion. "Sin" in 1:8–9 is this or that wrong act; "sin" in 3:4–10 is a life committed to antichristic ends. So, yes, everyone "sins" in the chapter-1 sense of the word, but only those fully rooted in and committed to the devil can "sin" in the chapter-3 sense of the word. To push the limits of the solution, a Christian woman, for example, might spend her entire life in dalliance with the dark, but when the final confrontation between Christ and the devil occurs, she will ultimately be found in the light. She literally cannot endorse the ultimate reign of darkness because she has at some point come to know—and thus be claimed—by the Light and the Life.

While this solution might seem radical, it is the only way to do justice to John's language without acceding to a fundamental incoherence. If John holds an internally consistent view that is fully and directly expressed in what is written here, it must be this one. Moreover, only a radical reconfiguration will suffice if we are to make sense of the dualistic language that follows. In verses 8–10 John describes two kinds of people: those who are God-born and those who are devil-born. In the final analysis one must have one's origin in one of those two places—there is no third option. Your DNA (σπέρμα, *sperma*; 3:9) is either from the Father or from the devil.[54] Your basic orientation toward the world is based either in the light or in the darkness. You are a practitioner either of sin or of righteousness. The arrival and the eschaton put all of humanity in sharp contrast.

53. Another possibility would be to posit an ideal and a reality that simply exist in tension, where reality is in chapter 1 and the ideal in chapter 3. But this approach seems like special pleading, given that nothing in the text indicates that John operates with anything like these two realms. In fact, where John posits two realms, the darkness and the light, he is deadly serious. The two do not vaguely coexist; they are at war and giving and taking ground.

54. See "Ecclesiology in 1–3 John: The Family of God" in the Theological Horizons section.

Where we now see grays, light and shadow, bright light, low light, and darkness, there will come a day when all is reduced to righteousness and rebellion.

Part of this sharply binary presentation is rhetorical: John's sermon is meant to force hearers to pick a side, as it were, to decide whether they are animated by the Rebel or by the Messiah. And it is how he introduces one of the focal points of the second half of the sermon: mutual Christian love. If there is one sign that one is born of God and lives in the light, it is love for believing brothers and sisters. If there is one sign that one is devil-born and a child of darkness, it is a lack of love for believing brothers and sisters (3:9–10).

1 John 3:11–18

11 For this is the message that you have heard from the beginning: love each other.
12 Don't be like Cain, who originated from the evil one and murdered his brother.
And why did he murder him? He did it because his own works were evil while his
brother's were righteous. 13 So don't be shocked, brothers and sisters, that the
world hates you. 14 We know that we have moved out of death and into life because
we love the church family. The person who does not love still lives in death. 15 Every-
one who hates their brother or sister is a murderer, and you know that no murderer
has eternal life residing in them. 16 This is how we know love: Jesus laid down his
life for us, and so we ought to lay down our lives for our brothers and sisters. 17 If
someone has the good things available in the world and sees a brother or sister in
need and doesn't care, how is God's love living in that person? 18 My little children,
let's not love in words or speech but in action and truth.

John begins verse 11 with "for," indicating that what follows explains what has come before in verse 10. That explanation again features the common refrain: "from the beginning." Up until now, however, what was from the beginning was the revelation of the uncreated Son of the Father. Only in 2:7 has John intimated that that revelation came with a message or word (λόγος, *logos*), but John's concern there was to affirm that nothing substantive of God's revelation has changed. Whatever the word was "from the beginning," it remains the same now, though clothed with new flesh, as it were. It would be tempting to suppose that here "from the beginning" refers to the announcement and reception of the gospel by John's hearers, but this would be a strange departure from John's consistent usage. Every time the phrase has been used, it has referred to cosmic origins and/or the uncreatedness of the Son (1:1; 2:7, 13–14, 24; 3:8). Here it is followed immediately by a reference to origins—Cain and Abel in Genesis 4—and a recognition that Cain had his own origins in the evil one, who himself "sins from the very beginning" (3:8). The language is highly associative and suggests that in some way, the message "love each other" is connected to—perhaps derived from—the unoriginated Son of the Father. The existence of the Second Person of the Trinity and his subsequent revelation-in-incarnation is the functional equivalent of God saying to the world, "Love each other." This radical statement prefigures and helps to make sense of the radical message that "God is love" below in 4:8. The logic is something like this: if a person has encountered the light that is the Son, reflected on who the Son is and what it means that the Son has come into the world, then such a person will recognize that the fundamental nature of God is agapic love and that God's primal, original message to the universe—love one another—is tantamount to a call for human beings to share in or conform to the nature of God.

The command in verse 11 logically supplies the negative command ("don't be") in verse 12, where the Greek has no imperative verb. Contemporary readers might be surprised to find that the reason for Abel's murder is that Cain's "own works were evil while his brother's were righteous," since Genesis 4 does not actually say that that is the case. In fact, the canonical story of the first murder is surprisingly vague. In the first century CE, Jewish tradition had gone some way toward filling out Cain's motives. The Jewish philosopher Philo notes that Cain's name is the Hebrew for "possession" and thus signifies that Cain attributes all of God's creative work to himself and that therefore Cain is filled with self-love (*Sacrifices* 1:2–3). If Cain is the symbol of self-love and if the ultimate expression of God's character to the world is "love each other," then it follows that Cain, like the evil one in whom he has his origin, is a rebel in rebellion, prefiguring the Rebel, who will inaugurate the rebellion. Fully embracing the anachronism, Cain is an antichrist.

Many modern translations omit the conjunction καί (*kai*, "so") at the beginning of verse 13 because the manuscript evidence is murky. Several of the best and oldest manuscripts have the conjunction, but a great many do not. Since the last Greek word of verse 12 is *dikaia*, it might be that copyists thought that the *καί* at the beginning of verse 13 was an error of addition and so omitted it. We have included and translated it to show that John's warning about hate in verse 13 is directly connected to the action of Cain in verse 12. That is, Cain is not simply an abstract type; he is a prefiguration of the kind of people who are actually now in the world who are acting to destroy those who walk in the light. Uncomfortable though it might be to hear, those who walk in the dark are Cain's children and therefore the children of the evil one: they are rebels; they have rejected light; they are antichrists and murderers. If this attribution seems hyperbolic, it should not; in verse 15 John specifically calls those who do not love, murderers, an appellation Jesus uses of the devil in John 8:44.

It is critical to recognize whom exactly the world and these murderers hate: the church family. More literally, John talks of loving (and subsequently of hating) "the brothers and sisters." Notice the lack of a possessive pronoun here. John is talking not about "our" siblings but about "the siblings." That is, he is talking about an objective set of relatives, namely, those who confess the Son, possess the eternal life (John 3:16), and share in union with Father and the Son and each other. These people share a familiality that is beyond the natural family relations brought on by blood. Loving this set of people shows one's origination in God; hating this set of people shows one's origination in the devil. In verse 15 the personal pronoun returns, reading "everyone who hates *their* brother or sister is a murderer." While the language differs, we might again hear an echo of Jesus's teaching in Matthew 5:21–22, where being angry with a brother or sister is tantamount to murder and judgment. As in Matthew, the point seems to be that everyone is a murderer because the darkness holds such sway, that hate is as calamitous as it is ubiquitous. The corollary, then, is that the church family is a special, unique set of people who have been rescued out from the world, who have the possibility of moving from hate to love, from being devil-born to God-born, from being rebels to righteous. The assumption is that just about everyone is a "murderer"; if we encounter someone who demonstrably loves the brothers and sisters of the church, there is a possibility that we have found a rare exception to the rule.

In verses 11–16 the sermon encourages hearers to self-identify. Do I love the church? Do I hate it? Am I a murderer because of my opposition to the brothers and sisters? Verses 17–18 demand a response. If John's persuasion has been successful, his hearers will want to show that they are indeed sibling-lovers and not sibling-haters. Verse 17 suggests that anyone who has the world's resources and sees a church sibling in need and shuts up his or her heart, does not have love abiding or living in them. The reversion to the use of μένει (*menei*), which we have variously translated as "living," "having union," "remaining," or "continuing," shows that John is again thinking of the interrelations between Christians as mirroring the union relationship had between the Father and the Son and the believers in 1:3. The outward manifestation of union with the divine, of possessing the eternal life, is love ἐν ἔργῳ καὶ ἀληθείᾳ (*en ergō kai alētheia*, "in action and truth," 3:18).

At this juncture it is critical to remember that this is a sermon and not an abstract statement of theological fact. John is looking for hearers to self-identify and respond. This matters because taking his words superficially rather than seriously can lead to unchristian judgment and condemnation. It is demonstrably the case that not every Christian acts charitably all the time. There will be eschatological revelation where the rebels and the righteous will be revealed and separated once and for all, but that revelation belongs to God and not to us. In the meantime, there are rebels who act righteously and righteous who rebel. John is preaching (1) to convince the former to stop merely acting and confess the Son and receive the divine life and (2) to remind and encourage the latter to reengage the light and reenter union with Father, Son, and church. John makes this appeal explicit in what follows.

1 John 3:19–24

19 This is how we will know that we have our origins in the truth and persuade
our hearts before him 20 whenever our hearts condemn us: God is greater than
our hearts and knows all things. 21 Dear friends, when our hearts don't condemn
us, we have confidence before God, 22 and whatever we ask from him we receive,
since we are obeying his commands and doing what pleases him. 23 And this is his
command: that we believe in the name of his Son, Jesus the Messiah, and love one
another just as he commanded us. 24 The one who keeps this command has union
with God, and God has union with them. This is how we know that he remains in
union with us: from the Spirit he gave us.

Having demanded a response from his hearers, John now encourages those who have doubts. He has been speaking in stark, eschatological terms: light and dark, righteous and rebel, God-born and devil-born. Surely many who hear may worry: in light of recent actions and accrued habits and practices, am I really one who is born of God? Have I loved enough? Walked close enough to the light? Could it be that I thought I was in the light but really am in the darkness? The beginning of verse 19, "This is how we will know," indicates that John anticipates what his hearers will experience. The first-person plural future tense allows John to demonstrate solidarity and an orientation to what will inevitably come to pass. Some will suggest that this use of ἐν τούτῳ (*en toutō*, "in this") must be referring back to loving "in action and truth," but this is logically unnecessary and out of keeping with John's use of the phrase.[55]

55. Iver Larsen ("The Phrase ἐν τούτῳ in 1 John," *Notes on Translation* 4, no. 4 [1990]: 27–34) argues that of the twelve instances of the phrase in 1 John, only 3:19 is anaphoric. He mitigates the claim somewhat, suggesting that it has an anaphoric and kataphoric aspect. My sense is that he is just noting that John is carrying through a pattern of thought and what has gone before is not logically disconnected from what follows. He will find no disagreement on that point. Nevertheless, it is critical for the logic of John's preaching in 19–24 that we do not find our assurance of being in God's family from the love "in action and truth" of verse 18. If we do, then there is no need for 3:19–24 at all, since assurance is therefore dependent on what

As before, this translation glosses ἐκ τῆς ἀληθείας (*ek tēs alētheias*, "from the truth") with "have origins in the truth," given John's continued concern with who or what we come from as the explanation for who we are. The God-born have origins in God and divine DNA, and the devil-born have their origins with the evil one and reflect his character and action (3:8–10). The Greek syntax here, especially in verses 19–20a, is ambiguous and, given the high theological stakes involved (i.e., Am I in God's family or not?), worth parsing finely.

First, both "we will know" and "persuade our hearts" (πείσομεν τὴν καρδίαν ἡμῶν, *peisomen tēn kardian hēmōn*) are in the future tense. This suggests that they be coordinated, with believers performing two separate actions in the future: (1) they will know or come to know that they are God-born and (2) they will remind or convince themselves that this is indeed the case. The verb πείσομεν can mean "pacify" or "set at ease," but John's preaching rhetoric has just condemned everyone in 3:18. Since no human being consistently acts according to the divine nature and since no one can claim to have constant union with God, hearts and minds will need convincing that they truly are God's children when they do not seem to be. This is because the "heart" is not merely the seat of affections or emotions, nor is it strictly the place of rational deliberation, which we would probably think of as "mind." In Hebrew anthropology the heart is the sum of the inner person—including conscience, affect, and deliberation. The goal is to know our origins, which will sometimes take persuasion; thus we translate "persuade our hearts" rather than "set our hearts at ease."

According to the NA[28] critical text, verse 20 begins with ὅτι ἐάν (*hoti ean*, "that if" or "that when"). This wording creates syntactic problems because verse 20 has a second ὅτι clause right after it. Compounding the issue, since we have read ἐν τούτῳ (*en toutō*, "in this" or "this is how") in verse 19 as future oriented, we should expect John—as he has in 2:3, 5 and 3:16—to use an explanatory clause. Thus, even leaving aside the problems of Greek sentence structure, it is difficult to know which ὅτι clause (or both!) functions as the explanation for how we will know we are from the truth and will persuade our hearts. Many have tried to ameliorate the problem by reading the first phrase in verse 20 as "(as to) whatever." This reading would make the phrase a second accusative of πείσομεν, meaning "and we will quiet our hearts before God as to whatever our heart condemns [in] us." While grammatically possible, note that it would strongly push against πείσομεν meaning "persuade" or "convince" because on such a reading John would appear to be saying that we should convince our heart

Christians *do* instead of what they *are*. See also Jobes (*1, 2, and 3 John*, 166), who builds her case on Larsen's work.

before God that it is right to condemn us.[56] Moreover, there is no manuscript evidence for this reading, and it is striking that we have already seen the very same awkward ὅτι construction in 3:2. The most probable solution is to accept that John's Greek is sometimes inelegant and to take the first ὅτι clause in verse 20 as explaining the circumstances that mark the time(s) when the second ὅτι clause becomes operative.[57]

In effect, John says, "We will know we are from the truth and we will persuade our hearts before him (and we will need to do this when our hearts condemn us) because God is greater than our hearts and knows all things." Our comfort proceeds from a remembrance that it is God—and not our hearts—who is determinative of our status. It is God who labored to bring us to birth in the divine life, not us. It is God's DNA that we have, not whatever our hearts might suppose. We must note that such a reading is essential to understanding the preceding and subsequent sections of the sermon. The human tendency is to want to make any assurance we have dependent on ourselves; this view is, of course, pride and folly. It leads to cycles of guilt and fear, the very attitudes that John expects to be absent from believers' lives! John exhorts us to live in keeping with our divine character: loving through action and truth. But there will be plenty of times when, if we are honest, our hearts will condemn us before God as not loving or as loving abstractly and thus not truly loving at all. When such condemnation happens, the solution is not to renew our efforts; this is a self-defeating strategy, as it puts on us the onus for confirming what God knows and has done. John provides a better way: remember that God is God, and let God be God.

Again translating ἐάν (*ean*, "if," "when") as "when," verse 21 describes the other sort of circumstance we will find ourselves in: the state of a clean conscience and therefore "confidence before God." Taking this clause as parallel to the preceding instance in verse 20 suggests a similar explanation about the time and place when the following action in verse 22 will be operative. The verbs here have switched to the present tense, but the parallel structure and the subjunctive mood in αἰτῶμεν (*aitōmen*, "we might ask") suggest that John is still entertaining notions of what will come to pass during regular Christian life.

There will be times when our hearts need no persuading and we are confident before God. During these times we will notice that we do in fact receive the things we ask of God. Translating the ὅτι as "since" is meant to capture the dynamic at work without suggesting some kind of lever we wedge against God,

56. This reading may help to explain why Bultmann adds a conjectural negating the πείσομεν (*peisomen*) clause. His interpretation would read, "and we will not persuade our hearts before God."

57. Conveniently, glossing "that when" as "whenever" solves the problem in English syntax and is the translation of the NRSV.

forcing God to grant our requests because "we are obeying his commands and doing what pleases him." Rather, when we are obeying his commands and doing what pleases him (note that this structure is a Hebraism: the second clause is a reformulation of the first, with the two basically synonymous), we will notice that we are confident before God. Obedience begets confidence, and confidence begets the sort of asking that leads to receiving. John will explain the dynamics further in 1 John 5:14–16, but for now it is enough to note that rather than obedience and confidence functioning as a twist on God's arm, so to speak, obedience brings us close to God's own heart—through union, we might add—and thus we find ourselves asking for the very things God is pleased to give.

When these times of confidence and asking and receiving arrive, the believer will be obeying a double command that echoes Jesus's teaching in the Synoptics: "Believe in the name of his Son, Jesus the Messiah, and love one another just as he commanded us" (Matt 22:37–40; Mark 12:30–31; Luke 10:27). As we noted above, John is conceptually committed to strong union between Father and Son—a trait shared in the Fourth Gospel. Thus, where Jesus's teaching in the Synoptics focuses on loving God and neighbor, for John, one loves God by acknowledging the authority, that is, trusting "in the name," of Jesus. Just as receiving the Son's message entails receiving the Father's message, so too does acknowledging the Son's authority mean submission and loyalty to the Father. They can be distinguished, but not too finely.

Verse 24 reiterates a main Johannine theme: trust in Jesus leads to union with Father and Son. We have again translated μένει (*menei*, "remain," "stay") as "union," since it certainly continues that theme from the first chapter. Even the grammar, where one remains "in him" and he remains "in us," suggests the sort of intermingling we have deemed "union."

The final clause of verse 24 introduces a new section of the sermon. Another way in which believers will know that they do indeed possess union will be "from the Spirit he gave us." This is the first of twelve explicit references to πνεῦμα (*pneuma*, "spirit," "Spirit") in 1 John, though we have argued that we may read the Holy Spirit into the anointing of 2:20. Nevertheless, it is frustratingly vague: How does the Spirit affirm our union with God? To begin, John's discourse on discernment in what follows confirms that John expected a community's testimony about the Spirit to be in some sense subjective and experiential. The word "spirit" can refer to the characteristics or quality of a person (à la "that woman's spirit") or even a community or an epoch (as in the German etymological sibling *geist* in "zeitgeist," the "spirit of the age"). Moreover, John's world is inhabited by many spirits, so it can be difficult to tell one from another.

But as we will see, it is not entirely subjective. In fact, if part of what the Spirit does in the renewed temple of believers involves anointing, we know from chapter 2 that such anointing involves initiating individuals as co-priests with Christ, reckoning and applying all that is needed to perform priestly duties. This initiation necessarily involves teaching and perhaps incipient doctrines. When the Spirit is in a place, orthodoxy (right belief) and orthopraxy (right action) will be too.

1 John 4:1–6

1 Dear friends, don't trust every spirit. Instead, evaluate the spirits to see if they
come from God, since many false prophets have gone out into the world. 2 This is
how you recognize the Spirit of God: every spirit that confesses that Messiah Jesus
came as a human being is from God. 3 Likewise, any spirit that does not confess Jesus
is not from God – indeed, this is the spirit of the Antichrist, which you have heard
is coming and now is already in the world. 4 Little children, you have your origins
in God, and you have overcome them because the Spirit in you is greater than the
one in the world. 5 They have their origins in the world and therefore speak from
the world's perspective, and the world listens to them. 6 We have our origins in
God. The person who knows God listens to us. The person who does not originate
from God does not listen to us. This is how we ascertain the Spirit of Truth and the
Spirit of Error.

The Johannine literature is replete with references to "spirits," spiritual beings whose influence manifests itself in human life. So, for example, Revelation 1:4 tells us that seven spirits sit before God's throne. In 16:13 three impure spirits come out of the mouths of the dragon, the beast, and the false prophet. Spirits animate the persons and communities they accompany and induce them to speak and do good or evil. 1 John is primarily concerned with the Holy Spirit, that is, the Spirit of Truth, and with the Spirit of Error or of Deceit, that is, the antichristic or diabolical spirit that might influence believers to travel down antichristic paths. Moreover, because institutions can have an animating spiritual being (e.g., the various angels of the churches in Rev 2–3), the warning here in 1 John 4:1–6 is about more than trusting individual people: it is about trusting institutions and communities too. When John speaks about "false prophets" at the end of the verse, he suggests that people animated by the Spirit of Deceit have gone about and influenced many people and places antichristically. Even after the false prophets leave, the Spirit of Error they serve remains, continuing the work of corruption. Rendering πιστεύω (*pisteuō*) as "trust" here rather than "believe" is critical because John is not concerned only with beliefs and doctrines false prophets might spread. He is concerned also about the actions that antichristic corruption engenders. It is not enough to have the correct beliefs: as we saw in the previous section and will see in the next, being loving is essential for having origin in the truth in the first place. This church, that business, this community leader, that servant—are they animated by the Spirit or by a spirit? How do we know whom we can trust?

Rather than trusting everyone and everything, John commands us to "evaluate" the spirits animating them. The Spirit of Truth confesses that Messiah Jesus came ἐν σαρκί (*en sarki*, "in flesh"). The translation here, that Messiah Jesus came "as a human being," is meant to flesh out, as it were, what John means by "in flesh." This teaching echoes John 1:14, where the Word σὰρξ ἐγένετο (*sarx egeneto*, "became flesh") and lived among us. This verse is the classic confession of the incarnation, that the eternal Second Person of the Trinity fully assumed human nature and lived in Israel as the man Jesus of Nazareth. This belief is always confessed by any person or institution animated by the Spirit of Truth. The confession, however, is not an abstract creed. Instead, it is the lens by which we know God. John 1:14 does not end with Jesus living among us. Instead, it continues, "We have seen his glory, glory like that of the one and only Son of the Father, full of grace and truth." The coming of Jesus is the revelation of the Father's glory and character. Where the Son comes, so come grace and truth, and therefore wherever the Father is, there too are grace and truth in plenitude. This is the concomitant orthopraxy (right action) that accompanies orthodox (right believing) confession. The Spirit of Truth will be revealed in people and places that have union with the Father and the Son, where the eternal life that Jesus lived is re-incarnated among Jesus's followers. In 1 John 4:7–14 John will specify this truth further by referencing agapic love. The Spirit of Truth confesses the Son's humanity and lives out his love. This is the full extent of how one evaluates the Spirit behind a person, people, or community: Do they confess the Son's humanity and instantiate it themselves?

If they do not, then the animating spirit is, as we see in 4:3, "not from God." In fact, it is antichristic, and this Spirit of Deception has gone out into the world corrupting wherever it goes. In verse 4 John resumes his epideictic discourse, reminding us that we are in fact animated by the Spirit of Truth. He calls his hearers "little children," reaffirming their belonging to the divine family and their origins in God. Here again we have overtranslated a bit, rendering ἐκ τοῦ θεοῦ (*ek tou theou*) as having "origins in God" rather than the simpler "from God." But the move is justified—John has just called hearers "little children," that is, children born of God. He reminds us that we have "overcome them." The semantic range of the verb νικάω (*nikaō*) is fairly fixed: it speaks of defeating, overcoming, vanquishing, or surpassing an opponent. In the Johannine literature the verb appears some twenty-four times, seventeen of which are in Revelation.

Of those seventeen, ten uses are in participial form, referring usually to believers who have in some way defeated the persecution or temptation or deception of the enemy. They are "overcomers" or, as in the CEB, "those who have emerged victorious" in whatever spiritual battles they have been engaged.

Overcomer language in Revelation suggests that when John speaks of "overcoming them," the "them" to which he refers is not primarily the false prophets of 4:1 but specifically the various people and institutions—surely the false prophets among them—that have been directed by the Spirit of Deception. Since John eschews specifics, we are left to imagine what these conflicts looked like. However, it would not be too much of a stretch—given the use here of "defeat" or "overcome"—to suggest that, at the very least, the problems narrated of the seven churches in Revelation might serve as a paradigm. If so, then the spiritual warfare John has in mind includes becoming loveless (Rev 2:4), confessing Jesus in a hostile environment (Rev 2:9; 3:8), facing physical persecution even to martyrdom (Rev 2:10, 13; 3:10), being deceived by false teachers and prophets in ways that lead to sinful behavior (Rev 2:14–15, 20), and becoming spiritually lazy on account of material wealth (Rev 3:15–17). By naming and defeating the Spirit of Deception by confessing the true, divine-and-human Messiah, John's hearers have avoided succumbing to these sorts of behaviors or being turned aside to erroneous teaching. These examples further suggest that if one wishes to identify places and people who have denied the whole truth about Jesus, one need only look for these kinds of habitual behaviors. In some way or other, the Spirit of Deception has found a foothold in these hearts and communities, and the results speak for themselves.

If John's hearers are tempted to take pride in their victory over the Spirit of Deception, they should be disabused: the overcoming happens "because the Spirit in you is greater than the one in the world." The Greek does not specify that the one greater than the world is in fact the Spirit, reading instead, "the one in you is greater than the one in the world." And since this "one" is "greater than the world," the only real options for identification are the Father, the Son, and the Spirit of Truth. The particle is the masculine singular, which would seem to militate against the neuter "spirit" as a potential referent. However, the question that John is entertaining in this section is basically, "Which spirit is in you?" And the "in you" language is suggestive, especially in light of its being used to describe the gift of the Holy Spirit in John 14:17, where Jesus tells the disciples that "the Spirit of Truth . . . will be in you." John's point is that some spirits are greater than others, and in this particular battle, the Spirit of Truth trumps the Spirit of Deception. This does not mean that we are going to "win" in any conventional sense, as victory in spiritual war can—again referring to Revelation—include martyrdom. The victories of the Spirit of Truth secure union with the Father and the Son and continual participation in the eternal life, a far cry from the spoils garnered by victory in martial warfare. This is both a reassurance and a warning. For hearers who recognize personal and communal victory over the Spirit of Deception, John's words bring comfort. For those who do not, his words sound the alarm. And so the sermon again demands self-identification and response.

Moreover, even as John's hearers have overcome the Spirit of Deception, the war has already been decided. In fact, many animated by the Spirit of Deception do not appear to know that they have lost. John continues, noting that those in thrall to the Spirit of Deception have developed a sort of network, an echo chamber of sorts. 4:5 reads, "They have their origins in the world and therefore speak from the world's perspective, and the world listens to them." The translation "speak from the world's perspective" glosses the Greek ἐκ τοῦ κόσμου λαλοῦσιν (*ek tou kosmou lalousin*, "they speak from the world"). Because their roots and origins are in the world, all that they say and do proceeds from the world's perspective, hence the translation. John and his hearers do not listen to this babble because it comes from those animated by the Spirit of Deception. But the world does listen because what it hears reinforces what the world already believes.

In verse 6 John contrasts the world's echo chamber with the one that operates under the animation of the Spirit of Truth, with its origins in the divine eternal life. Knowledge of God comes from the Spirit of Truth and results in someone who recognizes and listens to other people who have known God by the ministry of the Spirit of Truth. The language is simplistic but not tautologous. That is, when John speaks of the person who "knows God," he refers back to anyone who has embraced the whole truth about the Son, Jesus Christ. Knowledge of God comes from receiving union with the Son, which is orchestrated by the Spirit of Truth. Perhaps a bit reductionistic, but it is worth noting that the Son is in a very real way the criterion of Christian truth and knowledge. Confessing the incarnate, unoriginated Son is the beginning of Christian knowledge. It moreover creates a gap, a division in John's theology between worldly knowledge and Christian knowledge. The world, animated by the Spirit of Deception, and the church, animated by the Spirit of Truth, speak past each other.

1 John thus serves as a corrective to missional theologies that would seek to be overly accommodating to the dominant culture. 1 John fully embraces the Jewish notion of a temple-in-exile, a community of resident aliens operating in a foreign, hostile land.[58]

58. For more on church-in-exile, see Stanley Hauerwas and William H. Willimon, *Resident Aliens: Life in the Christian Colony*, 25th ann. ed. (Nashville: Abingdon, 2014).

1 John 4:7–10

[7] Dear friends, let's love each other, because love comes from God, and everyone who loves has been born from God and knows God. [8] Anyone who does not love does not know God, because God is love. [9] This is how God's love for us has been revealed in us: God sent his one and only Son into the world so that we could live because of him. [10] In this is love: not that we loved God but that he loved us and sent his Son as an atonement sacrifice for our sins.

1 John 4:7 begins an extensive section on what love is and how it functions among the God-born. We have broken it up into several pieces that feature John's familiar rhetorical method of preaching that demands self-identification and response, but really because the love theme is so prominent, the entire thought unit probably extends from 4:7 to 5:4a.[59] In these nineteen verses, John uses forms of the verb ἀγαπάω (*agapaō*, "I love") and the noun ἀγάπη (*agapē*, "love") thirty-two times. The extensive treatment of love probably derives from the need to distinguish the *agapē* operative in the Father, Son, and community of faith, from secular or perhaps even sectarian usage. Christian love, the love of God for humanity, indeed the love that is God, is monumentally more than "cherishing" or "esteeming" another. It goes beyond affection and even "seeking the good of the other."

The introduction to the section in 4:7, ἀγαπητοί (*agapētoi*), can be misleading, as its standard meanings "dear friends" or "loved ones" or "cherished ones" lack something that English cannot quite conjure. The hearers are not just friends—they are family, which John makes explicit at the end of the verse. *Agapē* originates from God, and everyone who has it has become God-born. The divine perfect passive γεγέννηται (*gegennētai*, "has been born") indicates that the birthing has already been completed, with the result that anyone who has experienced it has been birthed into the agapic family. Members of this family know or comprehend the Father, God, in a way that nonmembers do not, presumably because—as in a blood family—they possess an intimate knowledge of the Father's nature and character that is occluded from those who do not live with him. By this logic it is interesting that the command John gives—repeated here from 3:11, 18—is implicated in being God-born and knowing God. "Everyone who loves"

59. This subdivision of the text follows Raymond Brown's outline (*Epistles*, 512–13). Most prefer to break it up further because love is treated in so many ways, but Brown is right to use the frequency of the *agapē* lexis to demarcate the section as a whole. Attempting to circumscribe subunits is also fraught with absolutely no scholarly consensus; treating the text as a sermon rather than a letter helps make sense of the conceptual bleed.

uses the present participle to indicate a sustained action, a habitual practice, a way of life. If John's hearers have had this way of life inculcated, then why does John use the first-person plural subjunctive ἀγαπῶμεν (*agapōmen*, "let us love") to encourage mutual love as if it is not already operative?

In a sense, this question will help us avoid misinterpreting the whole section. John's love discourse is not meant to provide a path to assurance that we are members of the divine family, that we have been born of God. It is instead the rhetoric of persuasion, meant to shake his hearers into self-reflection and possible conversion. The use of the first-person plural subjunctive "let's love" instead of the second-person plural imperative (see 1 John 2:15) alerts us to this truth. John includes himself in the group of family members who need to be reminded from time to time to do what the family was born to do: love.

In verse 8 John deploys a familiar rhetorical move: he establishes the converse of what he desires for his hearers. Again, he deploys the present participle *agapōn*, but this time with a negation: the one who is not in the habit of agapically loving, who is not making this a practice, that person has no access to intimate knowledge of the Father. In stating the reason for this judgment, John offers what is now one of the most famous phrases in the Christian canon: ὅτι ὁ θεὸς ἀγάπη ἐστίν (*hoti ho theos agapē estin*, "because God is love"). Whatever one might think this statement means, even a cursory review of standard Koine synonyms for love indicates that John is talking about a special sort of love. Esteem, affection, warm regard are all fine things, but they are not God. In verses 9 and 10 John explicates what kind of love God is, and therefore what kind of love is natural to the divine family that has God's DNA by being God-born.

Using the familiar "in this" or "this is how," John again speaks of "God's love for us" (ἡ ἀγάπη τοῦ θεοῦ, *hē agapē tou theou*, with the subjective genitive) and how he has revealed it in verse 9. The translation keeps the passive voice, but this a divine passive; God clearly is doing the loving. Moreover, he did it "in us." This mention of "in us" is important because it reemphasizes that what God did was not only a historical act, but it was a historical act with a present manifestation. Jesus came *then*, but we have union and the eternal life *now*. Finally, he did it by sending his "one and only" (μονογενῆ, *monogenē*) Son into the world "so that we could live because of him." "One and only" and "live because of him" deserve a bit of attention. This is the only time "one and only" appears in 1 John, though it refers to Jesus four times in the Fourth Gospel. In typical usage it would indicate an only child (see, e.g., Luke 7:12; 8:42; 9:38). That cannot be the case in the Johannine literature because God has many children, the God-born. It might be that John is following the tradition of the Greek Septuagint, which renders the Hebrew יחיד (*yāḥîd*, "only," "solitary"), "beloved," in Genesis 22:2, 12, and 16. This translation would connect John's use of "one and only" with the Synoptic use of "beloved" at Jesus's baptism. This connection is possible but unlikely, since the Johannine literature is happy to refer to fellow believer Gaius with the adjective ἀγαπητός (*agapētos*, "beloved," "dear friend," 3 John 1), indicating that the adjective is not peculiar or specially used. More likely, the emphasis in μονογενής (*monogenēs*) should be on the *mono* ("one"), with Jesus the unique, the only Son among many sons and daughters. God has many children, but only one is uncreated, "uniquely gotten," as it were.

It is hard to miss the echo of John 3:16 in this verse, given the lexical overlap of ἀγάπη (*agapē*, "love") and μονογενής (*monogenēs*), the mention of the Son coming into the world, and the concern with life—the verb "to live" in 1 John 4:9 and the related noun "life" in John 3:16. In the Fourth Gospel, Jesus's message to Nicodemus centers on belief being the means by which people receive life through the Son. Accordingly, it might be the case that ἵνα ζήσωμεν δι' αὐτοῦ (*hina zēsōmen di' autou*) is making the same point here, that Jesus was sent into the world "so that we could live through him." However, the preposition followed by the genitive can mean "by" with a causal sense (e.g., Rom 8:3) leading to the awkward English: "so that we could live by him" or the smoother "so that we could live because of him." It is common now to assume the former meaning; John's soteriology is in some way mystical, and believers possess life through Jesus. This understanding is not entirely wrong, but it also does not best fit this context. When John wants to talk about the life believers have "through" the Son, he usually speaks of origins, of union, or of being "in" him (1:3, 6–7; 2:24; 3:6, 9). In verse 10 Jesus's being an "atonement sacrifice" clarifies what is meant by the revelation of God's love in verse 9. This is like Hebrew parallelism, where the repetition of an idea expands on it. The life we have in Christ is available because he acted as an atoning sacrifice, because he performed atoning temple worship on our behalf. While "through" can capture this meaning too, "because of" is more accurate and less ambiguous in English.

John's now customary "this is how" or "in this" indicates that verse 10 expands or clarifies what love is like—or at least the love shared by those in union with Father and Son in verses 7–9. John's analysis is uncompromising and stark: *agapē* is inhuman; it is not something natural to or originating in humanity, not even in the human pursuit of and love for God. Instead, *agapē* is manifested in the Father sending the Son as an atoning sacrifice for our sins. Forms of the verb ἀποστέλλω (*apostellō*, "send") occur three times in 1 John, all in this extended discourse on love (4:9, 10, 14). The Gospel of John features the verb twenty-seven times; seventeen of those uses specifically refer to the sending of the Son by the Father. Interestingly, the first use of "send" in this manner occurs in 3:17, functioning as a sort of clarification of God's intentional love in 3:16. Where in 3:16 God "gave" the only Son, in 3:17 Jesus explains that God "sent" the Son into the world to save it rather than judge or condemn it. *Agapē* is therefore missiological: in this case, it has an end, namely, the salvation of the world. While the Johannine writings evince the most extensive use of sending language, we should note that Paul thinks along the same lines. In Galatians 4:4–5 Paul confesses that God sent (ἐξαποστέλλω, *exapostellō*) his Son to "redeem those under the law" and provide us "adoption."

Sending language that is predicated of God is not unique to the New Testament, nor is the notion that what God sends is deliverance of some kind or another. Jeremiah 7:25 LXX suggests that the prophets are sent by God to correct Israel's misbehavior. The Psalms ask for God to send deliverance by various means as well (e.g., Pss 19:3 LXX/20:2 Eng.; 143:6–7 LXX/144:6–7 Eng.). It is just as common, however—indeed, perhaps more so—for sending language in the Hebrew Scriptures to refer to God's judgment or wrath. Perhaps what the Johannine literature suggests is that God's sendings may vary in purpose but that God has a special kind of sending, the sending of the only Son, which is agapic and especially revelatory. While God can send judgment, it is more in keeping with God's essential agapic nature to send the Son to save and deliver. God's first inclination, as it were, is to liberate, save, choose, redeem, ransom, or benefit in a "sonly" sending, though from time to time God judges that a different kind of sending is necessary.

As in 1 John 2:2, the reference to the Son as ἱλασμός (*hilasmos*, "atoning sacrifice") telescopes the entirety of the Son's mission, focusing on the crucifixion and the spilling of blood as God's act of ritual cleansing, the removal of disorder. We should not, however, let this text delimit the mission of the Son to the cross alone; John is not ignoring Jesus's life and ministry so much as he is describing *agapē*. And *agapē* reaches its climax, its fullest manifestation, in a Son who deigns to shed blood for the very world that demands his death. In this way, John's proclamation of *agapē* is preventative. So long as the cross is proclaimed, the church cannot water down the radical selflessness of "love." Love in the church cannot be used as a shorthand for warm feelings or affection or romance or even a disinterested seeking of another's good. It is nothing less than total self-abnegation of God.[60] In practice, it is impossible for our agapic actions to ever match the self-emptying of the Creator for the created. Only by sharing in union with the Father and Son can our love be godlike, for only through union can our love be God's love.

60. See "The Love of God" in the Theological Horizons section. For other theological treatments, see, for example, Jürgen Moltmann, *The Crucified God* (Minneapolis: Fortress, 1993), especially chapter 6, and Eberhard Jüngel, *God as the Mystery of the World: On the Foundation of the Theology of the Crucified One in the Dispute between Theism and Atheism*, trans. Darrell J. Guder (Grand Rapids: Eerdmans, 1983), especially part 5.

1 John 4:11–16

11 Dear friends, since this is how God loved us, we also are obligated to love each
other. 12 No one has ever gazed upon God. When we love each other, God lives in
us, and his love has reached its goal in us. 13 This is how we know that we live in
him and he in us: he has given us a share of his Spirit. 14 Now we, we have seen and
testify that the Father sent the Son to be the world's savior. 15 God lives in those
who confess that Jesus is God's Son, and they live in God. 16 And we, we have come
to know and trust in the love that God has for us. God is love, and those who live in
love live in God, and God lives in them.

Having captured the essence of God's self-giving love in the cross of Christ in 1 John 4:7–10, in verses 11–16 John draws some inferences about the lives of those who have known and experienced it. The conjunction is best rendered "since" because nothing that follows makes sense apart from the revelation of *agapē* in the preceding verses. Moreover, ὀφείλομεν (*opheilomen*, "we are obligated") in the second half of the verse connotes the responsibility to love mutually. But why is this an obligation? Most modern translations soften the blow in English, reading "we ought." It may be that at some time in the past "ought" carried the sense of "must," but at least in present, libertarian-minded contexts, "ought" implies a moral nudge this way or that but leaves the decision in the hands of the one nudged. The Greek is not so sanguine. Matthew 23:16, for example, uses the verb to speak of one's obligation to fulfill an oath. Paul uses it to discuss filial obligations in 2 Corinthians 12:14. Mutual love is not a polite suggestion; rather—and the first-person plural indicates that John is not exempted here—since God loved us by sending his Son sacrificially, we who believe owe the same sort of love to each other.

Whence the obligation? It might be that John's logic goes thus: God has given a gift of infinite value and thus accrued infinite obligation from us; we are therefore compelled to pay it back infinitely. Since the gift is *agapē*, the Christian is obliged to love. This is fine so far as it goes, but if John is really thinking in classical debt and credit terms, then the Christian obligation should be not to love other Christians but to love God. God is the giver, the one to whom we are indebted. Payments, therefore, go back to God. But if this is not John's logic of obligation, what is? Verse 12 provides the answer.

As we noted in comments on 1 John 2:5, the verb τελειόω (*teleioō*) indicates that God's love (again using the subjective genitive) is "vectored," or "goal-oriented." It has an end, a purpose. Here in 4:12 that purpose is revealed (or really, reaffirmed): God wishes to live with us, have union with us. Our translation of the perfect passive participial form of *teleioō* "has reached" is not as faithful to the

Greek as more common renderings such as "has been completed" or "has been perfected" that maintain the passive voice, but there are good reasons to read the form this way. First, it better reflects the goal-oriented sense of the Greek. Our translation is explicit about what John expects love to do. Second, this instance of τελειόω —just as in 1 John 2:5—can be read as a divine passive. God is *agapē*. So when the goal of *agapē* "has been reached," it is the case that God has been at work causing God's goal to be reached. We have again translated the conjunction "when," since John's is the language of expectation. We have an obligation to love each other; John now explains what happens when we do.

The beginning of the verse, θεὸν οὐδεὶς πώποτε τεθέαται (*theon oudeis pōpote tetheatai*, "no one has ever gazed upon God"), echoes verse 18 of the Gospel of John's prologue, which reads, θεὸν οὐδεὶς ἑώρακεν πώποτε (*theon oudeis heōraken pōpote*, "no one has ever seen God"). Aside from the word order, all that has changed is the swapping of θεάομαι (*theaomai*, "behold," "gaze") in the sermon for ὁράω (*horaō*, "see," "look") in the Gospel. The shift should recall 1 John 1:1, where John professes having eyes that "have gazed upon" the uncreated Son. The language of gazing or beholding is, as we argued earlier in comments on 1 John 3:2, critical because sight can be transformative. What we look on with longing or intensity can change us, and when that is the beautiful, it transforms us toward beauty. Ideally, then, human transformation could occur by our beholding the divine. But because our eyes cannot perceive God as God is, this sort of transformative gazing is—for now—impossible. How, then, can the kind of transformation God desires take place? John 1:18 claims that part of the solution is that the Son, who is in close union with God, reveals God. The other part of the solution is here in verse 12: the actualization of God's love among those in union with each other also actualizes union with God, which is God's ultimate purpose.

This revelation about union with God and others leads us to answer the question of obligation in verse 11. Believers are compelled to love agapically because they cannot access union with Father and Son otherwise. And since that union is God's purpose for the whole world, the God-born most fully become themselves in agapic communion. Perhaps an analogy will help here. A policeman is obligated to uphold the law because he gets paid to do so. This is credit and debt. He does not have to do his job, but he should. Consider instead a woman who loves justice passionately and takes a job as a police officer. She is obligated to uphold the law, but her sense of obligation is internal. Her joy is fullest when she participates in the justice that she loves. She is acting in accordance with her truest nature. So it is with the God-born.

Verse 13 introduces another "in this" or "this is how" clause pointing toward an explanatory ὅτι (*hoti*, "because," "since"). The need for explanation should strike us as odd, though. Verse 12 has already described how it is that God lives in us and we in God: through loving one another. Why, then, should we need an explanation for how we are to come to know that this has happened? "This is how we know that we live in him and he lives in us: he has given us a share of his Spirit." It would seem that, given the explanation of love in verse 12, all it would take to know that we have union would be to discern whether we are living agapically. Why should John bring up the reception of the Spirit? The most likely explanation is that human beings rarely, if ever truly and fully, express divine love. Our *agapē* is parasitic on God's; it is, apart from the revelation of the Son, unknown and possibly unknowable. If we are to measure our union with God in terms of how well our love mirrors God's own, we are left to a counsel of despair or rampant self-deception. Something else must seal our assurance of union, namely, the gift of the Spirit.

Admittedly, our translation adds "a share" where the Greek only has ἐκ τοῦ πνεύματος (*ek tou pneumatos*, "from his Spirit"), but this addition is only for clarity, since "he has given us of his Spirit" carries the same meaning, but obliquely. God's Spirit is inexhaustible, wild and unpredictable, like the wind. To say that God has given "a share" is not to say that the church has received such and such an amount or some percentage of the Spirit; the Spirit is unquantifiable. Rather, it is to say that the church has the Spirit of God in perpetuity. The Spirit's mark cannot be erased from believers. John has used ἐκ (*ek*, "out of," "from") to indicate origination, and here this pattern remains uninterrupted. We could even gloss to say, "He has given us to have origin in his Spirit." That is, what matters to John here is not any particular experience of the Spirit but instead the very fact of the Spirit's givenness. John uses the perfect tense to emphasize that this gift has been given. In doing so, he confirms here what Jesus in the Fourth Gospel said would happen: that a paraclete would be sent (John 14:26). What Jesus promised has come to pass, and it is this—not an experience or sign—that guarantees union with God. Even when our love does not measure up to divine *agapē*, the seal of our union remains. To again use an analogy: our union with the divine is like a lamp that has been plugged into the wall. The connection is constant, but the light is not. The electricity is there, but it's untapped as long as the light remains turned off. Similarly, the Spirit connects us to the divine life, but that life remains inactive unless it is "switched on" in agapic love among believers.

Verse 14 begins with the emphatic "Now we." Here the authors draw attention to themselves,[61] reaffirming that they are the ones who (using the perfect tense) saw back then and (switching to the present tense) testify now that the

61. There is some dispute over the "special we" in 1 John. Where the "we" echoes the opening confession about those who saw and heard and handled (as here), I take John to

Father sent the Son as the world's savior. Verse 14 again echoes John 3:16–17, thus forming a thematic inclusio of sorts that marks 11–13 off from 7–10 and 14–16.[62] It is startling, then, when verse 15 reaches back into the theme of who remains or lives in God, since that topic seemed to have been addressed in verses 11–13. It even sounds as if John is (again?) contradicting himself. In 4:12 he claimed that God lives in those believers who love each other. Here in 4:15 he sets out a different standard.

God now lives in those who confess that Jesus is God's Son. With the possible exception of 1 John 1:9 (see comments above), the verb ὁμολογέω (*homologeō*, "confess") uniformly denotes public, open acknowledgment. Such confession involves thought and act: one must believe that Jesus is God's Son, and one must hold that faith publicly. It takes the aorist subjunctive here, suggesting a one-time confession—possibly baptism—that results in union with God. John's Christology is now wide-ranging. He has endorsed believing that Jesus came as a fleshy human being (4:2). Earlier, confession meant recognizing the Son—presumably that the Son is true Son of the Father, in filial relationship (2:23)—and here that the Son is the man Jesus.

There are two major points of interest here. First, there is the question about what union with God really requires. Is it loving one another? A specific public confession? Certain convictions about the Son's humanity and divinity? With whom exactly does God live? The second point of interest is John's burgeoning doctrine of Christ. Both questions receive treatment in the theology sections of this work, but a few remarks may be made here.

Union with the divine—the status of remaining in God—is not coterminous with "being a Christian." Union ebbs and flows according to a believer's heart, mind, and actions. Loving in action and in truth brings union. Confessing Jesus as the Son of God brings union. Knowing and actualizing the Son's humanity in a community of believing and loving people brings union. One or all give us access to an actualization of the divine life to which we are connected. To suggest otherwise would require an unnecessary reduction of all of John's union teaching, or it would make being a Christian hopelessly out of reach. John preaches many aspects of union in the hope that his hearers will recognize those areas in

---

be referring to himself and his fellow authors—credible witnesses whose testimony should convince the sermon's hearers.

62. An argument could be made to treat verses 11–13 separately from 14–16. However, the frequency of the *menei* language causes thematic bleed, as it were. While the sermon's point shifts slightly at 14, there is still a continuation of the concern about what it is to remain in (or live or have union with) God. In any case, the larger unit extends from 4:7 to 5:4a, and arguing over some of these divisions borders on the pedantic.

which they are lacking and strive to reacquaint themselves with the joy that is the birthright of the God-born.

With respect to Christology, John's language—while not explicitly trinitarian by the standards of church tradition—is at least "binitarian." That is, at this point in the sermon, Jesus has been acknowledged as unoriginated (1:1–3), Son of the Father (2:23), fully human (4:2), the special, unique Son of the Father (4:7–10), and now, the Son sent by the Father to save the world (4:11–16). Taken in sum, it is not hard to suppose that John confesses the Second Person of the Trinity, though that language is, historically, not yet in use.

Closing the section, John repeats the emphatic "and we" used in verse 14, indicating that he is again referring to the authors of the sermon, to reaffirm their personal experience of the radical nature of God. They have "come to know and trust in the love that God has for us." We have translated the dative preposition as "for" here, to smooth the English. It might be the case that God has or holds or maintains a level of *agapē* in the community. If so, then the more wooden "the love God holds in us" would be preferable. But the context pushes against such a reading. What John and his compatriots knew was the love of God revealed in the Son, which was a love for the world. Since the dative works both ways, the smooth "for us" is a better fit.

This verse strongly echoes Peter's confession in John 6:69, where the same first-person plural perfect tenses of "trust" and "know" are used to identify Jesus as God's "Holy One." John perhaps is claiming here to have been either one of the twelve disciples for whom Peter spoke in the Gospel or perhaps a close associate of Jesus. John has already claimed a close unity between love, God, and the Son; trusting in the *agapē* God has for us is tantamount to trusting in the Son, who is its ultimate manifestation.

John now repeats, "God is love." Trusting in the love God has for God's people is just another way of saying one trusts in God. And subsequently, living in love is living in God, and God lives in those who live in love. In the twenty-first-century West, the watering down of "love" has turned John's radical confession into a bumper sticker. John does not talk of "love" as we do; he goes out of his way to define agapic love as the radical self-emptying, self-giving love that finds true and perfect expression only in the sacrificial sending of the Son. Because we have so elasticized the semantic range of "love," we are in danger of supposing that the divine life is being experienced among those who hold each other in great affection or kindness. Great affection and kindness are no doubt present in agapic community, but they are augmented or fleshed out by sacrificial self-giving. Agapic community hurts; it is uncomfortable. "Living in love" involves a commitment to pouring oneself out and trusting that others will do likewise. Such relationships are fragile because even though the true light already shines, the darkness yet holds sway. Believers who wish to live in love must take care; antichrists may try to come in and take advantage of agapic lovers, abusing and cannibalizing with little regard for the cross from which such love emanates.

Moreover, it is worth noting here that John assumes from the outset that union with others is the goal of living in love. This assumption implies communities of persons rather than individual, heroic, self-sufficient believers. If life rightly lived is self-sacrificial, then, well, there must be other people who receive the benefits of one's self-sacrifice.

1 John 4:17–18

17 This is how love has reached its goal with us – so we have confidence in the day of judgment – that we are just like Jesus is in this world. 18 Fear is not in love. Instead, mature love drives out fear because fear carries punishment. Whoever is afraid has not yet reached love's goal.

It is difficult to know how this minisection fits in logically with the rest of the love discourse. Confidence and fear do not seem to be in view either before or after verses 17–18. It is best to treat it as John drawing out yet another implication of the presence of *agapē* in the life of believers. Complicating things further, the Greek syntax of verse 17 is awkward in the extreme, our proposed solution even having been deemed "most unnatural" at one time.[63] The verse begins with the customary "in this" or "this is how." The reader assumes that an explanatory ὅτι (*hoti*, "that," "because," "since") clause will follow. And it does, but not until after a strange purpose clause introduced with ἵνα (*hina*, "in order that," "that"). Most modern translations try to elide the syntactic difficulty by treating the ἵνα clause as giving the purpose of the clause beginning with "this is how," with the following ὅτι clause further fleshing out the explanation. The problem with this approach is not only that it is just as awkward as any other solution, but also that it is nonsensical; "love has been perfected [in the past: the verb is in perfect passive] that we have [in the future: this verb is in the present subjunctive] confidence in the day of judgment." The first clause needs explanation: it is asking the question, "How has love been perfected in us?" Taking the purpose clause as the answer to that question is tantamount to saying, "It hasn't, but it will have been when we have confidence at the judgment day." The best solution is to treat the purpose clause as parenthetical, however "unnatural" it might be.

63. Brooke Foss Westcott, *The Epistles of St. John: The Greek Text, with Notes and Essays* (Cambridge: Macmillan, 1886), 157

John has already demonstrated a certain inelegance in his Greek syntax; it is no further mar to his reputation to posit it again here. A contemporary gloss would be: "This is how love has reached its goal with us: we are just like Jesus in this world. Moreover, because we're like that, we have confidence when judgment day comes." The purpose clause would come more smoothly after the ὅτι clause, but the meaning is nevertheless clear. This rendering is important exegetically because it prevents a major theological problem. On the standard reading, agapic love's maturity is dependent on our confidence at the day of judgment. But this is to get things backward. Our confidence at the judgment day comes from being just like Jesus in the world now.

The Greek of verse 17 does not feature Jesus's proper name. Rather, as in 2:6 and in 3:3, 5, 7, and 16, John uses ἐκεῖνος (*ekeinos*, "that one") to refer to Jesus. And again, we have translated the perfect passive of τελειόω (*teleioō*, "mature," "make perfect") in the active for reasons described above, which is serendipitous in verse 17, where the "with us" causes exegetical difficulties for more conventional translations. What is at issue is whether *agapē* is passive, reaching maturity in a community (with the Greek μεθ' ἡμῶν [*meth' hēmōn*] being rendered "among us"), or whether it is active, reaching maturity through community participation. Since John has consistently emphasized active participation in love, the latter is much preferred; by making love's activity explicit, the problem resolves itself in English, and the preposition with the genitive can remain translated normally as "with."

"Judgment day" probably refers to a climactic conclusion to the final hour that John warned about in 2:18, perhaps featuring an ultimate or penultimate antichrist who fully and effectively opposes the church until Jesus ultimately conquers. Once the Lord has returned victorious, he will sort out humanity, as it were, determining who has union with the divine life and who does not. John is preaching here: those who wish to be confident at that time can know that they will be so when they are as Jesus is in this world. The present tense of "to be" here is important. Whatever it means to be like Jesus, it is something that Jesus is now, presently, rather than what he was before crucifixion and resurrection. As Jesus is, so are we, but "in this world." There are almost as many interpretations of what it is to "be as Jesus is" in commentaries as there are commentators. Suggestions range from moral parity, incarnate humanity, making Jesus's story our story, agapic love, sharing Jesus's relationship to the Father, and so on. But perhaps John is vague here for a reason. In other places where he refers to Christ with the pronoun "that one," he has been fairly specific about what aspect of Jesus is worthy of imitation or instantiation. In 3:3, for example, he stresses purity or holiness; in 3:5, sinlessness; in 3:7, righteousness. Perhaps the vagueness here should recall again the prologue, which evokes something of the totality, a summing up of all it is to be the unoriginated, unique Son of the Father. That person remains in eternity and is manifest here and now because of our union with the Son and each other. Since this relation leads to confidence when Jesus comes as judge, perhaps it indicates that Christians will sense a sort of familiarity with the Son, a family resemblance, as it were, kinship even. Knowing that *this* is the one with whom we share union means fearlessness before his judgment. And this would make the best sense: when we are recognizably the God-born, sharing in the divine nature and agapic communion, it is indeed the case that love's goal has been attained.

Again John summons the converse of what has gone before to flesh out the point. Whereas mature love brings confidence in the day of judgment, faulty love gives way to fear in verse 18. The word for punishment here, κόλασιν (*kolasin*, "punishment"), has a history of usage in the LXX that refers to punishment earned against and meted out by God. So, for example, Antiochus's execution of Andronicus for the murder of Onias in 2 Maccabees 4:38 is understood as the Lord repaying Andronicus with the punishment he deserved. In the Septuagint reading of Ezekiel 43:10–11 God will judge Israel's faithlessness with punishment. The word appears only twice in the New Testament, the other place being Matthew 25:46, where Jesus uses it to refer to eschatological punishment. Here, then, the "punishment" that inspires fear is likely eschatological punishment on the day of judgment. John is therefore calling on his readers to self-identify again. When you think about the return of Jesus in judgment, does it inspire confidence or fear? If fear, then there is something wrong with your *agapē* because fear is not in it. In fact, John amplifies the statement with a Hebraism. Not only is fear not in love, but mature love drives fear away. The verb βάλλω (*ballō*, "cast out," "drive out") anthropomorphizes the love that has reached its transformative goal. It is a strange metaphor, one that makes more sense in light of the following clause, ὅτι ὁ φόβος κόλασιν ἔχει (*hoti ho phobos kolasin echei*, "because fear carries punishment"). The verb ἔχει typically means "has" or "holds" and most translations gloss it as "implies" or "involves" or even "expects." John probably means that every object of fear carries with it an attendant harm. The fear of water carries with it the harm of drowning. The fear of fire carries with it the harm of being burned and so on.[64] In context, the fear of judgment day carries with it the harm of divine punishment. So the entire metaphor works like this: doubts about one's standing at judgment day prowl around like burglars, trying to infiltrate the mind's home. Mature *agapē* functions like a guard dog, driving or chasing the intruders out. The logic, though, is subtle. Mature love, the self-giving divine love that sent the Son to save the world, is what God is. If so, then familiarity with

64. Following Jobes, *1, 2, and 3 John*, 205.

God's essential nature chases fear away. What has one to fear from the Son who gave himself up in death out of love? The notion is absurd. The very apprehension of the nature of mature love categorically excludes the possibility of punishment or harm from the one who is mature love. Only someone with defective love, a love that is lesser, cheaper, more pedestrian, could worry about judgment from the Son of the Father.

John ends verse 18 with a warning: Whoever is afraid [of judgment day] has not reached love's transformative goal. The rhetoric is frightening; it evokes cataclysm and the end of history. Who would not be frightened of such a clash? The answer, of course, is someone who has not yet delved the depths of God's ridiculous, unmatchable love. The hearers of the sermon are forced to self-identify and respond. Those who can face the notion of the end of days with anticipation and confidence can be sure that they have correctly grasped the wondrous love of God. Those who tremble must decide to reengage God's love, rehearse and reignite the story of the atoning sacrifice God sent into the world to save the world. Incarnate that story in and among others who share it. And in that process, come to recognize or remember what God is like and why there is no need to fear.

1 John 4:19–5:1

19 We love because he loved us first. 20 When someone claims, "I love God," while
hating a brother or sister, that person is a liar. For if we aren't loving the brother or
sister we have seen, we aren't able to love God whom we haven't seen. 21 So this
is the command we have from him: those who love God must love their brothers
and sisters too. 5:1 Everyone who believes that Jesus is the Messiah is God-born. And
everyone who loves the parent loves the parent's child too.

Inattentive hearers could be forgiven for assuming that verse 19 preaches a love of reciprocity. It could be that our love is a response to God's love. But this would be a mistake because it would necessarily misconstrue agapic love for something else. Agapic is active, not a response; it must take the initiative, or it is not really self-giving at all. Perhaps our *agapē* is imitative of God's love. It is no doubt true that our love must imitate God's, but that cannot be what John means here because he uses "because"; God's love is somehow the cause of our love, not merely its template. It might then be that God's love is the origin of our love. God's surplus of self-giving love brought the world into being, sustained it, and then created space within it for us to spawn love as well. Our love is parasitic and predicated on God's. Again, this is surely true, but it is not John's meaning. Remember that God's love has a transformative goal. It is meant to change us.

And when it has changed us, we find that we have become loving too. We have become God-born through his love. God's love has made us God's children with God's DNA. And because we have that heritage, we have that nature too. God's love makes lovers of ordinary human beings.

In verse 20 we have continued to translate the conjunction with "when" rather than "if." Used with the subjunctive aorist of λέγω (*legō*, "say," "claim"), John is expecting the hypothetical he lays out to come to pass at some point or another. Inevitably, someone will claim to love God "while hating" a Christian sibling. We have glossed the present subjunctive "hate" with a present participle to ensure that the nowness of the Greek comes through in English. John is highlighting hypocrisy here. At the same moment that this person claims to love God, he or she is simultaneously hating a so-called brother. The latter act gives the lie to the former claim. The following coordinating conjunction "for" indicates that John will now explain why this is so. He hearkens back to the claim that no one has seen God in 4:12. And since no one has seen God, loving is difficult; it is not easy to love something one cannot experience directly. Humanity, however, tends to think the opposite. It seems much easier to "love" something far off and intangible than to love those with whom we are proximate. The orphans in a foreign country are easy to "love." A monthly payment, a yearly letter, and the satisfaction of knowing that our love has gone across the ocean into the life of someone we have not and never will meet. Loving the prickly widow in the next pew over, however—that is much more challenging.

John assumes the opposite to be the case. Loving the prickly widow makes it possible to love the orphan (and God) too. Loving the widow costs something. It requires patience and endurance. It will involve discerning her needs and desires and finding ways to meet those—even if she never reciprocates. It will mean building up genuine affection when to do so feels unnatural, as well as locating the hidden traits to which one's natural affections might respond. How much easier to simply love an invisible "God" whose invisibility makes such terrestrial demands on us impossible. It is more like loving an idea than a being. Surely this is a simpler task!

But it is not; verse 5:1b explains why. The given translation, "everyone who loves the parent loves the parent's child too," hides some of the awkwardness of the Greek. To begin with, John does not use the standard words for parent or child (as he has earlier in ch. 3). Instead, he uses participial forms of "beget": τὸν γεννήσαντα (*ton gennēsanta*, "the begetter," "the one who begot") and τὸν γεγεννημένον ἐξ αὐτοῦ (*ton gegennēmenon ex autou*, "the one begotten from him," "the one born from him"). The begetter clearly stands in for "God," and so it has been proposed that "the one born from him" refers to Jesus the Messiah. Presumably, the etymological relationship between the earlier μονογενής (*monogenēs*) and γεννάω (*gennaō*) is meant to carry the day, but this tie-in is insufficient. The Gospel of John uses various forms of γεννάω eighteen times. In all but one of these instances the texts are speaking of humans other than Jesus. Of the nine other occurrences in 1 John—including a reference to the God-born just below in 5:4—all refer to the God-born, not to Jesus. The remarkable consistency of Johannine usage, along with the persistent focus on the family of God ("brothers and sisters," "God-born") in this section, suggests that "the one born from him" is in fact a Christian brother or sister. But this raises the question why John uses participial forms of γεννάω rather than familial nouns like "father," "child," or "little one." John uses the begetting language to emphasize the filial resemblance between God and the God-born. They share in the same stuff, as it were. The apple has not fallen far from the tree. Love the one, and you will naturally love the other; you will be loving something very similar.

This background gives us the solution to the riddle in 4:20. Love of the seen, known child of God guarantees love of the unseen, unknown father of the child—because they share a nature. There is a resemblance between them. If you cannot love the prickly widow in the next pew, how can you possibly love the Father who begot her, whose nature she shares? The one who claims to love God and not the widow, who loves the far-off orphan but hates that one's spiritual family, this one does not love "God" or the "orphan" at all. If such people love anything, they love the idea of God that they have conjured, not the Father who sent his Son to save the world. And such a love must fall far short of mature *agapē*, for it is instantiated not in action and truth but in—at best—a weekly tithe and good feelings during a prayer. There is nothing self-sacrificial about such a love, nothing radical or self-giving. It is instead a covert form of self-love, a fictive object of affection that indulges the self and cohabits peacefully alongside the hatred of one's brothers and sisters.

We have skipped over 4:21–5:1a and now return to them. Taken together, the two verses repeat—with alterations and reversed order—the twofold command of 1 John 3:23: believe that Jesus is the Messiah, and love each other. In 3:23 the command is to believe "in the name" of the Son, "Jesus the Messiah." It may be that by the time John writes, Χριστός (*Christos*, "Messiah"), especially for Greek-speaking Christians, had become a part of Jesus's proper name. So while we assiduously translate it "Messiah," a case could be made for leaving it as "Christ" in 3:23. That is not the case in 5:1a. The ὅτι (*hoti*, "that") clause explains the content of what is believed, namely, that Jesus is the Messiah. In John 1:41 Andrew tells Peter, "We have found the Messiah [Μεσσίαν, *Messian*]." Then follows an editorial clarification: "which is translated 'Christ' [Χριστός, *Christos*]." *Messias* is the Greek transliteration of the Hebrew משיח (*māšîaḥ*, "anointed"), which explains the need for translation to *Christos*. The Johannine literature has a strong Hebraic understanding of messianic expectation; for this reason, to be God-born, you must know Jesus not just as the Son but also as Messiah, the anointed one of Israel. Jesus is Jewish; he has a Jewish tradition, a Jewish mission, and a Jewish religion. We are not called to believe in an ahistorical, supernatural, invisible, imaginary Christ. No, the command is to believe in the Jewish Messiah who rightly fulfills a Jewish mission of sacrifice and redemption. 1 John 4:21 completes the reiteration of the double command from 3:23: as we have argued extensively above, love for God demands love for the spiritual family, as the former is impossible apart from the latter.

1 John 5:2–4a

2 This is how we know that we love the children of God: whenever we love God and practice his commands. 3 This, then, is love for God: that we observe his commands. God's commands are not difficult, 4 because all the God-born defeat the world.

John's customary, explanatory "in this," or "this is how" leads to yet another infelicitous Greek construction. Our translation continues the custom of treating "this is how" as pointing forward, in this case to the clause beginning with ὅταν (*hotan*, "whenever"). This is the most natural, straightforward rendering of the text. As it happens, it also appears to create a tautology. Above, in 4:20–21, John seemed clear that love for God is predicated on love for one's spiritual family. Here, love for God's children appears to be known in love for God and practicing his commands. Either John is hopelessly confused, or there is some kind of loving dialectic in place, where love for God issues and is known in love for the spiritual family and vice-versa. The best solution to the apparent tautology is to remember that when John uses the word *agapē*, he is using it over and against common contemporary usage. He is engaged in lexical genesis—the extension of the meaning of *agapē* to something more than what it had meant before. He is, to put it bluntly, coining a new word.

Since the *agapē* that originates with God is novel and different, it is difficult to grasp, especially for hearts and minds attuned to the world's fractured and inert iteration. Thus, much of what John does in the agapic discourse of 4:7–5:4a is set up criteria that serve as guideposts. When so-called *agapē* does *x* or does not do *y*, then we may be sure that it is faux love, the world's corrupted imitation of the divine. The primary criterion—I borrow the term from Brown, who uses it similarly here—for divine *agapē* is the sending of the Son by the Father as an atonement sacrifice.[65] But that action was once for all and therefore strictly

65. Brown, *Epistles*, 537.

inimitable. How then can Christians actualize the same love that drove Jesus to the cross in the here and now? As we have seen above in comments on 2:3–6, it is significant that John does not formalize *agapē* beyond the sending of the Son. There is no list of ethical do's and don'ts, no hard specification of yes to this and no to that. *Agapē* shifts and metamorphizes according to cultures, contexts, and communities. But like "living in the light," there are some ways of walking or being that just cannot be agapic.

In the present case, we know we are loving the God-born with divine *agapē* when we are also loving God and regularly practicing God's commands. The verbs ἀγαπάω (*agapaō*, "love") and ποιέω (*poieō*, "do," "make") come in the subjunctive because they follow the conjunction ὅταν (*hotan*, "whenever"); what interests us here is that they appear in the present tense. The question John answers is this: How do I know that the love I have for my spiritual sister *right now* actualizes divine *agapē* instead of worldly *agapē* or filial love or romantic love or something that is not love at all? Rather than answer the question with a strict inventory of internal modes of being, John suggests asking a different question. Rather than worry about the agapic nature of your love for your spiritual sister, instead ask whether you are regularly loving God and regularly practicing God's commands. In fact, John goes on to collapse that distinction in 5:3, where love for God—here the objective genitive ἡ ἀγάπη τοῦ θεοῦ (*hē agapē tou theou*, "love for God")—just is doing what God commands. If you are in the habit (for comment on ποιέω [*poieō*] and "practice," see 1 John 2:15–17 above) of observing and doing God's commands, your love for your sister will be divine and not worldly. Referring to 4:20–21 above, if you wonder whether your love for God is divinely agapic, reflect not on your love for God but on your practice of loving your spiritual family. That you do the latter confirms the authenticity of the experience of the former. Love and action, love for God and love for the God-born, all mutually implicate one's love as divinely agapic.

If all this seems overly complicated and difficult—nay, impossible—to perform, 5:3c-5:4a softens the blow somewhat. There is an assurance that God's commands are not difficult or laborious. At the simplest level, John might say to someone who worries overmuch about his or her *agapē* that if maintaining love for God and others is troublesome and wearing and wearying, then you are doing it wrong. βαρύς (*barys*, "burdensome") is not common in the New Testament and spans a wide semantic range. With respect to following rules or commands, 1 John 5:3 strongly echoes Matthew 11:30, where Jesus's yoke is easy and his burden is light, and Matthew 23:4, where the religious elites tie up heavy (βαρέα, *barea*) loads on the backs of ordinary people and do not help with the carrying. Given the concern here with loving spiritual brothers and sisters, it is interesting that the Septuagint uses this word to describe the heaviness of the people on Moses because they require so much of him (Exod 18:18; Num 11:14, both rendering Hebrew כבד, *kabed*). Both are probably implicated here, since obeying God's commands and loving the spiritual family are so bound up in John's thought. We might imagine the once-indefatigable believers striving to serve and meet the needs of the family, assiduously attending to the scruples of Torah, only to find themselves exhausted and empty. How could such effort not be burdensome or difficult? What does John envision?

Verse 5:4a will help flesh out his meaning. John again uses the verb νικάω (*nikaō*, "defeat"), as he has in 2:13–14 and 4:4. The language of 4:4 is important. There, the reader will remember, John warns of the spirit or spirits of deception, those that go out—as here—into the world corrupting people and institutions antichristically, that is, instilling false beliefs and wayward practices. Defeating such demonic forces involves personal and communal transformation; union with the eternal Son who fully assumed human nature enables apprehension of the light and the ability to live within it. Winning the spiritual war depends on being changed into a people who live in dependent union with Christ.

Victory language explains how John's explanatory clause in 5:4a makes sense of 5:3b: God's commands are not difficult because they flow naturally from those who simply trust in Jesus, living in union with him and with other believers. Remember, the "commands" are not specified and change according to time and context. But they are not altogether relative either, for they lead to loving action and are based in a right understanding of who Jesus is and what he is like.

The divine commands are analogous to the rules of relationship that govern healthy, stable family life. Some of these rules are stable and mostly fixed—for example, do not lie to your spouse. But such a stark command necessarily gives under the pressures and circumstances of the relationship. There are times where it is probably better to remain silent than tell the whole, unvarnished truth to one's spouse. This is a judgment call, one that balances the need for truth-telling with the need for spousal care and a safe, loving space of communication. But it is not difficult to know what to say or not say *if* one intimately knows one's spouse. The regular intimacy of the relationship itself can nurture an intuitive, almost automatic ability to know what is or is not appropriate to maintain the status quo. Of course, life is not always like this, but the analogy holds: transformation into the children of God, who know God as Father and enjoy union with him and the Son, is not unlike the familiar intimacy of a healthy spousal or parental relationship, where the rules of conduct are somewhat unfixed and yet intuitive and easy. Thus John can rightly say that God's commands are not difficult, and if we wonder whether our *agapē* is worldly, we need only consider whether we know and are intimate with Christ and with our fellow believers.

1 John 5:4b–12

4b Now this is the victorious power that has defeated the world: our faith. 5 Who,
then, defeats the world if not those who believe that Jesus is the Son of God? 6 This
is the one who came through water and blood – Jesus Christ. Not in water only
but in water and in blood. And the Spirit is the one who testifies, since the Spirit is
truth. 7 Indeed, three are testifying:[66] 8 the Spirit and the water and the blood, and
the three are as one. 9 If we accept the testimony of human beings, the testimony
of God is weightier. For this is God's testimony: God has testified about *his Son*.
10 Those who believe in God's Son have the testimony within themselves, but those
who don't believe God make him out to be a liar, because they haven't believed
the testimony that God gave about his Son. 11 Now this is the testimony: God has
given us eternal life, and this life is in his Son. 12 Those who have the Son have life;
those who do not have God's Son do not have life.

Most translations render the noun νίκη (*nikē*) in 4b woodenly, as "victory," but this makes no literal sense in conjunction with the participial form of "defeat" that follows. Bluntly put, "victories" cannot "defeat" anything; they are, instead, the result of one party defeating another. In this case "our faith" has defeated the world. But this too is ambiguous. Not only could πίστις (*pistis*, "trust," "faith," "belief") be rendered "faithfulness"—namely, our fidelity or persistent effort defeats the world—but even if "faith" is taken as a metonym for something like "Christian religion," it still would not answer the question of how such a way of believing and acting has "defeated" the world. Moreover, the participle is in the aorist, indicating (as per our rendering) that the victory has already taken place. This also is puzzling, as much of John's rhetoric has involved spiritual warfare that takes place in the present. Where definitive victories have been

66. Older English translations based on the Textus Receptus such as the King James and New King James Bibles feature the so-called Johannine comma, a variant version of verses 7 and 8 that reads: "For there are three that bear witness in heaven: the Father, the Word, and the Holy Spirit; and these three are one. 8 And there are three that bear witness on earth: the Spirit, the water, and the blood; and these three agree as one." Interestingly, these words do not appear in any of the ancient Greek manuscripts and feature only in the Latin tradition, beginning in the late fourth century. Most think that the textual tradition began as an interpretive gloss in the margin that was copied as original. The circumstantial evidence is as compelling as the textual: this verbiage is found nowhere in the works of the Greek fathers who participated in the trinitarian controversies. Since, for example, Athanasius was familiar with 1 John, it would have been beyond odd for him to omit this language in his arguments against Arius. For a concise presentation of the evidence, see Bruce Metzger, *A Textual Commentary on the Greek New Testament*, 2nd ed. (Stuttgart: German Bible Society, 1994), 647–49.

cataloged (e.g., 1 John 2:13–14; 4:4), John has used the perfect tense of νικάω (*nikaō*, "defeat").

The Johannine literature makes more use of νικάω than any place else in the New Testament. It is almost always used to depict spiritual warfare: either direct conflict with the evil one (e.g., 1 John 2:13–14; Rev 12:11) or conflict against human agents under demonic influence (e.g., 1 John 4:4; Rev 2–3). Only here in 5:4b and in John 16:33 is it used to speak of defeating "the world." In John 16:33 Jesus ends his farewell discourse by encouraging the disciples to "take heart," since he, Jesus, has "conquered the world" (ἐγὼ νενίκηκα τὸν κόσμον, *egō nenikēka ton kosmon*). Jesus is explaining to the disciples that in the near future, he will be gone, and they will face persecution. But this prospect should not leave them hopeless because at such a time Jesus will have already defeated the human powers that have sought to destroy him and will have sent the Spirit to comfort and empower them in the truth. What is not said and is made explicit only in retrospect is that the victory itself comes through crucifixion and resurrection—Jesus's "glorification" in the Gospel of John. In terms of light and darkness, Jesus—the true light—enters the domain of darkness, exposing and opposing it at every turn. The world—the domain of darkness—strikes back, shaming and killing Jesus in a barbaric form of execution. But even this extreme response is not enough. Jesus is raised from death, sends his Spirit, and creates a permanent and expanding foothold on the earth—the church—that lives in the light and anticipates a time when the light is all in all. On this view, "our faith" in 5:4b is the ongoing trust in Jesus that results in participation in him and his victory. The "victory" is better understood metonymically as the triumphing power of Christ, accessed by spiritual union, that was inaugurated in simple trust in Jesus and continues into the present and the future.[67]

The rhetorical question in 5:5 confirms such a view nicely. Our wooden rendering—"if not those who believe"—is somewhat archaic but hews closely to the Greek. Syntactically, it is worth pointing out that Ἰησοῦς (*Iēsous*, "Jesus") is the first word in the explanatory clause, giving emphasis to the name "Jesus." This accords with John's insistence on faith in the incarnation: it is believing in the human man Jesus as Son of God that confers victory. In other words, it is *this man* and not some other figure, force, or spirit who lives and has power.

John's claim is a bold one because it is exclusive, even scandalous. To suggest that just one being—the Son of God—has the power to defeat the world is already strange; John lives in a world that assumes many gods, many powers, and

67. While he is somewhat oblique, Rudolf Schnackenburg (*Johannine Epistles: A Commentary*, trans. Reginald Fuller and Ilse Fuller [New York: Crossroads, 1992], 229–30) appears to espouse the substance of this view.

many forces. On Luke's telling, the apostle Paul capitalizes on this assumption to try to introduce the God of Israel to educated, pagan audiences (Acts 17:22–31). In such a context monotheism itself is peculiar, but John's further claim, that the one God's unique, uncreated, unoriginated Son has come as a real human being, extends the radicality of the gospel. In verses 6–12 John explains why his perhaps as-yet-undecided hearers can countenance it.

Verse 6 emphasizes that Jesus is the one who came "through water and blood." Much hangs on the translation of the preposition διά (*dia*, "by," "through") because this is the first time in the sermon that John has mentioned water and only the second time that he has mentioned blood (see 1 John 1:7). The immediate co-texts offer little in the way of a hint about what John might mean. In the larger Johannine corpus, water features prominently and often takes on a symbolic cast. The water can represent baptism (John 1:26–33), the Spirit (John 3:5; 7:38–39), eternal, divine life (John 4:7–15; 5:7; Rev 7:17; 8:10–11 [as death, life's opposite]; 21:6; 22:1, 17), and spiritual cleansing (John 13:5–10). There is, of course, some overlap here: life and spiritual cleansing have strong associations with the coming and presence of the Spirit, and given the nature of Jesus's baptism, baptism and Spirit become strongly associated as well. Just as with water, blood features symbolically in the Johannine literature. It can represent human birth (John 1:13), eucharistic wine (John 6:53–56), cleansing from sin and glorification (1 John 1:7; Rev 1:5; 7:14), and death as sacrifice or ransom (Rev 5:9; 12:11).

In only one other place in the Johannine corpus are water and blood mentioned together: John 19:34, where a Roman soldier pierces the crucified Jesus's side with a spear, and "blood and water came out." This clause is suggestive for two reasons. First, the Fourth Gospel uses ἐξέρχομαι (*exerchomai*) for "came out," and here 1 John uses the same verbal root ἔρχομαι (*erchomai*, "come," "go") to describe Jesus's coming. Second, in both John 19 and 1 John 5 blood and water are anarthrous, the lack of an article indicating that they should be treated as a single object, as it were, rather than separately. John emphasizes this significance in 5:6 by subsequently treating them separately with articles. The point is that whatever water and blood mean, they can be thought of as separate things, but in the Son's coming they must be understood as a unity. Likewise, at the crucifixion, Jesus's side produces a unity, a mingling of water and blood, not one without the other.

The crucifixion in John's Gospel should be treated as a birth scene, where the co-mingling of water and blood signals the spiritual birth of God's human children.[68] One of the more interesting aspects of the crucifixion account in the Fourth

68. Thomas Andrew Bennett, *Labor of God: The Agony of the Cross as the Birth of the Church* (Waco, TX: Baylor University Press, 2017), especially chapters 1 and 3.

Gospel is how it changes the relationship between the disciples and God. Before Jesus's crucifixion God is "Father" only to Jesus. After the crucifixion and resurrection, Jesus tells Mary he is going to "my Father and your Father" (John 20:17). Similarly, during the crucifixion scene, Jesus's mother becomes the mother of the beloved disciple (John 19:26–27). The crucifixion—the labor of God—changes the family relations between Jesus, the Father, and Christians irrevocably. Such a reading makes good sense of this text as well. If we understand blood to allude to humanity and human birth—as in John 1:13—and water to allude to the divine, eternal life mediated by the Spirit, we can understand the unity of water and blood as a reference first to the incarnation, in which the divine spiritual life is mingled with the life found in human blood, and second to the union with the divine that all blood-born believers may experience once they have become God-born at the cross. "Water and blood" represent divine life and human life united.

In terms of John's overall argument here in chapter 5, verse 6 alludes to something unique about Jesus: he was born through blood, that is, as a normal human being, but he also came through Spirit, bearing the eternal, unoriginated divine life to the world. This is what separates Jesus from every other divinity, power, or force, what gives Jesus immediacy and immanence and also power and transcendence. For this reason believers do in fact defeat the powers of darkness, though they are mere human beings: by trusting in Jesus, they enjoy union with his human and divine nature, sharing in blood and water.

John's secondary emphasis in verse 6b, "not in water only but in water and blood," is necessary. The idea that spiritual powers or gods or demonic spirits could come to the world was not strange in the ancient world. There was little in the way of what we think of today as atheism—the ancients simply assumed that there were spirits that had some congress with the physical world. As Christianity emerged, many of the earliest heresies adopted some form of docetism, the notion that Jesus was not a real human being. The specific doctrines are variegated, but the uniting thread posits a thoroughgoing dualism, that the human and the divine cannot mingle or be united. Whatever Jesus was, he was not human as we are human. In John's terminology, he did not "come through blood." John and his friends know the opposite to be the case. They, after all, saw, heard, touched, and handled. It is therefore essential to John's sermon that Jesus came not only through water (i.e., spiritual, divine, eternal life) but also through blood (i.e., genuine human body and life).

Because his claims are radical, in 6c John invokes legal terminology—"testifying"—to defend them. In this he is following the pattern of Jesus as depicted in the Fourth Gospel. There, Jesus's authority and identity are challenged by several groups: the followers of John the Baptist (3:26), Jewish people offended by his ministry (5:16), the Pharisees (8:13), and Jews curious as to Jesus's messianic identity (10:19, 24). In each case, Jesus's authority and identity are vindicated by the testimony of witnesses. So, in John 3 John the Baptizer offers testimony on Jesus's behalf to convince his followers. In the majority of cases, however, Jesus is left to defend himself, as it were. In John 5 the Father is said to witness on Jesus's behalf through the signs and wonders that Jesus accomplishes. Because these signs and wonders are in keeping with the will of the Father, Jesus claims that the Father has authored them (John 5:36). Jesus then goes on to suggest that the Father's word in the Scriptures/Torah also testify to his authority and identity (5:37–47). In John 8 Jesus again claims that his enemies do not know the Father and so do not hear his testimony about the Son. In John 10 it is again Jesus's doing the Father's works that are the Father's testimony.

In effect, Jesus's authority and identity cannot be confirmed apart from a prior recognition of the nature and character of the Father as revealed in the Hebrew Scriptures, especially the law of Moses. If those hostile to Jesus had read rightly, they would know a Father-commanded work when they saw one. But because they have badly misunderstood the nature and character of the Father, they cannot see that the kinds of signs Jesus performs could have come only from God. Moreover, if they could see that, then they would also see that Jesus's claim of God as Father and the even more clearly blasphemous claim that "the Father and I are one" (John 10:30) are both true and testified to by the Father himself.

All this serves as necessary background to the claim here in 1 John that the Spirit now gives witness to the authenticity of the through-water-and-blood Jesus. In John 15:26–27, Jesus anticipates the same kind of battle over authenticity and Christian faith that will take place after he has gone. He reassures his followers that he will send the Spirit and suggests that "the Spirit who comes out from the Father" will continue the same sort of testifying that the Father has been doing during Jesus's ministry. It bears repeating that this testimony is indirect—it depends on knowing God rightly through the Scriptures and then recognizing that self-same God's works in present contexts.

All of which brings us to verses 6c–12, where John invokes a chain of testimony that begins with the Spirit. The Spirit, having been sent by Jesus from the Father (John 15:26), is, by definition and origin, "the truth." The Spirit's "testimony" is the present equivalent of the Father's testimony about the Son during Jesus's earthly ministry in the Fourth Gospel. Those who possess a right understanding of the God witnessed to in the Scriptures will see that the sort of life on display in John and his friends is the same blood-and-water life that was present in Jesus and is the life of the Father. Verse 7, a clause beginning with another ὅτι (*hoti*, "for," "that"), should be read as "further specification" rather than an explanation.[69] John has claimed one witness, but just as Jesus claimed more than one

69. So Brown, *Epistles*, 581.

witness against his interlocutors in the Fourth Gospel, so must other witnesses be called here. To call three witnesses is, in Jewish tradition, necessary for cases to be determined according to Deuteronomy 19:15. Just as Jesus pointed to the Scriptures, his signs and wonders, and John the Baptist to prove the Word of the Father, so John here shows that even in the absence of those witnesses, three witnesses continue testifying. The present active participle of testify indicates that even though Jesus himself is not present, witnesses continue to testify on his behalf now and into the future.

Verse 8 claims that the three witness are the Spirit, the blood, and the water, and that "the three are as one." The construction here is awkward, and a wooden translation might read, "the three are into the one." The Fourth Gospel features similar phrasing in 11:52 and 17:23, but in neither of those cases does the numeral have a definite article. John 11:52 speaks of gathering the dispersed children of God "into one." The force of the preposition there is of convergence, drawing disparate entities into oneness. This is likely the force here: three otherwise disparate witnesses give independent testimony that converge into one testimony: that Jesus is God's Son. This, in conjunction with our previous consideration of what "Spirit," "blood," and "water" signify, produces a powerful argument. Invoking the Spirit means drawing on a right reading of the Scriptures concerning the nature and character of God and showing that Jesus manifests that nature and character. Blood signifies the Son's humanity, that Jesus was flesh and blood like the rest of us, just as those who saw, heard, and handled have said. And water signifies the divine life of God, a nature foreign to those who have not been God-born but familiar to those who have, a life that opens new possibilities for life here and now and points to the fullness of the life to come.

Verse 9 introduces a new witness: the Father of the Son. It is interesting that the verse begins with a contrast introduced by thc conjunction εἰ (*ei*, "if"). The contrastive conjunction indicates that the previous three witnesses—the Spirit, the water, and the blood—are mediated to us by human testimony. And this conclusion makes sense. While the Spirit is certainly not human, our understanding of the Scriptures comes from the Spirit through human mediators—teachers, mentors, and so forth. Likewise, the testimony of Jesus's human life comes through human witnesses—John and his friends who actually knew the man Jesus of Nazareth. The testimony of the water, the divine life, is communicated by those believers who have experienced it and wish to see it shared.

John tells us now that, however compelling the Spirit, the water, and the blood are, the testimony of the Father is weightier. Older translations read μείζων (*meizōn*) as "greater," since it is the comparative adjective, but this reading ignores the immediate context. Here, as Jesus does in John 5:31–40, John is comparing the veracity of witnesses. In John 5 Jesus admits that his own testimony would not be valid according to Deuteronomic law, so he first invokes John the Baptizer. This human witness is valuable, but Jesus then points to an even more trustworthy witness, the Father himself. God, being infinitely more truthful than even the holiest human, has a testimony that is more convincing or, as per our translation, "weightier."

The following conjunction is again forward pointing and causal, introducing the unspoken question of what God's testimony is. It points to the next ὅτι (*hoti*, "for," "that"), which is explanatory, represented by the colon in the above translation. John's point is that God's testimony concerns not just a man, not himself, but a son of a father. This is filial testimony, God revealing more than a prophet or a priest or a king. Jesus comes as Son, as Son of the Father. This is a critical christological point. While Jesus certainly does function as a prophet, priest, and king, John here suggests that his primary identity according to God is filial. Understanding the content of God's testimony in this way helps make sense of the seeming tautology that follows in verse 10.

In verse 10 John appears to set up something like a tautology. Those who believe in Jesus have God's testimony within themselves, and those who do not believe God's testimony about Jesus make God to be a liar. It seems that one must believe in Jesus first in order to receive God's testimony. Or perhaps upon believing in Jesus, God's testimony is simultaneously or perhaps coterminously obtained. Either way, it seems as though God's testimony is unavailable to those who do not believe. If you do not believe, then you do not have the testimony. If you have the testimony, you have believed. The conundrum is resolved through careful attention to the use of "son" in this section. God's witness is about his Son, not some other kind of person or being. As we have been arguing, the sending of a Son—a person who shares union with divine and human life and fully instantiates the nature and character of God in a human being—makes sense only on a particular understanding of God's nature and character.

Indeed, such an understanding was in John's day—and remains now in ours—quite ridiculous. But John knows that God has been testifying about his special Son from the beginning. Everything God has done with and to and through Israel has been screaming, "I have a Son!" to anyone who had the ears to hear, as Jesus put it. God's words and actions and laws have been saying, "I am radically gracious and faithful, I will give of myself endlessly to give you life and sustain it, and I will share this selfsame nature with you fully and without reservation." Such a God would be expected not to send a priest or a king or an angel or even just a spirit. Such a God would be expected to have and give a singular Son fully bearing his nature and character. What John says is simple: if you hear God giving testimony about a Son and not something or someone else, that is who you are looking for and that is the one in whom you will believe. If you think "God" gives testimony about anything else, you are making God a liar. Misknowing, mishearing, or misunderstanding God's testimony means not recognizing that it is and has always been about God having a Son.

The beginning of verse 11, "Now this is the testimony," functions as a Hebraic intensification, repeating and expanding on verse 9c: "For this is God's testimony: God has testified about *his Son.*" Whereas up until now the focus has been on God's filial testimony, now John expands and fills what it is for God to have borne testimony about a Son. Not only has God always and everywhere testified about having a Son, the sort of God who would have and send a special Son would also share that Son's (and his own) life, the eternal life. Thus, the expansion of God's testimony in verse 9 here in verse 11: "God has given us eternal life, and this life is in his Son." If God is radically agapic, that is, self-giving and self-sharing—as John has taken pains to suggest—then of course God's testimony is and always has been a testimony of giving his divine, eternal life to the world through his sending of the divine, eternal-life-possessing Son.

The fourfold repetition of forms of ἔχω (*echō*, "have," "possess") with accusative forms of ζωή (*zōē*, "life") in verse 12 is distinctly Johannine, occurring in fourteen verses in the Gospel of John. In all of these, the life is either explicitly or implicitly "eternal life" and is granted by the Father to the Son (5:26) and is accessed by human beings through belief (e.g., 3:16; 6:40), through following Jesus (8:12), or by consuming Jesus's "flesh and blood" (6:53–54). Here in 1 John the phrasing occurs in three verses, but here in chapter 5, in successive verses, 12 and 13. Whereas the phrasing in the Fourth Gospel mentions "having eternal life," here the emphasis is on "having the Son." This makes sense logically because John's preaching in this section has been centered on the essentiality of trusting not just in any version of Jesus, but in the eternal Son of the Father, who fully assumed human flesh and shares union with us and with the Father. This is the Son that all faithful, true testimony—human and divine—has referenced. On John's view, there is no other access to the divine life; one must trust in Israel's Messiah or else one will not have access to life and will be in danger of finding one's rootedness in the devil. The possibilities are stark and uncompromising, all the more so since the final hour is at hand and the evil empire is being swallowed up in the light.

1 John 5:13–21

13 I have written these things to you so that you can know that you have eternal
life – you who believe in the name of the Son of God. 14 Now this is the confidence
we have before God: when we ask for something in keeping with his will, he listens

to us. [15] And since we know he hears us when we ask, we know that the things we
have asked from him are ours. [16] When you see your brother or sister sinning (in
a way that is not to death), pray, and God will give them life (to those whose sin
is not to death). There is "to death" sin; I do not say you should pray about that.
[17] All disorder is sin, but not all sin is "to death." [18] We know that none of the God-
born sin. Instead, the God-born protect themselves, and the evil one cannot touch
them. [19] We know we are from God, while the whole world finds itself in the evil
one. [20] We know, then, that the Son of God has come and given us comprehension
so that we can recognize the true God. And we are in the true God, in his Son, Jesus
Christ. This man is the true God and eternal life. [21] Little children, protect yourselves
from idols!

The final section of the sermon begins with several notable features. Verse 13 closely echoes John 20:31, the raison d'être of the Fourth Gospel, which was written "that you may believe" and "have life in his name." In 1 John 5:13 the goal is slightly different. Here John writes "so that you can know that you have eternal life." This goal fits with John's rhetorical strategy: he has repeatedly put his hearers on the spot, forcing us to self-identify as in the light or not, in union or not, a spiritual young adult or not, and so forth. We have preserved the Greek word order, where "you who believe in the name of the Son of God" is a dative present participle unpacking the "you" at the beginning of the verse. This description comes after the more important programmatic statement about knowing that one has eternal life. This is the first time John has reverted to the first-person singular ἔγραψα (*egrapsa*, "I have written," "I have been writing") since 2:26 and, combined with the purpose statement, it clearly demarcates verse 13 as the beginning of the end of the text. Nevertheless, what has come before is still in mind, since John repeats the "have" + accusative of "life" from verse 12. This does not mean, however, that "these things" should refer only to the previous section, 5:4–12, any more than the Gospel's purpose statement should refer only to the prior pericopes regarding Jesus's resurrection in chapter 20.

Verse 14 recalls both 2:28 and 3:21–22. The connections are lexical and thematic: the noun παρρησία (*parrhēsia*, "confidence") is used in both, and both involve the believer's status before Christ (2:28) and the Father (3:21–22). Moreover, the verb "ask" is used here in 5:14–15 and in 3:22 to refer to prayer, and in both places John expects God to answer. The verse begins with the familiar καὶ αὕτη ἐστίν (*kai hautē estin*, "and this is"), which leads in our translation to the colon, followed by the also familiar conditional ἐάν (*ean*), translated here as "when," as in 2:28 and 3:21–22 above. We have glossed κατὰ τὸ θέλημα αὐτου (*kata to thelēma autou*, "according to his will") as "in keeping with his will" to preserve the Johannine emphasis on union between the believer and God; this rendering keeps the present section concordant with the teaching in chapter 3, where the believer-in-union possesses a sort of synergy with the Father. In such a state what is asked is obtained, as here. There may be a chiasm in verses 14–15—"a touch of style in this laborious and prosaic section":

we ask
    he hears
    he hears
we ask.[70]

Of course it is impossible to know whether this form was intentional, but we should not miss the underlying logic. When the believer is sharing in the divine life, relations with God are harmonious and mutual. There is almost a rhythm to the back-and-forth of knowing, asking, receiving.

John then assumes in verse 15 that God's hearing us is synonymous with us receiving what we ask. The Greek phrasing here makes for an awkward English construction. A wooden translation would be "we have the things asked that we have asked from him." Our gloss "the things we have asked from him are ours" hews closely to John's diction, but it obscures his continued use of the verb "have," which likely represents an attempt to retain a thematic and lexical connection to the discussion of "having life" in the previous section. This textual link indicates that those who have eternal life are the ones who can expect to be in sync with God's desires and can therefore expect to have their prayers answered.

Just as the continued use of "have" connects verse 14 and 15 to the previous section, so does the future active of "ask" in verse 16 provide a textual link to what has come before. The high degree of lexical repetition signals to the hearers that John's concerns here are not thematically disparate, even if they might sound that way. That is, praying for sinning siblings is a part of sharing in the divine life, just as living and praying in keeping with God's will is. In a way, John's associative language conjures an image of ideal Christian life, wherein the believer's access to union through Christ results in certain states of knowing and prayer.

Exegesis of verses 16 and 17 is fraught, given that here too we appear to encounter a reiteration of John potentially contradicting himself concerning the issue of Christian sin. To begin with, it is critical to continue translating the conjunction ἐὰν (*ean*) as temporal rather than conditional (i.e., "when" rather than "if"). This rendering puts John's teaching here in chapter 5 in harmony with the teaching in 1:8–9, where all—even those in union with the divine life—sin. John

70. So Brown, *Epistles*, 609–10.

anticipates a situation that will occur among believers, a situation in which it becomes clear to one Christian that a spiritual sibling is ἁμαρτάνοντα ἁμαρτίαν μὴ πρὸς θάνατον (*hamartanonta hamartian mē pros thanaton*, woodenly, "sinning a sin but not to death"). The use of the verb and its cognate noun is a Hebraism, intensifying the force of the verb. This practice is not uncommon in the LXX (e.g., Lev 5:6) nor indeed in the Johannine literature—see the previous verse![71] John's syntax brings home a harsh reality of Christian life. The present-tense participle and the addition of the cognate noun suggests that while it might be surprising, it is nevertheless the case that while we are in active, mutual union with God, other believers will be persistently sinning. The qualifying "not to death" functions parenthetically (as suggested by our use of literal parentheses in the above rendering) to remind hearers that there is sin and there is sin-to-death.

The Johannine corpus uses θάνατος (*thanatos*, "death") in a variety of ways. It can refer to physical death (e.g., John 11:4; Rev 2:10), but much more often it signifies the state of someone who does not possess eternal life. So, in John 5:24 the one who has eternal life has moved or transferred from death into life. Perhaps tellingly, 1 John 3:14 echoes this phrase—maybe even quotes it—in the only other place in the sermon featuring θάνατος. The reader will recall the section in 1 John 3 that equates hating a spiritual sibling to murder and claims that anyone who does not love "lives in death." This context suggests that here, "death" should be understood as the spiritual state of those who categorically reject the eternal divine life and union with the Father through the Son. The reader will also recall exegesis of 1 John 3:4–10, where we argued for an apocalyptic reading of "lawlessness" and "righteousness." Rebellion is John's way of talking about those who fundamentally oppose the light and life, who take the side of their true father, the devil, who have their origins irrevocably in the darkness. It is probable that John is reinvoking that notion here.

He makes two assumptions. First, believers in union with Christ will be able to tell the difference between those who sin and those who sin-to-death. Second, the antidote to sinning is not "righteousness" or "repentance" or "forgiveness" but, in verse 16, "life." We will treat each in turn. "Ask" appears in the future tense, not the imperative, but still carries something of a command. The entire sentence begins with the temporal conditional; thus, John is looking forward to something that will happen and describes the proper response. The implied future in our translation captures both the future orientation and the slight imperative, "When you see . . . pray." We could just as easily translate, "When you see . . . you will pray." In either case, John assumes that having eternal life grants the believer a perceptive advantage, an ability to discern between a fellow believer who strug-

71. Contra Smalley, *1, 2, and 3 John*, 300.

gles with sinning and someone fundamentally hostile to the invading reign of God. This discernment could be subtler than what we might expect. Indeed, the New Testament authors frequently warn against poseurs—enemy agents, as it were—who infiltrate the church with the intention of destroying it (e.g., Matt 7:15; John 10:12; Acts 20:29). Given John's warnings and commendations earlier in the sermon, his teaching here suggests that faith communities must count as leaders some whose obvious, intimate union with Christ gives them the vocation—to say nothing of the credibility—of identifying and ejecting predators. John makes this understanding clear at the end of verse 16, repeating that "there is 'to death' sin" and, in the present indicative, "I do not say you should pray about that." It is worth noting that he does not forbid such asking, but instead merely refrains from recommending it. Perhaps John is placing a humble limit on his own ability to divine what God might redeem and what God might not; thus, even if praying for a rebel appears hopeless, some might continue asking in faith and, on a rare occasion, God might see to it that the rebel lives.

The second linguistic oddity—that the remedy for sin is "life" rather than repentance or righteousness—becomes much less strange in light of the distinction between sin and sin-to-death. In John's theological imagination, union with Christ is the eternal, divine life of God experienced and enacted amid this world. But such union is threatened by persistent reversion to the so-called life of the old age, which, John has already noted, is really a kind of death-in-life (1 John 3:14). To use a more contemporary metaphor, union with Christ could be likened to an electronic device plugged into an electrical socket. Instead of electricity, Christ supplies the believer with eternal life; however, just as an electrical socket might be defective or switched off, the union conduit to eternal life in Christ can be derailed by a believer's continual traipsing about in the dark. Still, it is nevertheless telling that John does not suppose that strenuous moral effort on the wayward believer's part is what will bring such a one back from the dark or resupply this one with life. No, God does these things on God's own, in response to the faithful prayer of a spiritual sibling.

Verse 17, it must be admitted, is somewhat tedious. One suspects, however, that the repetition is John's rhetorical attempt to emphasize the difference between sin and sin-to-death. And, it turns out, the historical bewilderment of commentators over his supposed contradictions concerning sin in the lives of believers indicates that he was right to do so. The novel diction in 17 is ἀδικία (*adikia*, "wrongdoing," "unrighteousness," "disorder"). We do well to remember that the only other time in the sermon that John uses ἀδικία is in 1 John 1:9, where it describes Jesus cleaning up our "disorder" so that we can be pure before God. John is just recognizing what is obvious. Not even the most stalwart believer or community is fully in keeping with the divine ordering of things. Sure, there is a tremendous amount of light, but there are a few, hopefully faint and receding, shadows as well. John's logic is explicit even if the coordinating and contrastive καὶ (*kai*, "and," "so," "but") is not: a good gloss of 17 might be, "All disorder is sin, but *such* sin is not 'to death.'"

With the standing distinction between sin and sin-to-death, verse 18 is clearly deploying the latter. John has not the diction to make the lexical contrast that we have, so instead he belabors the point, piling on seemingly contradictory statements to drive home the differences between sin and sin-to-death. The opening "we know" is rhetorical, inviting the hearer to self-identify as one who is with John and his compatriots. This self-identification extends into the following clause, where "none of the God-born sin." Our translation rolls together the πᾶς (*pas*, "every," "all"), which describes "those born from God," and the negating οὐχ (*ouch*, "not") to make the more direct and felicitous English "none of the God-born sin" rather than a wooden "every person born from God does not sin." From a syntactic standpoint, some might wish to translate the present-tense ἁμαρτάνει (*hamartanei*, "sin," "sinning") as "continuing to sin" or "persisting in sin" (so, e.g., the NLT's "make a practice of sinning"). Unfortunately, John already has a phrase with this implication, namely, ποιέω (*poieō*, "do") + ἁμαρτία (*hamartia*, "sin"; 1 John 3:4, 8–9). The impulse to overtranslate the present tense here likely arises from a desire to make sense of John's seeming contradictions. Without the crucial sin/sin-to-death distinction, verse 18 sounds confusing at best and incoherent at worst—but it is neither. Those whose origins are in God, who share union with Christ and the divine eternal life, are simply incapable of rebellion; they are not able to reenvision the world according to the darkness, according to the devil's deceptive, murderous intents. The Spirit of Deception has been banished, and they are essentially ordered according to the light. The God-born could not sin any more than those liberated from Plato's cave could continue believing that the shadows present the truly real or Nietzsche's Übermensch could submit to the morality of slave religion.

The following clause in verse 18 is notoriously controversial, in part because of its grammatical ambiguity. The difficulty begins with the shift from the perfect passive to the singular aorist participle, "the one who has been born" to "the one who was born." While the Johannine writings occasionally use the aorist tense when speaking of someone born of God (e.g., John 3:5; 1 John 4:7), the participial construction is always in the perfect except here. Is John giving an example of what a person who is born from God does, or as many have read it, is he perhaps referencing Jesus as the only-begotten? The NRSV, TNIV, and NASB explicitly choose the latter route. This reading is made more possible because some of our best and earliest manuscripts read αὐτόν (*auton*, "he," "him"; NA[27]) rather than the reflexive ἑαυτόν (*heauton*, "himself"; NA[28]). So the TNIV reads, "the One who was born of God keeps them safe," using the plural English pronoun rather than the singular to preserve gender inclusivity.[72] The biggest problem with such a reading is that nowhere else in the Johannine corpus is Jesus referred to as "the one born from God." Rather, every time Jesus's ontological relation to the Father is explicitly mentioned, it is as the singular Son, the "one and only" (John 1:14, 18; 3:16, 18; 1 John 4:9).

It is usually on theological grounds that the plainest reading of this clause is treated as suspect. On this reading, "himself" is read as reflexive, and "God-born" is thought of as referring to a specific believer. So the NKJV's "he who has been born of God keeps himself." The difficulty with such a reading, it is said, is that it makes believers responsible for ensuring that, as per the final clause of the verse, "the evil one cannot touch them." This is apparently problematic because the overwhelming consensus of the Johannine literature is that it is God or Christ—not Christians—who is responsible for security from the enemy. In John 10:28–29 both Jesus and the Father ensure that no one can snatch the sheep away. 1 John 3:8 declares it Jesus's mission—not ours—to destroy the devil's works. Jesus prays to the Father in John 17:15, asking the Father to protect his followers "from the evil one." This is all true, but there is also a strong Johannine penchant for believers overcoming" or "conquering" (e.g., 1 John 2:13–14). The power to have victory over temptation or faithfulness in the face of suffering is surely from the Spirit, but it is manifested in the lives of believers-in-union with Christ (see the numerous examples in Rev chs. 2 and 3). Fortunately, the knot unravels itself once we recognize that John is talking about sin rather than sin-to-death. First, he states that the God-born do not participate in the rebellion, that is, sin-to-death. The contrastive construction conveys what they do instead, namely, remain alert, watchful, on guard, because enemy action is afoot. This is the final hour, the beginning of a new age, and the evil one is sending antichrists to disrupt the advance of the light. Believers are incapable of rebellion, but it is a persistent threat *from outside*. The natural response is vigilance—the sort demonstrated by the young adults and parents of chapter 2—which ensures that "the evil one cannot touch them."

Verse 18 began with "we know"; verse 19 and 20 do the same. As in 18, this is a rhetorical ploy, inviting hearers of the sermon to identify themselves as John's coreligionists and affirmers of his teaching. Verse 19 continues the thought pattern. There are two opposing forces: those who are from God, and everyone and everything else—the whole world, which finds itself ἐν τῷ πονηρῷ κεῖται (*en tō ponērō keitai*, "sourced in the evil one"). The verb κεῖμαι (*keimai*) is difficult to translate here, as it usually means to lie down or recline (e.g., Luke 2:12). It

72. So recently, Jobes, *1, 2, and 3 John*, 237–38, and Lieu, *1, 2, and 3 John*, 230.

could be that John is leaving exactly how the whole world is lying unsaid, that is, lying under the power of the evil one. Most modern translations take this route; indeed, every other Johannine use of this verb has this standard meaning. However, every other time John uses it, he is also referring to an actual physical object—this is the only metaphoric usage of the term. If we read the καὶ (*kai*, "and," "so," "but") as coordinating yet another set of contrasting clauses, then it makes sense to read, "while the whole world finds itself in the evil one" (so BDAG s.v.). In either case the whole world is under enemy control, but for John the more concerning issue is that the whole world has—for now—the evil one as its source and foundation. As the light advances, the world "finds itself" in this position. What was once an obscured origin, an unquestioned status quo, is revealed by the clear counterorigination of the church and the God-born. The presence of the church and its reordering in the light clarify that the whole world is in danger of rebellion and, having been so put on notice, must transfer allegiance, believing in the name of the Son for a share in the eternal life.

The "we know" that begins verse 20 is followed by a conjunction, here functioning to emphasize that the final piece of knowledge is in keeping with those in 18 and 19 and follows conceptually. That is, it is the revelation of the Son of God that makes knowledge of the God-born and devil-born possible and certain. Likewise, the fact that "we know" about sin and sin-to-death and about our divine origins and DNA, and also that we possess union and eternal life—all of this depends on the prior recognition of the Son and thus right understanding of God. And this is exactly what John affirms in what follows as he builds to his penultimate climax, the confession of Christ as "true God." The Son of God has come and given διάνοιαν (*dianoian*, "mind," "thought," "comprehension"). This is a relatively rare word in the New Testament; it is notably added to the Shema by Jesus in Mark 12:30, meaning "mind" or "thoughts." Here it is meant to convey understanding or comprehension. Knowing the person and character of the Son gives Christians a framework or matrix for understanding the truth about the divine. That is, God must be known "Christly." The nature of God—absolutely committed, self-giving love—is received in Christ so that it can then be clearly seen of the Father. Thus we have translated γινώσκωμεν (*ginōskōmen*) as "we can recognize" rather than "we may know." Lots of people claim to recognize what God is like; only Christians have the right framework in place. I do not mean that, say, a Jewish follower of Yahweh might not understand God as absolutely committed, self-giving love, but it is to say that those in union with Christ cannot know God otherwise. We have made τὸν ἀληθινόν (*ton alēthinon*) explicit. Rather than "the one who is true" or "the true one" we translate "the true God." If this rendering robs John of some of his poetry, it has the benefit of being clearer. The verse continues to reaffirm union: "we are in the true God, in his Son, Jesus

Christ," hearkening back to the very beginning of the sermon. It ends with a powerful summation: "This man is the true God and eternal life." The pronoun οὗτος (*houtos*) could be left ambiguous ("this one" or even "this") but doing so is unnecessary. The previous sentence ends with the masculine singular designation, Jesus Christ. The plainest reading is for the pronoun to refer to him. It is nevertheless a shocking restatement of the beginning confession of the sermon. John uses the demonstrative pronoun οὗτος (*houtos*, "this one") rather than αὐτός (*autos*, "he"), but he has done so elsewhere (1 John 2:4, 5, 22; 5:6), usually to emphasize personhood. Since John has made a practice of confessing Jesus as a real human person, we have translated "this man." It is interesting that in what follows John does not say that Jesus has or gives eternal life, but that he just is eternal life. He is the divine life but also a man. True God, true life, and true humanity. Such a formulation foretokens the doctrine of recapitulation[73] and, as above, confirms that only by "plugging in" to Jesus can normal people have access to true God and true life.

The end of 1 John has perplexed commentators for its seemingly abrupt pivot toward idols. John once again invokes the diminutive "little children" here for emphasis as much as affection, hence our treating it as an exclamation. Though the diction is different, note that John continues to borrow from the semantic field surrounding guarding, protecting, and keeping watch. In verse 18 John states that the God-born protect themselves, which makes them untouchable to the evil one. Here he ends with specificity. The God-born must primarily be on guard against idols. While John has not talked about idols specifically, one of the major themes of his sermon has been about recognizing the true God by knowing the true Son. If we treat "idols" metaphorically, the sermon has been about little else. Over and over John has professed the importance of Jesus—the one who comes through water and blood, divine and human, the Son of God, the promised Messiah. The one who reveals and gives access to the Father and to divine eternal life. What is an idol but trying to access that God and that life by any means other than Christ? This is the final hour; antichrists are trying to deceive and offer fake Jesuses and fake truths to advance the rebellion by disrupting the righteous.

A final note. John ends with this exclamation because, although it is written, 1 John is not a letter in the classic sense. It is, like Hebrews, a sermon. There is no greeting and no farewell. Instead, there is a message that entreats believers to

73. In one of the earliest examples of atonement theology, Irenaeus of Lyons suggested that Jesus functions as a "new Adam," the divine human being who fixes, corrects, fully instantiates, sums up, or "recapitulates" the image of God that has been broken by sin and death. By being in Christ, believers receive the perfected *imago Dei* and prepare to be received up into divinity.

reaffirm their faith and allegiance and beckons the unconvinced to convert. To the covert enemies who have infiltrated the church, it is a devastating condemnation and warning. It ends with a plea, but a plea to beloved "little children," in whom John has the utmost confidence.

2 John 1–3

1 The Elder, to a chosen lady and her children: I love you in truth, and not just I, but
everyone who has come to recognize the truth. 2 Such love comes from the truth
that lives in us and will be with us into eternity. 3 Grace, mercy, peace – from God
the Father and the Son of the Father, Jesus Christ – be with us in truth and love.

2 John is structured as a letter with a greeting, body, and farewell—which does not make it any less enigmatic than John's sermon. To begin with, "The Elder" is an odd way to identify a sender, especially if "elder" is meant to mark out a specific office in the church, as in, say the pastoral letters. Contrast with Paul's practice. While he might name himself as "apostle," that description is always appended to his name (e.g., 1 Cor 1:1). Such a comparison could mean that 2 John was written anonymously, but this conclusion is unlikely, since the addressee ἐκλεκτῇ κυρίᾳ (*eklektē kyria*, "chosen lady") is likewise unnamed. Rather, just as the early readers of the Fourth Gospel would likely have known the identity of "the beloved disciple," so would they know "the Elder" to be John and the "chosen lady" to be the patroness of a local congregation. Both designations are hotly contested by scholars, of course. In the wake of historical-critical studies there is a built-in skepticism about attributing an anonymous letter to a disciple of Jesus, despite fairly early attestation.[74] There are basically two schools of thought concerning "chosen lady": either it refers to a specific Christian woman or it is a metaphoric reference to the church or churches that received the letter. We will, contra most contemporary commentators, contend for the former view.

The Latin translation of the fragments of Clement of Alexandria treat 2 John as a letter "written to a Babylonian lady, by name Electa." Here "Electa" would have to be understood as a Latinized name derived from the Greek ἐκλεκτῇ (*eklektē*). This idea is unlikely, since it would make "lady" a title, which would necessitate the use of a definite article. Moreover, it would mean that in verse 13 John is speaking about another woman with the same name, which seems bizarre. Others have suggested that "lady" is a proper name and "chosen" or "elect" is an adjective describing her. Still, we should expect a definite article—

74. See Introduction, subsection "Authorship," for more on the authorship of 2 John.

and John is certainly capable of supplying one, as he does in the greeting of 3 John: Γαΐῳ τῷ ἀγαπητῷ (*Gaiō tō agapētō*, "to my dear friend Gaius"). Another solution is to treat *kyria* as the feminine form of *kyrios*, the "lady" to one's "lord." If so, John is engaging in a fair bit of politesse, and there must be a reason for it, since, as we just saw, he is happy to name his recipient in 3 John 1. Some argue that the "internal evidence" of 2 John suggests that John is writing to a group of people rather than an individual and that this view pushes against "chosen lady" being an individual.[75] But this argument is unconvincing, since "chosen lady" is immediately followed by "and her children." John is quite obviously sending this letter to a group; it just may be that he is addressing it to a specific leader or patroness out of respect.

Luke 8:1–3 and Acts 16:14–15 suggest that it was quite common for wealthy women to host churches in their homes and provide for members of the early church. 2 John 10 warns against bringing false teaching "into the home." Interestingly, verse 10—as most of 2 John—is addressed to a plural "you" but refers to a single home. It is therefore quite possible that a local congregation is somehow hosted or supported by a wealthy, influential patroness and John is addressing her as he would someone of her station. On this view, the "sister" of verse 13 is a fellow patroness, possibly a leader in another nearby church, and the "children" are those who gather in her home. Supporting this view is the fact that John, himself a leader in the church, addresses congregants as "little children" (e.g., 1 John 2:1, 12, 14, 18, 28), indicating that on his metaphoric view of the family of God, congregants are the spiritual children of elders and leaders. Commentators are keen to point out the many contemporaneous instances of referring to the people of God or churches in the feminine, but in the Johannine literature, only in Revelation 19:7–8 is feminine imagery used of the church, and there it is bridal imagery ("the wedding celebration of the Lamb and his wife") instead of mother/father and children.[76] John's use of family imagery for the church is intentional and theologically fraught. Christians are the children of God (e.g., 1 John 5:2), and God's parenthood is mediated by other Christians who live in deep union with the divine life. So in 1 John, John sees himself as father to believers within his sphere of influence, even as he includes himself among them by frequently using first-person plural pronouns and verbs. Moreover, John 19:26–27 provides a near precedent. In this incident during the crucifixion, Jesus appoints his mother to be the mother of the beloved disciple. Spiritual motherhood and fatherhood supersede blood relations and, to our point here, are enfleshed in other Chris-

75. So, for example, Smalley, *1, 2, and 3 John*, 317–18; Kruse, *Letters of John*, 204.

76. We omit reference to the New Jerusalem "adorned as a bride" in Revelation 21:2, as it is referencing a place rather than a people, those who compose the church.

tians. So we have every reason to believe that wealthy, influential, spiritually mature women could "mother" believers within John's sphere of influence. And accordingly, John affords them the utmost respect for their service, provision, and sacrifice.

A final note. Johannine writings do evince a way of talking to a church, but it is not—at least not straightforwardly—metaphoric. In Revelation, when John prophesies to the churches, he addresses his words not to a "chosen lady" but "to the angel of the church in Ephesus" (Rev 2:1). If John is in the habit of referring to a congregation with feminine imagery, it is passing strange that he does not do so to any of the seven churches to which he writes. Moreover, if he is in the habit of addressing a guardian angel or angelic keeper when addressing a group of believers—and Revelation 2–3 gives us evidence that he is—then why would he revert to a different, wholly unattested metaphor in 2 John 1? The Johannine literature has a much stronger preference for the classical New Testament diction—ἐκκλησία (*ekklēsia*, "assembly," "church"—when speaking of or to churches (e.g., 3 John 6, 9–10; Rev 2:7, 11, 17, 29; 3:6, 13, 22) than it does for feminine imagery; why disrupt the pattern? In every Johannine epistolary context, John names his recipient, whether Gaius or an angel or, as here, a patroness/leader. Despite the preponderance of recent commentators who opt for a metaphoric reading of "elect lady," a fresh reconsideration of the classical view is surely warranted for the reasons laid out above.

Introductory matters in Greek letters frequently include multiple participial phrases and dependent clauses that make for an awkward, extended English syntax. That is the case here, where we have elected to translate "I love you in truth," whereas the Greek extends the sentence with a relative pronoun "*whom* I love in truth"). The same holds for verse 2, where the introductory sentence extends out with a prepositional phrase ("from the truth") and a descriptive participial construction ("that lives in us"). Stylistic choices aside, John's repetition of "truth" is notable because he uses it in ways that are, on the surface at least, bizarre. For example, love comes from the truth that lives or remains in us. Standard contemporary notions of truth tend to associate "truth" with "what corresponds to the real world." This is a broadly scientific idea: what is true is the set of facts about reality, and knowing the truth means being able to confirm these facts. It should not be difficult to see that whatever John means, it is not that. No set of confirmable facts can elicit love, and certainly not the *agapē* love John attributes to God and the church. We would do well to recall the words of 1 John 2:18–23, where believers are said to have a special anointing from the Holy Spirit that grants special access to the "truth." And really, throughout 1 John it was repeatedly noted that the Holy Spirit conflicts with and exposes the Spirit(s) of Deception. Perhaps John's use of "truth" necessarily invokes some account of the

Spirit's indwelling, or perhaps even the Spirit as such. Hilary of Arles suggests, "By 'truth' John is referring to the Holy Spirit, because love is always the work of the Spirit."[77] This solution is surprising, but it does offer a convincing fit with what John actually says. If "truth" is really "Truth," and a sobriquet for the Holy Spirit, then it is less difficult to see how it animates love and lives in us forever.

Furthermore, such a reading strongly echoes 1 John's union language. The union that exists between John and the patroness and her church is the same union that John has with the Father and the Son. If such union is mediated by the Spirit, then it makes sense that the Spirit is truth. The trinitarian implications of this move should be clear. Since 1 John 4 has already claimed that God is love, and we are here claiming that the Spirit is truth and that truth elicits love, it is not much of a conceptual leap to unite God and Spirit. If we saw "binitarian +" theology between Father and Son in 1 John, 2 John 1–3 opens the door to something very close to the classical Nicene confession; sans the philosophical acumen perhaps, but certainly pointing toward triune divinity.

An added benefit to reading truth-as-Spirit comes in verse 3, where grace, mercy, and peace come from the Father and the Son but are "with us in truth and love." Triunely, grace, mercy, and peace come from the Father and the Son but are actualized in the life of the believing community as love that springs from truth.

The formal greeting "grace, mercy, peace" strongly echoes other New Testament and early Christian letters. The standard Pauline formula is "grace and peace," where Paul adds the Christian virtue of grace to the Jewish virtue of peace, or shalom. Several New Testament letters feature "mercy" as well (e.g., 1 and 2 Timothy, 1 Peter, Jude). The Septuagint often uses ἔλεος (*eleos*, "mercy") to translate the Hebrew חסד (*ḥesed*, "faithful love"), perhaps most famously in the call-and-response Psalm 135 (LXX/136 Eng.), where every verse features an affirmation of God's commitment to God's people. Significantly, John includes himself in those who will have the grace, mercy, and peace from the Father and the Son; he is stating a truth rather than offering a blessing. That is, because God is gracious, faithfully loving, and shalom-giving, it is appropriate to use an indicative future verb—"will be"—to claim that those gifts will be present in the community and that they, by the Spirit, will not be limited by geographic separation.

2 John 4–6

4 It brought me great joy when I came upon a group of your children walking in
truth, just as we were commanded by the Father. 5 But now, friend, I'm begging

77. A. Hamman, ed., *Patrologia Latinae Supplementum*, vol. 3 (Paris: Garnier Frères, 1990), 126.

you – not as if writing a new command to you, but one we have had from the beginning – that we love each other. [6] Now this is love: that we walk according to his commands. Just as you have heard from the beginning, this is the command that you can follow.

Verses 4–6 almost require glossing in order to transition into smooth English; in this translation we have tried to strike a balance between Greek syntax and word order and readability. In verse 4 we have "came upon" in order to specify the circumstances of John's letter. Many commentators wish to supply a backstory to the writing of 2 John that we do not have. On the standard telling, 2 John is written to a local congregation that is dividing or in danger of schism, and John has found that some of the Christians are hewing to apostolic doctrine and others are not. Thus, translations will talk of John "finding some of your children" doing right, with the implication that John has been checking up on them and that "some" are doing wrong. The Greek allows for but does not demand such a reading. In the absence of any historical (or textual!) evidence, it is better to translate as we have. The verb εὑρίσκω (*heuriskō*, "find," "discover") can mean to chance upon something or to discover something after a search; our translation leaves the matter open-ended. Likewise, where we have "a group," a wooden translation would read "from the children of you," a roundabout way of saying "some" or "a group from among your children." However, there is nothing about the Greek that indicates that John might not be talking about all the Christians in the congregation. Insofar as someone might want to use the text of 2 John to spin a tale about the historical situation John is writing into, there is nothing here to suggest anything other than that John has encountered some (or all) of the Christians under the lady's care and that when that happened, they were living in the Spirit of Truth.

Where we have translated "friend," the Greek text has the vocative κυρία (*kyria*, "lady"). "Lady" does not fit with contemporary forms of address in English; even "my lady" or "dear lady" sounds stilted and anachronistic. Given the obvious familiarity between author and recipient, we have elected "friend" as a way to indicate affection. However, we have then translated ἐρωτῶ (*erōtō*, "I ask," "I request") as "I'm begging you" to capture some of the status difference between John and the patroness. This deference is suggested by the oblique way John makes the request: he insists that the command is neither new nor even from him—it is given "by the Father." Moreover, the command is "from the beginning." We noted earlier in 1 John that this phrasing suggests a connection to the uncreatedness of the Son and the beginning of creation. The call to love each other, then, is not John's command to the patroness and her congregation; it is God's first word to all creation, sourced in God's own reciprocal agapic love between Father and Son as actualized in the Spirit.

The repetition of "from the beginning" and the use of ἐντολή (*entolē*, "command") four times in three verses strongly suggests that John wants the patroness and her church to locate ultimate authority in God and not in John. However trustworthy John might be, he is a mediator and messenger—not a commander. The final phrase of verse 6—ἵνα ἐν αὐτῇ περιπατῆτε (*hina en autē peripatēte*, "that in it you should walk")—is difficult because it is not clear from the grammar what "it" refers to. It is a feminine pronoun, so it could refer to "command," "love," or even "truth." Since the section is already rife with repetition, the most likely candidate is the closest antecedent, "command." Then, to smooth the English, we have glossed "this is the command that you can follow." Such a reading has the added benefit of again avoiding making John's teachings tautologous. For this would surely be the case if the commandment is to walk in love, since "loving" was just defined as "walking in his commands." Instead, we have a polite but emphatic entreaty to recognize the agapic nature of God's love and to share in that love with other Christians. But why the immediacy? Why the urgency? In verses 7–11 John identifies the threat.

2 John 7–11

7 Look: many deceivers have gone out into the world. They don't acknowledge Jesus
Christ coming as a real human being. This is the sort of person who is a deceiver
and antichrist. 8 Check yourselves so that you don't lose what we've worked for
but instead receive your full reward. 9 Anyone who runs off ahead and doesn't stay
with Christ's teaching doesn't have God; the one who stays with the teaching has
both the Father and the Son. 10 Don't invite anyone who comes to you and doesn't
bring this teaching into your home or even greet them, 11 for anyone who greets
them partners in their evil work.

Verse 7 begins with a conjunction translated either "that" or "because." Given the severity of what John is about to say and the repetitious, emphatic nature of what has gone before, we have translated "Look," which captures in English the transition to the grave warning that follows. As in 1 John, we have translated ἐν σαρκί (*en sarki*, "in the flesh") "as a real human being," since that rendering best captures the sense of the idiom. And here John raises the stakes to the highest level: anyone who denies Jesus's humanity is ὁ πλάνος καὶ ὁ ἀντίχριστος (*ho planos kai ho antichristos*, "the deceiver and the antichrist"). As in 1 John 3, it is hard to say whether John expects an apocalyptic final enemy of Jesus to come at some point, but if so, he is keen to ensure that Christians now be on the lookout not just for this ultimate foe but for that foe's minions and prefigurations. We do well to recall the "Spirit of Error" from 1 John 4:6. The world features many spirits, and some are bent on guiding antichrists to come and deceive the church.

The participle "coming" in verse 7 is interesting because it comes in the present tense. This might have a forward-looking aspect, with John subtly referencing Jesus's imminent return. It could also simply be a reference to "how Jesus comes," that is, as a human being. Either way, the point John makes is that when Jesus arrives—present, past, or future—he does not come as something sub-, super-, or nonhuman. He comes as one of us, even if glorified. Jesus's coming as a human has important implications for soteriology and eschatology because it indicates that Christian glory is somehow human but also divine, fully us but also fully God. In the same way that the incarnation featured the fullness of God emptied into a human person, our humanity will remain intact even as it is emptied into full divinity.[78]

Verse 8 begins with βλέπετε ἑαυτούς (*blepete heautous*, "look to yourselves," "look after yourselves"). The contemporary gloss "check yourselves" might sound a bit too colloquial, but it has the benefit of maintaining the visual metaphor of the Greek in a way that "guard yourselves" would not. Some translations favor "watch yourselves," but this wording is too passive. John is recommending group vigilance.

Notice the switching between the first and second person in this verse. The first verb, "look, check yourselves" is second-person plural. The third verb, εἰργασάμεθα (*eirgasametha*, "we worked," "we've worked for"), is first-person plural. The last is again second-person plural. This alternation suggests three things. First, John does not strongly distinguish between the patroness and her people and himself. She and her people are in some way him and his people. In the tradition, this notion has come to be the confession of the church's catholicity, the idea that whatever differences we might have, all Christians belong to the same divine family. This conviction is why we can read 1–3 John as just as much "to us" now in the twenty-first century as we can read it as "to them" in the first century. They are us, and we are them.

The second implication is that we all rise and fall together. Whatever sort of personalized, heroic notion of Christian discipleship we might entertain, it is certainly not shared by John. John worries that the patroness and her church might lose what *he too* has been working for, not what *only they* have been working for. We might be reminded of the apostle Paul's teaching in 1 Corinthians 3. There, he expects to be rewarded for the success of the Corinthian church. As a third implication, he rejects any notion that the church is Paul's or Apollos's or anyone else's other than God's. This is a strange way of thinking about earning and receiving

78. See "Transformation: Soteriology and Purgatory in 1–3 John" in the Theological Horizons section.

rewards for those of us who live and breathe within the structures of cosmopolitan, global capitalism. It does not fit on our ideological spectrum—there is not any ownership, but everyone earns, and they earn together. One would have a hard time assigning the spiritual economy a "Marxist" or "capitalist" or "socialist" designation, as there seem to be features of all. This conclusion should not be surprising, however, because John knows something that the global marketplace does not: there is an unseen world of spirits and Spirit that animates people and institutions. There is, moreover, a different sort of life, the divine eternal life, that does not belong to the world's regimes, even if it must overlap them and nestle uncomfortably within them.[79]

Verse 9 introduces a novel character, ὁ προάγων (*ho proagōn*, "the one who goes ahead"). There is nothing pejorative about the Greek itself, for it could designate a leader, but for readers of Johannine literature, it might be negative. John's works are so replete with "remain," "stay," "live," "abide" language (esp. μένω, *menō*) and "from the beginning" language that the very idea of being a spiritual pioneer, leader, or innovator might receive a negative cast from the outset. For this reason, it is not too far a stretch to gloss "anyone who runs off ahead."

There is a question of what to make of the genitive construction in the phrase τῇ διδαχῇ τοῦ Χριστοῦ (*tē didachē tou Christou*). It could be a subjective genitive, that is, "Christ's teaching," meaning the instruction that Jesus gave or gives by the Spirit. It could also be an objective genitive, meaning "the teaching about Christ." This latter option would nicely restate the conviction of verse 7 that Jesus was truly human, but it would be a strange departure from regular Johannine usage. Every time "teaching" appears in the Johannine corpus, it refers to the content of instruction possessed by someone. So in John 7:16–17 Jesus references "my teaching." Then in Revelation 2 the teachings of Balaam and Jezebel are disparaged and condemned. Theologically, the subjective genitive makes better sense as well: John possesses no authority on his own; what authority he has comes from his credible reporting on what, according to the beginning of 1 John, he has seen, touched, handled, and, crucially, heard. Furthermore, in the Gospel, Jesus tells the Jewish leaders that "his teaching" comes from God. Thus, John claims to be the latest in an unbroken chain of Spirit/truth that goes from God to Christ to John to the patroness and her congregation. At every step the Spirit mediates and enlivens the transmission of what partially constitutes the Spiritself.

In verse 10 John's warning reaches a shocking climax: the rejection of Christian hospitality to those animated by the Spirit of Deception or any antichristic

79. In the Theological Horizons section see "The Unseen World: Spirit and Spirits in 1–3 John" and "Transformation: Soteriology and Purgatory in 1–3 John."

spirit. The Greek begins with the conjunction εἴ (*ei*, "if," "when"), as in several places in 1 John. It is misleading to translate this word "if" (indeed, I have elected to omit it altogether) because there is no uncertainty about whether deceivers and antichrists will try to infiltrate the church. They assuredly will; the only question is when. While the imperative "Don't invite" does not come until the second clause in the Greek, it fits more naturally at the beginning of the sentence in English syntax. The Greek positioning reemphasizes the kind of person John is warning about, including the depth of their evil and the insidious way they operate, but it does not come across in awkward English renderings. Better to capture the flavor of the warning by repositioning the clauses.

Another point of translation: we have rendered the coordinating conjunction καὶ (*kai*, "and," "or," "even") as "or even" to highlight the escalating severity of the church's proper response. Where we have "or even greet them," a wooden, literal rendering would be "and 'Good day!' to them don't say." This teaching might seem exceedingly harsh—antichristic even—given contemporary focus on, for example, the Sermon on the Mount and heightened recognition of the importance of hospitality in Jewish and Christian ethics.[80] But such a judgment would require ignoring John's language. These people are not innocent, misinformed, or well-meaning. They are fundamentally opposed to the true Christ, and they seek to infect the church and destroy it from within. In John's day—as in many places in ours—the church was under existential threat that could seem strange to those who live in the post-Christendom First-World West. Until Christians meet those who want nothing less than the end of Christianity, such warnings will seem overwrought, even backward and tribal. What makes the patroness's situation most alarming, however, is that these wolves pretend to be sheep; they mouth most of the platitudes and seem to want to assimilate. Thus identifying the wolves takes priority and with it communal vigilance that no true Christian begins to adopt wolfish ways and beliefs.

John completes the thought and runs through the full implications of failed vigilance in verse 11. Even a "good day" to a wolf makes us complicit in its schemes. Note that John again talks about "work." There is everything John and his compatriots have been working toward and there is a counterwork, an antichristic work that the wolves are building up. The reason that even a welcome makes us complicit in evil is that what is normally perceived as kindness

80. See Hans Boersma, *Violence, Hospitality, and the Cross: Reappropriating the Atonement Tradition* (Grand Rapids: Baker Academic, 2004), for a balanced and helpful treatment of the extent and limits of biblical hospitality.

and tolerance *normalizes* antichristic attitudes. It makes a wolf less threatening, someone "just like us." It sets the stage for an insidious infiltration that will undo everything John's cohort has set out to accomplish.

On reflection, then, it might seem odd that the buildup in verses 4–6 to this extraordinary warning has been the command to "love each other." But this is the case only when we import into our notion of "love" the saccharine content it carries in contemporary usage. Since English does not differentiate lexically between various sorts of loves, the *ḥesed*/agapic nature of the love John teaches is easy to overlook or supplement with something foreign to its nature. God's love is demonstrated by God's unrelenting commitment to protect—to save—the world. This commitment is so faithful and unyielding that the Son willingly obeys the Father's sending to incarnation, crucifixion, and exaltation. To put it another way, God's hospitality to his children demands their fierce protection. What God has saved God cannot lose, and if this commitment to preserving them means that the patroness and her people must be harsh or rude, so be it. The preservation of the truth and the protection of the church override any inclination it might have to tolerate or show kindness to thoroughly antichristic enemies.

2 John 12–13

12 I have a lot to write to you, but I'd rather not commit it to paper and ink. Instead,
I'm hoping to come to you and speak face to face so our joy can be full. 13 Your
chosen sister's children send you their greetings.

In 1 John 1:4 John says that when people embrace the message of union with the Father and the Son that he and his friends share, then "our joy [is] made complete." The same language is used here but with an interesting twist. Part of the joy of union with Father and Son is actualized when Christians are physically together, which perhaps explains why John places such an emphasis on Jesus's humanity and the importance of union mediated by the Spirit. There is something inexpressible about the way that physical presence can draw people into union with each other and how that union can lead to the deepest sort of joy. Insofar as we are God's children and share God's DNA, our physical togetherness functions as a replacement of sorts for the Son's current physical absence. We long for that union but can experience the joy of it here and now when we gather in love.

John ends in a typical fashion, closing the letter with a promise to visit to help fill in all the rest of the details while bringing the greetings of another patroness and her congregation.

3 John 1–2

[1] The Elder, to my dear friend Gaius, whom I love in the Spirit. [2] My dear friend, I pray you are in good health and that all the things of your physical life are going as well as your spiritual life.

3 John, like Paul's letter to Philemon, is a personal letter to a specific individual and, as such, might seem to be a strange candidate for inclusion in the Christian canon. As we will see, though, its inclusion creates a theologically generative tension with its antecedent, 2 John.

The letter begins with a greeting that is typical of Greco-Roman epistolary, with John identifying himself as the elder, followed by an effusive address to Gaius. Where we have translated "my dear friend" and "whom I love," the Greek uses cognates of *agapē*. More controversial will be the translation—really, the gloss—"in the Spirit" for ἐν ἀληθείᾳ (*en alētheia*, "in truth"). The move is not only justifiable, but probably much preferable to standard readings that ignore John's pneumatology. We have seen how closely John identifies the Spirit and truth in 1 John, and we have also seen that Hilary of Arles simply conflates the two entirely in his commentary on 2 John in order to make sense of how love can proceed or be generated by truth. There is, moreover, evidence internal to 3 John as well. Verse 12 features a highly suggestive mention that the truth "speaks highly" of a man named Demetrius. It is difficult to know how else to understand such a statement unless the truth is a person with agency. And there would seem to be no suitable candidates for the personhood of truth other than the Holy Spirit. We will address the grammatical issues below; let it suffice here to note that John understands his relationship to Gaius to be deeply sharing in love and truth such that, from a theological standpoint, we must conclude that they share union together in the Spirit's power. John and Gaius are as close as John and the Father and the Son.

The translation of verse 2 is intended to highlight the way John parallels the flourishing of Gaius's ἡ ψυχή (*hē psychē*, "soul," "spirit," "inner being") with his desire for Gaius's physical or material flourishing. He signals the parallel by using the same verb, εὐοδόω (*euodoō*, "prosper," "succeed," "go well"), to refer to πάντων (*pantōn*, "everything," "all things") and to Gaius's soul/spiritual life. Since Gaius's soul is in superior condition—he is, after all, in union with the Father and the Son—the kindest thing John can say is that he prays for all the physical things in Gaius's life to go just as well. This parallel explains why he also wishes for good health. Apart from the spiritual, Gaius presumably needs to have his material needs met, business dealings prosper, family life secured, and good health besides. If all these areas can have the quality of his connection to God and to John, Gaius will flourish in every possible way.

3 John 3–4

³ For I was overjoyed, brothers and sisters, coming and confirming your faithfulness, how you're walking in the truth. ⁴ I have no greater joy than hearing that my children are still walking in the truth.

John's grammar in verse 3 probably indicates a fair bit of coming and going; John uses the aorist to describe his having been overjoyed, but then switches to present-tense participles for "coming" and "testifying" or "confirming" (ἐρχομένων, μαρτυρούντων; *erchomenōn, martyrountōn*). John probably meets friends and acquaintances of Gaius on a more-or-less regular basis, and they keep bringing the same reports: examples of σου τῇ ἀληθείᾳ (*sou tē alētheia*, "your truth"). The question is what it would mean to "testify to your truth." The Greek word can carry a similar connotation to the English "true" when we speak about someone "remaining true to us," that is, faithful, constant, truthful. And this is probably the meaning here, though it is clarified by the following phrase to mean continued faithful action (and, later in the letter, continued hospitality and generosity). Many translations read "your faithfulness to the truth," but we can hew more closely to the Greek by, ironically, omitting "to the truth," since "walking in the truth" follows so soon after.

In verse 4 we have added "still" to walking in the truth to emphasize the continued present tenseness of John's language. John's declaration is interesting because it helps to explain what constitutes "full joy." For John, joy comes in union with the Father and the Son and fellow believers by the Spirit. This context is consistent across the Fourth Gospel (e.g., John 15:11; 16:20–22), 1 John (1:3–4), 2 John (v. 12), and here in verse 4. The only thing that changes is the way that union is manifested. In some cases it is physical presence. In others it is across distance but mediated by the Spirit. Here is an example of the latter case, where stories about faithfulness sustain or manifest the union shared between John and Gaius. They cannot speak or see each other as frequently as they might like, but they are made present in letters and tales as the Spirit reconfirms in John's heart what he knows to be the case in his head.

This language should echo for us the initial confession in 1 John, that union with the unoriginated, uncreated Son of the Father began by seeing, hearing, touching, and gazing. These physical, relational actions inaugurate union, but that union is sustained by the Spirit in their absence and then reincarnated, as it were, in new examples, new instances of seeing, hearing, touching, and gazing. The point is that while there might be something mystical about union with the divine and with each other, it is not all mystical. Just as John bears concern not just for Gaius's spiritual health but his physical health and material needs, so does John acknowledge the human, physical aspects of union that bring joy.

3 John 5–8

5 My dear friend, you are being faithful in what you are accomplishing for the fam-
ily – even though they are strangers. 6 They gave examples of your love here in the
church, and you will do a good thing when you have aided them on their journey
in a manner worthy of God. 7 They started their journey for the sake of the Name,
and they don't take any help from nonbelievers. 8 We ought, then, to be hospitable
to such people, so we can be coworkers for the truth.

In verse 5 John uses two "doing" verbs, ποιέω (*poieō*, "do," "make") and ἐργάζομαι (*ergazomai*, "work," "accomplish"); a wooden reading would be, "you are faithfully doing whatever you do/accomplish." There may be an echo here of John 6:28–30, where the crowd asks Jesus, "What should we do [ποιέω, *poieō*] to accomplish [ἐργάζομαι, *ergazomai*] God's works?" Jesus responds that they should believe in the one God sent. The crowd then responds, "What miracle will you do [ποιέω, *poieō*] so we can see and believe in you? What are you accomplishing [ἐργάζομαι, *ergazomai*]?" In the Gospel, the crowd wants to know what they have to do or accomplish to be "part of the family," as it were. But they have put the cart before the horse, and so Jesus corrects them: You do not "do" anything to be in or with me, you simply believe. But this is not an economy that the crowd is familiar with, nor is it one they want to embrace. They immediately turn on Jesus, demanding that Jesus "do" something, demonstrate an "accomplishment" that will make him worthy of their trust.

Gaius "does" it differently. He demonstrates that he is a "family man" by being hospitable to other believers. But belief/trust comes first. Notice that one of the marks of being in the family in verse 7 is refusing to receive the "help" of "nonbelievers." John actually uses the term ἐθνικός (*ethnikos*, "gentile"), but we have translated "nonbeliever" because John thinks not in terms of Jew versus gentile (which the more literal translation might imply) but in terms of "believer" and "everyone else," or according to an older patois, "Christian" and "pagan." While what is here is probably not a strong anti-Pelagian theology, it is suggestive of how John thinks about the relations between right believing and right doing—you cannot have one without the other. The crowds want to do right before they trust right. And then they demand that Jesus do right before they can trust right. Gaius believes and does. Thus, if it had been the disciples rather than the crowd asking Jesus what "walking in the truth" looks like, Jesus might have been able to point to someone like Gaius, who makes hospitality and generosity to God's family a high priority.

We have again glossed the language of "testimony" or "witness" in verse 6, preferring instead to clarify what John's metaphoric language is bringing. That is, there was not a trial in John's church where witnesses came forward and testified about Gaius's good character. Instead, people in the church who had journeyed in and through Gaius's area of influence told John and the church what had happened to them, that is, how Gaius had "loved" them, that is, shared shelter and resources with them to help them on their way. The Greek ἐνώπιον ἐκκλησίας (*enōpion ekklēsias*, "before the assembly," "in front of the church") sounds overly formal and court-like in English, so we have translated "here in the church" to capture a more family/community sense.

Although the Greek does not explicitly use "journeying" language in verses 6 and 7, there can be little doubt about what is meant. The verbs προπέμψας (*propempsas*, "those who were sent out") in verse 6 and ἐξῆλθον (*exēlthon*, "they went out") in verse 7 are both frequently used of missionaries and missionary delegations in the New Testament and the Greek Apocrypha. So, for example, in 1 Esdras 4:47 the king aids all who "were going out with" (προπέμψωσιν, *propempsōsin*) Zerubbabel to rebuild Jerusalem. In Acts 15, after Paul and Barnabas report on the conversion of the gentiles, a delegation of witnesses "were sent out" (προπεμφθέντες, *propemphthentes*) by the church (v. 3). Paul hopes "to be sent" (προπεμφθῆναι, *propemphthēnai*) to Spain by the Roman church after he passes through (Rom 15:24). The verb ἐξέρχομαι (*exerchomai*, "leave," "go out") is strongly favored for departing language in the Johannine corpus, often with a sense of mission (esp. in the Fourth Gospel). Taken together, the language of 3 John strongly implies that even without knowing them personally, Gaius had shown hospitality to itinerant Christian missionaries. Thus, "aided them on their journey" and "started their journey" is a much more helpful English rendering than "sent them out" or "when they left."

As is his habit, John uses a subtle—or perhaps not-so-subtle—shift in verb tenses to convey his desire in 6b. He begins with the future "you will do good" or "you will do a good thing" and then shifts to the simple past with the participle "aided them on their journey." The syntax does not quite work in English, so we have shifted to the perfect "have aided them," but John's meaning is clear: he very much hopes that Gaius will again furnish these missionary Christians with shelter and resources to help them on their way. Like the patroness of 2 John and Philemon, to whom Paul appeals, a status gap very likely exists between John and Gaius. But that status gap holds only according to the cultural standards outside of the family of God. Indeed, just as Paul reminds-by-not-reminding Philemon that he owes him "his own self" (Phlm 19), so John has already noted how much joy it brings him to find his "children" walking in the light. However rich or powerful Gaius might be according to Greco-Roman standards, he is John's spiritual son and brother to the missionary band.

3 John 6b asks Gaius to provide aid "in a manner worthy of God." The appeal depends on the extent to which John and Gaius share a notion of God's character. In the Gospel of John, God is described as giving and sending: God gives and

sends John the Baptizer (1:6), the Son (3:16–17; 16:27), whatever we ask (11:22), teaching (6:45), and the Spirit (3:34). God's gracious constancy, the uninterrupted desire to provide for the divine family, suggests that a "manner worthy of God" means lavishly furnishing whatever needs the missionaries might have—perhaps going above and beyond basic needs as God has done in Christ and the Spirit.

Since he mentions "God" in 6b, it is likely that ὑπὲρ τοῦ ὀνόματος (*hyper tou onomatos*, "for the sake of the Name") in verse 7 likewise refers to God the Father rather than Jesus. While the Johannine literature does place a large emphasis on Jesus's name, there are also numerous instances of reference to the name of the Father (e.g., John 5:43; 10:25; 12:13, 28). If this is the case, it is a Hebraism, one that we know early Christian authors continued.[81] It is not a minor point: John is here explaining the motivation that drove this group to go out spreading the good news, and it is likely that they are doing so in imitation of the gracious giving and sending of the Father. From a theological perspective, John knows Yahweh as the gracious Father of Jesus Christ, so it is quite likely that John understands the whole history of the Father as one of gracious giving and sending. The coming of the Son is just the latest in a series of giving/sending actions.

Where we have "and they don't take," the Greek has a plural present participle. John's point is that the missionaries have a standard practice that began when they set out and continues into the present: they don't take help from τῶν ἐθνικῶν (*tōn ethnikōn*, "foreigners," "gentiles"). While John himself is Jewish, he thinks of believers as God's family, a sort of nation or tribe unto itself. This tribe comprises Jews (like John) and gentiles (like Gaius), which does not matter; believers have God's DNA, and this familial connection is primary. Whatever other characteristics believers have (ethnicity, gender, etc.), they are secondary in terms of identity. As such, "foreigners" or "gentiles" is shorthand for those who are not Christian or, per our translation, unbelievers.

If Gaius and his people accede to John's request, they συνεργοὶ γινώμεθα τῇ ἀληθείᾳ (*synergoi ginōmetha tē alētheia*, "can be[come] coworkers for the truth"). The notion that Christians mutually participate in God's work is strongly established in the Pauline corpus. Paul describes ministry partners as "coworkers" eleven times and, in 1 Corinthians 3:9, describes himself and Apollos as work partners of God. This is probably an extension again of the notion of Christians as members of the divine family. It is less the case in the twenty-first-century First World, but most of human work has taken place "within the family," as it were. The Greco-Roman household was not only an estate housing relatives, servants, and close friends, it was also an economic association. The vineyard—a

81. See, for example, *Didache* 10:2. Brown (*Epistles*, 711) points also to Ignatius of Antioch's letter to the Philadelphians.

common motif in Jesus's parables—had a similar composition. Yes, there were an estate and a wealthy landowner, but the work was shared in the family and provided for local laborers as well. That Jesus usually invokes the vineyard as a stand-in for the kingdom of God is particularly suggestive; the Christian family, by promoting the gospel and sharing union with the brothers and sisters, is like a vineyard producing wine and grapes and sharing in the largesse.

Still, it might seem strange to be coworking "for the truth." In English this sounds as though "the truth" is the boss and Gaius and the missionaries are the laborers. This understanding might be to personify "truth" overmuch, but it captures the Johannine flavor of what the church is to be about. The era of the darkness has passed its zenith and is being replaced by the era of light. Wherever the Spirit of Truth goes, the darkness gives way, and the true ordering of the universe according to the nature and character of the Father and the Son is revealed. The Christian community is united in promoting the reign of this true ordering, and whenever Christians aid one another in doing so, they become coworkers or colleagues or colaborers.

3 John 9–10

9 I wrote something to the church, but Diotrephes – who craves leadership – isn't
acknowledging our authority.[82] 10 So when I come, I will point out what he is doing,
spreading evil nonsense about us. Not satisfied with that, he also refuses hospitality
to the family, stops those who want to do so, and tosses them out of the church!

82. The NRSV translates ἐπιδέχεται (*epidechetai*, "receive," "admit") as "acknowledge authority," following the notes of Bauer in BDAG. Margaret Mitchell ("Diotrephes Does Not Receive Us: The Lexicographical and Social Context of 3 John 9–10," *JBL* 117 [1998]: 299–320) argues that the existing parallels do not support what amounts to a gloss. However, her review of the relevant literature, especially the passages in Polybius about receiving or rejecting letter carriers, suggests that John's concern is about what the rejection of his letter by Diotrephes *meant*. That is, Diotrephes wants to be first, to lead, to be in charge, so he rejects John's letter because he does not want to acknowledge John's spiritual authority over him. This is not a matter of historical reconstruction—which we take to be impossible—but a matter of making sense of the language. John's accusation that Diotrephes is ὁ φιλοπρωτεύων αὐτῶν (*ho philoprōteuōn autōn*, "one who desires to be first among them") has no logical connection to Diotrephes's action—not receiving John and his cohorts—unless doing so is a rejection of John as spiritual authority. The action is symbolic; rejecting John's letter means rejecting John. For this reason the NRSV gives two different renderings for the verb in verses 9 and 10. Our translation follows this convention. In verse 9 the literal "not welcoming us" is tantamount to rejecting John's authority, so we make that explicit. In verse 10 literally "not welcoming the family" does both—it refuses hospitality to fellow believers and does so because it rejects John's leadership or spiritual fatherhood. The rendering "isn't acknowledging our authority" in verse 9 best conveys the sense of the language in English, even if it must spell out what the Greek only implies.

From a rhetorical standpoint, John clearly wishes to make a strong contrast between Gaius and Diotrephes. Gaius is a leader of the church, but he understands John's position of authority such that John can confidently request favors. Diotrephes is ὁ φιλοπρωτεύων αὐτῶν (*ho philoprōteuōn autōn*, "one who desires to be first among them"). Diotrephes, per our translation, "craves leadership"—and likely power too. People speak well of Gaius, and he continues living in the truth. Diotrephes spreads evil nonsense (λόγοις πονηροῖς φλυαρῶν ἡμᾶς, *logois ponērois phlyarōn hēmas*, "is spreading evil nonsense about us") that does not accord with the truth. Gaius welcomes and shares with family he does not know; Diotrephes rejects letter carriers and missionaries alike in order to reject John's authority and brandish his independence. Gaius's church participates in God's work, while Diotrephes excommunicates those who wish to do so.

Commentators of the past often took swipes at John's inelegant Greek, but the parallels here between Gaius and Diotrephes reveal cunning rhetorical skills. In everything John praises Gaius, he swiftly condemns its opposite in Diotrephes. The tactic is strongly reminiscent of the rhetoric of 1 John, where stark possibilities—light and dark, rebellion and righteousness, truth and falsehood—forced hearers to self-identify. Am I in the light? Do I hew to the truth? Am I a part of the antichristic rebellion? John's rhetoric here sets Gaius up to face the same brutal choice and will make it explicit in the final section of the letter.

Before moving on, however, we must take note of the "cardinal sins," as it were, that John highlights in Diotrephes's behavior. The second, spreading lies and rejecting truth, should not be surprising. Nor should the third, the accusation of being inhospitable, since John has been adamant about loving the brothers and sisters in real, concrete ways. But the first might. John has had little to say about power in 1, 2, or 3 John. It is presumed of the Godhead throughout the Gospel and the sermon, but never as anything other than a vehicle for God's gracious, loving redemptive purposes. While John assumes a kind of spiritual authority, he too refuses to wield it, preferring to encourage, persuade, or woo people into remaining with the light. So it might seem jarring for this to be the first attribute he singles out as demonstrating Diotrephes's break with God's reordering of the universe.

But to think this way would be to forget that John has been formed by Israel's Scriptures, where leadership and the power that comes with it are consistently and incisively critiqued. The prophetic tradition is blunt about it, calling out kings and priests who betray the people they are meant to serve. But the narratives are not any less sparing. Even the best of Israel's leaders—Moses, David, and Solomon—are shown to be corruptible and weak, vainglorious, self-pitying, self-indulgent wrecks. Furthermore, their sins are shown to have a much greater effect on the people than the sins of regular folk. This difference should be intuitive, since leaders' decisions are by definition the sort that have consequences for their followers; wise, benevolent guidance produces better results for those within one's sphere of influence than foolish self-interest. John, of course, has witnessed this dynamic firsthand in the betrayal and execution by the religious and political leadership in Jerusalem of the one who was from the beginning; it is no wonder, then, that seeing someone *want* power—power that corrupts and violates—horrifies him. If anything, power should be something reluctantly taken up, a necessary evil, not something to which one aspires or grasps.

3 John 11–12

11 Dear friends, don't imitate what is evil, but what is good. Anyone who does good
has origins in God; anyone who does evil has never seen God. 12 Everyone speaks
highly of Demetrius – even the truth itself. We also speak well of him, and you know
that our witness is true.

Verse 11 strikes a chord that should remind us of the rhetoric in 1 John. Having laid out the two ways, as it were—the way of Gaius and the way of Diotrephes—John offers Gaius and his friends the opportunity to reaffirm that they are and will continue in the light. In this particular circumstance, that reaffirmation means continued union with John, sharing shelter and resources with spiritual family, and continuing in love with one another. The use of μιμέομαι (*mimeomai*, "imitate"), from which we get the English cognate "mimic" and, in its noun form, "mimesis," should indicate that John is not talking about abstract notions of "the good" and "the evil." Rather, he is talking about their visible instantiations in Gaius and Diotrephes. Gaius and Diotrephes can be imitated, "the good" cannot. Recognizing the importance of imitating an actual person rather than an abstract form helps us see that John rejects dualism; he has done so in his confession of Jesus coming as a human being, and he does so again here. We cannot perceive "the good" as such, anymore than we can see God; instead, we can see Jesus, John, and now Gaius—those whose union with the Father produces tangible, visible incarnations of God in the here and now.

For this reason John can claim that anyone who does evil has never "seen" God, while suggesting that those who do good have their origins therein (again translating ἐκ τοῦ θεοῦ ἐστιν [*ek tou theou estin*, "is from God"] as speaking of rootedness or origination). In the coming of Jesus, John and his cohort "saw" God and gained origin in God; in Gaius's walking in love, others see it now; and Diotrephes's evil reveals his God-blindness. This episode gives some flesh and blood to the more abstract commands to love in 1 John. That is, this is what love "looks like" in Gaius's community. It will look different elsewhere, but we should be vigilant for suggestive markers: hewing to the truth, hospitality for the family, reluctance to coerce and, perhaps, even to lead.

In verse 12 John suggests that the truth itself testifies to Demetrius's good character. This should be taken as a reference to the Spirit as in 1 John 5:6, where the Spirit's testimony about Jesus is true because "the Spirit is truth." We have seen that the Spirit is ubiquitous in the Johannine literature, coequal to Father and Son in importance and divinity, and John sees the Spirit literally at work, helping discern other spirits and demarcating truth and error. John simply assumes that believers will be sensitive to what the Spirit indicates. That many in today's church do not probably says more about us than about John's language here. The Spirit is a person. The Spirit is the truth. And the Spirit continues to reveal, here to Demetrius's benefit.

3 John 13–15

[13] I had much to write to you, but I'd rather not commit it to pen and paper. [14] I hope
to see you shortly when we'll speak face-to-face. [15] Peace to you. The family sends
its love. Greet the family there by name.

Structurally, the end of 3 John is almost identical to the ending of 2 John. Here John uses the past tense to speak of the "much" he has to write, and he uses θέλω (*thelō*, "will," "wish") instead of βούλομαι (*boulomai*, "wish," "intend") to indicate his desire to avoid writing it down. The content, however, is the same: a standard closing to a Greco-Roman letter, complete with a desire to visit, well-wishing, and final greetings. We have elected to translate the two uses of φίλος (*philos*, "dear friend") as "family," to reflect the Johannine sense of the believing community as more akin to a family/household and have glossed "sends greetings" with "sends its love" to be more congenial to colloquial English.

Theological Horizons of 1–3 John

The Trinity

Theological Epistemology: Knowing God

"anyone who says, '"I have come to know him"'

It is well known that smoking cigarettes is harmful to one's health. The studies are in, the science is settled, and yet people continue to smoke, knowing full well that they are putting themselves in danger of an early death or a low quality of life in advanced age. It is clear that while knowledge has something to do with informing human action, there are other factors at play. Ancient philosophers dubbed this problem "akrasia," that is, acting in a particular way despite one's better judgment. The sciences have improved our understanding of akrasia, so now we can say with some certainty that addictive behaviors dramatically alter our very neural pathways, even damaging our assumed freedom to act in particular ways.[1] So the person addicted to certain types of substances *may not have*

1. See Hamed Ekhitari and Martin Paulus, *Neuroscience for Addiction Medicine: From Prevention to Rehabilitation—Constructs and Drugs* (Amsterdam: Elsevier, 2016), 19–32, for a helpful overview of current research in neurotoxicity, the study of neural damage induced by substance abuse/addiction. Brain imaging captures the neural changes wrought by abuse of addictive substances, though precise effects differ at the molecular level according to the particular drug. Thus, cocaine produces different effects than methamphetamines, though both produce psychobiological damage, prohibiting fully functioning brain systems. See also the more general *Neuroimaging in Addiction*, ed. Bryon Adinoff and Eliott A. Stein (Chichester: Wiley-Blackwell, 2011), which provides a global overview of neural plasticity and how addiction generates neural pathways in the brain.

a choice but to indulge in those substances. These are murky waters to be sure, for it is not uncommon for, say, a heroin addict over time to break addiction by religious adherence to the twelve steps in a community of accountability and encouragement. It is therefore difficult to say when substance abuse is a foregone conclusion and when choice is reintroduced into the addict's life. Whatever else can be said, there is a process of mind change, in which neural pathways are realigned through a combination of mental and physical practices that replaces a self-destructive pattern of life with one that offers the possibility of mental, emotional, physical, and spiritual wholeness.

John assumes something like the obverse of harmful, akratic addiction to be the end goal of God's gracious gift of the Son. What John's sermon envisions as whole human life is the sort of knowledge that is accompanied by a particular pattern of living—one that is obedient to the Son's commands. Whereas akratic action defies the clear judgment of one's knowledge, this obedience to the Son is the result of one's knowledge and trumps contrariwise inclinations. In fact, if the church fathers are to be believed, this knowledge ultimately usurps and even transforms those inclinations entirely, such that obedience to the Son becomes as natural as breathing or, to carry on the previous example, the addict's substance abuse. It becomes simply the new furniture of one's daily life.

Therefore, "knowledge" in John's telling is not "a set of facts to which one assents." Nor is it merely the experience of seeing, handling, touching, or, more colloquially, "having gotten to know someone." Neither of those definitions would explain the tight unity between knowing the Son and obeying his commands. There are many people we know; there are only a few whose commands we follow. However, the nature of the Son we are "getting to know" might itself compel a particular sort of obedience. How might this be?

We have already suggested that John's theology of light implicates a kind of aesthetic revealing of the structure of the cosmos, a beauty. And even cursory reflection on the nature of beauty reveals that, wherever and however it is encountered, it is compelling. There is a reason that knights are willing to fight dragons for the sake of the maiden's kiss. Perhaps the Son possesses a kind of being that, once intimated, compels in particular ways. Some of Clement of Alexandria's teaching on knowledge of God is helpful. He explains: "The person who does not have knowledge of the good is evil. For there is one good, the Father, and not knowing the Father is death, just as knowing Him is life eternal, through communion with the power of incorruptibility. And to be incorruptible is to share in the divine nature."[2] The kind of knowledge Clement speaks of is surprisingly in keeping with John's claims of having union with the Father and

2. Clement of Alexandria, *Stromata* 5.10 (PG 9:97).

the Son (1 John 1:3). "Knowledge" is participatory; it is itself a type of sharing a particular form of life. It is perhaps analogous to what we mean when we say, "Cain *knows* farming." It suggests a deep intimacy that has developed through consistent participation. To know farming—as opposed to, say, knowing how to farm—suggests apprenticeship, trial-and-error, reflection, commitment: a cluster of attitudes, experiences, and patterns.

Likewise, John's language conjures not merely one's holding certain beliefs or recognizing some facet or facets of God's character, but instead a regular intimacy or sharing in the divine nature. At this point religious knowledge of God begins to intersect with atonement theology. If "John knows God" is at least analogous to "Cain knows farming," the points held in common begin to break down at the point of ontology. It is not that Cain's nature is actually connected to a particular plot of land. But John has already claimed that his nature is connected to the divine life. He shares union with Father and Son, that is, actually lives God's life. This obscure, but not incomprehensible, claim is reflected in Clement's "power of incorruptibility." The second-century father Irenaeus developed image-of-God theology to explain exactly how this union with God might be the case, suggesting that human beings possess God's image but only in a fractured, broken condition. Through Christian faith, the Spirit of God applies to us the perfect image—held in the human nature of the Son—healing, sewing up, reconstituting, or in Irenaeus's patois, "recapitulating" it.

Some explanatory remarks are necessary. First, what exactly is meant by "image of God"? J. Richard Middleton has suggested that the image of God is something like a divine vocation, a right kingly rule that God has given to human beings, the mission of which is to extend God's gracious regency to the world.[3] God rules the universe by giving humanity a special commission to extend the principles of that rule into new environs and circumstances. The brokenness of the image is the distorted, corrupted way in which that vocation has actually played out in human life and society. The Spirit's work, then, is to reorder the inner workings of the human person so that (in the case of a woman) she produces the right sort of regency. Or to put it another way, the Spirit reshapes thought patterns, emotions, and psychological states so that, in her royal capacity, she responds to the vicissitudes of her domain exactly as God would. Or in yet another way: she lives and acts in her own community the way the Son lived in his while he was here. Because the woman programmatically expresses the divine vocation, it must be that she shares in the divine life itself.

Christian theology has traditionally explained this "possession of the divine

3. J. Richard Middleton, *The Liberating Image: The* Imago Dei *in Genesis 1* (Grand Rapids: Brazos, 2005).

life" in dualistic terms. Dualism is the belief that at least part of the human person is an immaterial object, a "soul." Since the Spirit is invisible, it seems to make sense that the Spirit operates on the invisible part of the person. Thus, what it is to have a repaired image of God is to have a soul that has been cleansed from sin and healed from its ravages. While this wording is helpful insofar as it goes, much of contemporary neuroscience and philosophy of mind has become skeptical of the existence of souls, suggesting instead that what was once relegated to the soul is really the domain of the inner workings of the human brain. If so, then it is worth considering whether something like Irenaeus's theology of the healed *imago Dei*—and, by extension, John's theology of the knowledge of God—can still be gospel in a world without souls.

One supposes that it can. Often misattributed to John Wesley, seventeenth-century English philosopher Ralph Cudworth once remarked, "I mean by holiness, nothing else but God stamped and printed on the soul."[4] Replacing "soul" with "brain" yields something of the same meaning: the neural pathways, the ruts and grooves of human thought, must be reshaped until they form the human analogue to the mind of God. This refashioning is, again, mysterious, but, again, not incomprehensible. We can wonder whether the glorified Lord has a glorified brain with glorified neural pathways.

The ontological underpinnings, whatever mechanisms produce God's eternal will, are, and will remain until the end of days, ineffable. But the coming of the Son shows that whatever we are to make of "God's brain," the human brain can bear its stamp or imprint truly, if limitedly. This imprint, in the end, is how one "knows God" and why anyone who truly knows God follows his commands. Since God's commands are simply the vocational outworking of God's gracious kingship to the world, the person who shares union with God's nature lives them out easily and consistently.

Concomitantly, such a view suggests what contemporary theologians call a kenotic Christology, which is the ontological view that the Second Person of the Trinity had to "empty himself" of some of what it is to be God in order to "fit" in human flesh. The Second Person's being emptied of certain divine powers or attributes is conceptually needed because, as many have noted, Jesus is in Nazareth, but God is everywhere. If God is everywhere, then Jesus cannot be God if Jesus is not everywhere. We can do some hand-waving about the mediation of God's presence through the Spirit to the world in order to show that it is the Third Person—not the Second—upon whom God's omnipresence in the world

4. Ralph Cudworth, *The Life of Christ the Pith and Kernel of All Religion: A Sermon Preached before the Honorable House of Commons, at Westminster, March 31, 1647* (Westminster: BiblioBazaar, 2010).

is predicated. But we still must have a way to make sense of Jesus being "fully God" and "fully human." The best solution is to suggest that the Second Person forgoes some of what God can do in order to be truly human.

Trinitarianism in 1–3 John: Ambiguity in Speech about the Persons of the Godhead

"in this we know that we have come to know him"

It is difficult to say whether "his commands" in 1 John 2:3–6 refers to commands given by the Father or by the Son, though it may not ultimately matter, thanks to John's theology of the union shared by the two. It is worth being reminded again of the Fourth Gospel, where Jesus claims, "Those who love me will keep my word, and my Father will love them, and we will come to them and make our home with them. Whoever does not love me does not keep my words; and the word that you hear is not mine but is from the Father who sent me" (John 14:23–24). Words from the Son are the Father's, and words from the Father come through the Son. Any strict distinction is to misapprehend the revelation of "what was from the beginning" to those who handled, heard, and touched it. And this point is important from the perspective of trinitarian confession.

Christian worship often features some ambiguity in, for example, prayer that is "to God" but references the nature and character of Father, Son, and Spirit. There is often what we might deem "conceptual bleed," where it is not entirely clear which of the persons of the Godhead is being addressed in the interstices of our speech. Such patterns of ambiguity in worship, prayer, and preaching appear even in 1–3 John. Notice that 1 John 2:3–4 appears to be speaking about God and God's love. Then, at the end of verse 5, John gives us a concrete way to know whether we are "in him." But who, exactly, are we in? the Father? the Son? If the thought is coherent, then the answer ought to be God the Father. But then in verse 6 we learn that if we are to claim to still be "in him," then we "ought to walk just as he walked." Given the opening of the sermon as a whole, and the importance of the handling and seeing, the referent here would naturally be the Son, who did in fact walk before John and many others. So in this section "he" and "him" begin as referents to the Father and end as referents to the Son, without any change in the overall theme of the section.

From a nontrinitarian point of view, it would appear that the sermon conflates Father and Son, failing to sharply distinguish between the two, and confusing the hearer. A better—and Christian—way to hear the text is to confess something of the doctrine of perichoresis, or coinherence. Trinitarian doctrine distinguishes God's nature and God's persons, with the three persons being known individually while sharing oneness in nature and will. One of the ways that this unity-in-distinction is conceivable is by recognizing the mutual interpenetration of the persons, such that the Father and the Son are so intimately involved in cycles of gifting glory and will and love that it is difficult to know—from a human perspective—how they are still conceptually distinguishable (though conceptually distinguishable they are).

It may be helpful to think about this entire section as a reflection on the relationship between God's being and God's action. Notice that John is concerned with a kind of true knowing of God, that is, a vibrant and robust experience of who God is in Godself, which is tied to the knowledge and experience of what God did in and through Jesus, who "walked" among us. It is tempting for human beings to sharply distinguish between these two divine aspects, thinking that how Jesus walked intimates to us something of what God is like. This approach is true insofar as it goes, but it risks positing an essential distinction between the economy of God realized in the person and work of Jesus and the eternal nature of God's being. It is against just this sort of hard and fast distinction that Karl Barth warns: "God's essence and work are not twofold but one. God's work is His essence in its relation to the reality which is distinct from Him."[5] It is who God is to share life and union. Because there is a universe that is external to God, it is in God's nature to spill out from the Godhead in gracious, life-giving initiatives. Christian confession gives primacy to the notion that as Jesus's walking among us holds pride of place in the economy of God's life-giving initiatives to the world, the incarnation is—in terms of divine action—no different than the outpouring of the Spirit at Pentecost or YHWH's adoption of Israel as a special people. To put it crudely, these are just the sorts of thing that happen when a being like God encounters a world like ours that is external to Godself. By linguistically occluding the distinction between the Father and the Son in this section, John may be hinting at a fundamental unity between God's being and God's action.

Speech about the Godhead may sharply define economic functions—that is, it is the Son who undergoes crucifixion rather than the Father or the Spirit—but such conceptual clarity is, as we have seen, more difficult to maintain at the ontic level. Thus, Christian worship often features some quite necessary ambiguity. Knowing God, being "in him," walking as he walked—such a juxtaposition is therefore helpful but, if left unchecked, can also become dangerous. When insufficient attention is paid to the distinctions between the divine persons, Christian faith lapses into unqualified monotheism and loses the endless differentiation that accounts, economically, for the variegation in the created order and the importance of the collapse of differences in acts of gracious love. Still, rigid and relentless distinction opens Christian faith to charges of tritheism or subordina-

5. Barth, CD I/1, 371.

tionism. John strikes just the right balance. There is some ambiguity about Father and Son—which is especially true when listening to the sermon out loud—but there is also marked clarity, such that in this section walking as Jesus walked enfleshes knowledge of and obedience to God the Father.

John's example, therefore, should offer a pattern for worship, one that strikes a balance between two extremes on a pendulum. At the one end, worship would rigidly delineate the persons of the Godhead by economic function. At the other, worship would treat the persons of the Godhead interchangeably. The former would endanger us of sharply separating being and act and invite accusations of tritheism. The latter would endanger us of modalism, supposing that "Father," "Son," and "Spirit" are just masks for the same person. Orthodox, trinitarian worship should oscillate somewhere in between.

From God Is Love to Nicaea: Incipient Trinitarianism in 1 John

> "Anyone who does not love does not know God, because God is love."

Perhaps more than any other New Testament text, John's confession that God is love has radically altered human religious thought. Even so, it is more profound a confession than we might think. While original to John, the Jewish thinking behind *agapē* is spelled out in 1 John 4:10, where, as we noted in the exegesis, John explains what sort of "love" it is that God is and has. And that love is the self-emptying, gracious sending of the Son as an atoning sacrifice for the world, an extreme, uncompromising sort of love if ever there was one. But in so doing, John reveals that when he says, "God is love," he is simply translating the Hebraic notion of God's *ḥesed*, God's loyal, loving commitment, into the Greek-speaking Greco-Roman world.

Just as the Jews had always known YHWH to be the covenanting God who never quit on his people, so the revelation of God in Christ shows that this commitment was always intended to go beyond the Hebrew people to include the whole world. And because that task was so massive and monumental, God could accomplish it only by giving the unoriginated Son, the substance of Godself, into the world to be with it and redeem it. The sending of the Son demonstrates a depth to God's loyal love that is and was shocking and shameful: surely the Creator of the universe is too glorious to give Godself over to the world to be denigrated and killed? What sort of majesty is God demonstrating here? In one sense it is merely the logical conclusion of truly loyal love: if the only way to save the beloved is to give oneself over to death, then that is what God must do if God is to remain true to who God is.

But how can any of this make sense? How can the Father send the Son? How can the Son taste death if the Father is life, and yet God still be one? Surely there are at least two gods here? One implication of John's "God is love" language is that God, though one, is also at least two. It carries out the implication of God's fundamental nature being hesedic loyal love. By its very nature, love is not an action or attitude that one being can do alone. Love—at least any love that is most perfectly revealed by sending the Son to save others—is directed not at the self but at the other. With this understanding of love, we can say that God the Creator, in eternity past before there was any creation, must have a Person within Godself at whom God can direct God's Godliness. The logic was always implicit in Israel's confession of God's covenantal nature, but in the Old Testament *ḥesed* is always described as something God has, not God's nature itself. But John, having gazed on and touched the eternal Son, knows that love is not just something God does. It is not even the thing God loves doing most. It is God's inner being; it is the source and engine of the universe. If God is love, God cannot be God unless God is at least Father and Son, eternally bonded in the giving and receiving and regiving of self-emptying, edifying love. The Father must exist in eternal self-abnegation, pouring out glory and honor and joy onto the Son, who must exist in eternal joyful obedience and deflection of glory and honor back to the Father. And for these two to truly be one, the Spirit must eternally unite the Sender and Sent, the Glorifier and Glorified. The Father's eternal sending of the Son must be united with the Spirit's power eternally raising, glorifying, and exalting the Son to the Father's right hand.

John has told us in simple language that God is love, and love reaches its greatest economic manifestation in the sending of the Son to die for us. If that is "love," it just cannot be God unless God is three and one, one being in three persons eternally bound up in a limitless, gracious union of love. Unqualified monotheism of the Jewish or Muslim varieties cannot say "God is love" truly; Johannine Christianity can and does. The reason is that self-love, even that of a perfect being, is not the right sort of love, for love must go outside the self to really be itself.

Christology

Christ the Co-priest: The Fulfillment of the Temple

"We have a co-priest before the Father, Jesus Christ."

1 John, and really Johannine literature as a whole, is not rightly understood apart from a strong theological reckoning of Christ and the church as eschatologi-

cal fulfillments of temple worship. Jesus does not replace the temple—though historically we must acknowledge that the destruction of the Jerusalem temple in 70 CE required that Yahweh worship continue without the trappings of the temple cult—but instead is the fullest expression of everything the temple was always meant to be.[6] That is, 1 John pictures Jesus and believers as co-priests, participating in rites of temple worship in and through the life patterns of the church community.[7] But how does co-priesthood work, and why is it required?

The darkness of which God has no part and in which the universe is mired is the darkness of an oil slick: it slops and sticks and stains, and even the holiest believers at their most alert are in danger of contamination. So it is that John must reassure his "little children" that, though he warns to give them every chance to live out of sin's reach, some darkness very well may creep in, and yet, thankfully, it does not have the last word.

John remains ambiguous, however, about whether Christians will know that sin has veiled their eyes and insinuated itself into their lives. As we noted above, John's claims about the light and the darkness do not preclude—in fact they practically demand—that many in the darkness will honestly suppose themselves to be in the light. If sin is this radically corrupting, then it is not impossible—in fact, it is highly likely—that some Christians may have a foot or a leg swallowed up in the shadows and truly not know it. 1 John 2:1–2 offers trinitarian hope for just such persons. We have a "co-priest," that is, a "paraclete," Jesus himself, with the Father. Before examining what exactly "co-priest" means, it is worth pausing to note that John has not qualified the Paraclete's paracletic activity with our confession or repentance. Whatever else confession and repentance do or do not do, they do not imperil either the fact of Jesus Christ, the truly righteous one, or his participatory ministry on our behalf.

In John's extended metaphor, the striving Christian, the Christian who confesses and seeks the right-ordering of God's light, is ultimately like a priest who periodically seeks forgiveness in and through the rituals of the temple cult. In this capacity, the Christian has help, a cominister of sorts, whose unique status

6. For examples of the burgeoning literature on this point, see for the Fourth Gospel, for example, Paul M. Hoskins, *Jesus as the Fulfillment of the Temple in the Gospel of John* (Eugene, OR: Wipf & Stock, 2007), Alan R. Kerr, *The Temple of Jesus' Body: The Temple Theme in the Gospel of John* (London: Sheffield, 2002), and Mary L. Coloe, *God Dwells with Us: Temple Symbolism in the Fourth Gospel* (Collegeville, MN: Michael Glazier, 2001); and for Revelation, see Andrea Spatafora's *From the "Temple of God" to God as the Temple: A Biblical Theological Study of the Temple in the Book of Revelation* (Rome: Editrice Pontificia Università Gregoriana, 1997).

7. I have made this case in "Jesus and the Believer as Co-Priests: The Temple Cult and Paraklētos in 1 John," presented at the 2016 Annual SBL Conference, San Antonio, TX.

as the Father's Son garners him the right to coparticipate in the ritual, thereby ensuring its success. It is not clear exactly how this happens.

The Jewish theologian Philo, writing roughly contemporary to the writings of the New Testament, suggests that the vestments worn by the high priest act as a "paraclete," a "joint minister," and represent the whole cosmos before God. In *On the Life of Moses* 2:134, Philo indulges in a figurative interpretation of the priestly garments, demonstrating how the appearance of various accoutrements contributes to an overall representation of the cosmos. The robe "reaching to his feet," for example, is an "imitation of the air," and its "scarlet dye" is "the emblem of fire." Everything that makes up the universe in ancient cosmology is represented: the four elements, the heavens and the earth, even the stars making up the constellations—all are in some way signified. Even the world's wise order according to God's reason—elsewhere known in Philo as the Logos (2:127)—is represented in the priest's chest plate. Thus fortified, the priest enters God's presence in the temple. Philo notes the significance of this union between the priest and the cosmos: "For it was indispensable that the man who was consecrated to the world's Father, should have as paraclete, his son, the being most perfect in all virtue, to procure forgiveness of sins, and a supply of unlimited blessings" (2:134). Philo uses the metaphor of a father and son to characterize God's relationship to the world.[8] Because the universe is structured according to God's divine wisdom, or "perfect in all virtue" as he says here, it is like God's son, bearing the Father's own visage and character. And this son, this perfectly ordered universe, functions as the priest's paraclete as the priest seeks amnesty for Israel. We cannot help but hear an echo of this thinking in 1 John 2:1–2, where our co-priest Jesus is himself an atoning sacrifice that is sufficient for the right ordering of the entire universe. How fitting too that Jesus is known as Son to the Father in precisely the same way that Philo thinks of the universe as God's son. Philo recognizes that whatever needs to be accomplished through the rites of temple worship, the high priest is inadequate to perform alone. He is not sufficiently representative of the universe and, on his own, would not be able to perform an efficacious service. The world must be with him, jointly performing the prayers and sacrifices as God's worthy son and representative of all that has been created and is not human. In a similar

8. Contra Jintae Kim ("The Concept of Atonement in 1 John: A Redevelopment of the Second Temple Concept of Atonement" [PhD diss., Westminster Theological Seminary, 2003], 77–78), who wrongly suggests that "son" refers to reason in *On the Life of Moses* 2:133. While grammatically possible, this understanding ignores Philo's almost identical phrasing in *On the Special Laws* 1:96, where the father/son metaphor is used of God and the universe. Kim suggests that this usage is not parallel because in this case the world is acting as the priest's "fellow ministrant." A better reading would be (as below) to admit the parallel usage and recognize the conceptual overflow of "fellow ministrant" for Philo's use of "paraclete" in the present text.

vein, believers by themselves are never quite fit to render priestly worship with God. They need a co-priest, Jesus, to offer them cleansing and to be in himself an atoning sacrifice for all cosmic disorder.

John calls Jesus ὁ χριστός (*ho christos*, "the Christ," "the Messiah"). This title draws our attention to Jesus's messianic status. Interestingly, ὁ χριστός follows the use of χρῖσμα (*chrisma*, "anointing") in 1 John 2:20. The words are easily recognizable as cognate, and both connote a special choosing and vocation. The real question is the exact relationship between the Christian's anointing and Christ's singular status as "the anointed one." Given the theme of temple fulfillment, the strong connection to ordination and purification texts in Exodus LXX, and our "co-priesthood" with Jesus, it appears that John conceives of our priesthood as deriving from Jesus's in much the same way that Aaron's sons would have derived priesthood from their father: by familial connection, or blood. The ordination ritual itself involves oil, but only those of Aaron's family have the right to the rite, as it were. As in ancient Israel, one must be a member of the family first, and only then is one initiated into the familial vocation.

But readers will remember that John began his sermon with a confession about the eternality, the unoriginatedness of the eternal life that was manifested in human being in Jesus. It would be incorrect, therefore, to assign Jesus merely the title of "high priest" or "first high priest" of the fulfilled temple, for to do so would be to accord him too little *divinity*. John's Christology, then, appears caught on the horns. Vocationally and relationally, Jesus functions as co-priest with believers, being in himself atonement for the cosmos and guarantor of right worship. In terms of essence or being, however, John testifies that Jesus shares the divine life and reveals it to humanity, offering all the chance to join into divine union with both Son and Father.

So who, then, is Jesus? And how are we to conceive of him? As elsewhere in the New Testament, John's language and conceptual horizons push us to embrace Jesus as the *Deus Homo*, the God-Human, the one who joins humanity with the divine as a mother bears a child into a family. John is not, of course, at all specific about how this comes about, though the example of the divine high priest in Hebrews demonstrates that such a notion is not foreign to other early Christians.[9] We may therefore speculate a bit about John's theotic priesthood

9. Richard Bauckham ("The Divinity of Jesus in the Letter to the Hebrews," in *Jesus and the God of Israel* [Grand Rapids: Eerdmans, 2008], 233–53) does invaluable service, demonstrating both the divinity and the humanity of the author's notion of Jesus's high-priestly status. In Hebrews 3–6 the author goes to some length to explicate Jesus's high-priestly humanity—that he was "just like us," as it were. In 7:1–3, however, the notion of Melchizedekian priesthood is understood to be "without father, without mother, without genealogy, having neither beginning of days nor end of life, but resembling the Son of God" (Heb 7:3 NRSV). By connecting

here. In the fresh, fulfilled temple that is the church, Jesus the priest ministers with all who, by confessing him, become a part of his family and therefore part of his familial, priestly vocation. Jesus, however, unlike Aaron and the Levitical priesthood, shares in the eternal, divine life of the Father. By entering into the divine family and vocation, believers share in the divine life in Christ, just as the Levitical priests shared in the family of Aaron. Fulfilling our priestly role of ministering to and for the Father, then, is an act of theosis, of sharing fully in the divine life, of union with God.

From the perspective of biblical theology, it might be that 1 John and Hebrews are not so far apart. While John emphasizes the practices of love and living in the light, a temple theology lurks in the background, and Jesus's divine priesthood conjoins believers with the Father. Thus, Jesus's priestly ministry does not replace the temple so much as fulfill everything the temple was always aiming at.

Soteriology in 1–3 John: In Jesus's Name

> "Your sins are forgiven through Jesus's name."

In 1 John 2:1–2 John characterizes Jesus's death as an atoning sacrifice. If we are to import the logic of Old Testament sacrifice, then, we might expect to learn that our sins are forgiven "through Jesus's sacrificial death" or "on account of his atonement sacrifice." How strange, then, that John suggests that all the sins of the children of God have been forgiven "through Jesus's name" (1 John 2:12).

The phrasing is not unique to the Johannine literature; it crops up also in Acts (10:43). However, its use is different in 1 John and the Fourth Gospel than in Acts. Luke uses "Jesus's name" to connote a particular kind of authority; for example, one's sins are washed away in baptism if one resorts to "calling on his name" (Acts 22:16). Jesus has the right and power to make this thing so, and thus it is so.

If we remember that for John sin is something more like cosmic disorder than a list of one's personal infractions of the divine law, we may also conclude that forgiveness implies more than a verdict of not guilty. Rather, "forgiveness" will include revelation—seeing rightly what is light and what is dark—as well as sharing in the divine life. Therefore, we translate διὰ τὸ ὄνομα αὐτοῦ (*dia to onoma autou*) as "through his name" rather than "on account of his name." For

Jesus's priesthood to Melchizedek's, Hebrews professes Jesus's coeternality with the Father and "true divinity."

John, faith in Jesus is partially constituted by recognizing this man and his life as God and the possessor of God's eternal life.

It is telling that the Fourth Gospel's summary statement in 20:31 uses similar language: "But these things are written so that you may believe that Jesus is the Messiah, the Son of God, and that by believing you may have life in his name." The statement capstones the pericope in which Thomas—having seen and handled the resurrected Jesus's wounds—professes, "My Lord and my God!" (John 20:28). Thomas draws the conclusion that this man is the complete manifestation of the nature and character of Israel's God. In keeping with an earlier theme in the Gospel of John, "Jesus shares fully in the divine activity of giving life and judging (5:25–26), the two characteristic activities of God in Scripture that are now exercised through, and entrusted to, the Son."[10] Reckoning Jesus's "name" as a cipher for his person and character in the Gospel and now here in 1 John, Christians are invited to remember that they are made right, put to order, and ennobled to see God and the cosmos as they are and will be by looking at everything *through* the name of the Son. Jesus's life and person are like a lens and a torch, both correcting one's sight and illuminating the darkness, allowing one to truly see. Thus, we receive full and unfettered forgiveness—the complete transformation of our lives—through his name. Jesus is the access point to light and life; we gain immeasurably by seeing and living through him.

It may be that 1–3 John, and really the Johannine literature as a whole, acknowledge something of Abelard's exemplarism. While it is sometimes caricatured in contemporary discourse,[11] part of Peter Abelard's theology of atonement involves the subjective effect of Christ's passion on us. That is, by meditating on the way Jesus lived and died, the sheer magnanimity of his love compels us also to love more fully and deeply. But note that this subjectivism is predicated on an objective fact about Jesus, namely, that he lived *this* life and died *this* way. That is, agapic love is not truly, fully known until the advent of the Son. The Son reveals agapic love and the eternal life in and through his own being with us. There is an objective aspect to exemplarism: Christ is revealed as the divine Word, and in Christ and only in Christ is the deity truly known. To put it another way, we cannot follow Christ or be inspired by him until we have come to see and know who he was and what he was like.

When Jesus becomes our lens and light, something outside of us has changed us. So it is that 1–3 John can admit of a kind of objective exemplarism, a view

10. Thompson, *John*, 430.

11. For a relatively recent take that delves into the nuances of what Abelard actually says, see Denis Kaiser, "Peter Abelard's Theology of Atonement: A Multifaceted Approach and Reevaluation," *JATS* 26 (2015): 3–28. If nothing else, Kaiser proffers an extensive bibliography that contextualizes different approaches to Abelard's so-called exemplarism.

on which the objective revelation of Christ atones by enlivening our hearts and minds to what true love and true life look like.

In the Flesh: Incarnation and Christology in 1–3 John

> "Every spirit that confesses that Messiah Jesus came as a human being is from God."

Central to John's teaching is that he and others actually knew and met and lived with a human man named Jesus. For this reason he begins 1 John by focusing on tactile verbiage: seeing, gazing, hearing, and touching. Ancient religion postulated that the cosmos was populated by many spirits and gods. But in the wake of Plato's philosophy it also affirmed a strict separation, a dualism, between seen and unseen. While it was assumed that there was some congress between the spirit-world and the physical one, the two remained separate, unmingled. So any claim that God had come to the world would have been met with a shrug: of course the gods (or The God, if he exists) can visit the world and see what is happening. But the early Christian claim was obscene: God did not just visit the world; God came into the world as a human being. In the ancient schema, such a claim was a scandalous mixing of two types of being. The result was a spate of heresies over the first few centuries of Christian faith that tried to obviate its absurdity. On these views Jesus only appeared to be human, or the Logos wore a human skin like a costume, controlled it like a puppet. Either possibility was more plausible than a true God-human. How could such a thing even be possible? Much of early Christology involved trying to make sense of Jesus as truly God and truly human according to various ancient anthropologies. So, for example, if a human being was composed of soul and body, what kind of soul did Jesus have? All orthodox Christologies acknowledged that his body, the stuff out of which he was composed, was truly human; the question was what made up Jesus's soul, and how could it be shown to be human and divine? These were the concerns out of which Christian theologians and philosophers developed the so-called hypostatic union: one soul with two complete, interpenetrating (or "perichoretic") natures. The interpenetrating part was important: the two natures could be theoretically distinguished but were so thoroughly fused that they produced one mind or one soul.

Most contemporary philosophy finds these arguments primitive and quaint because most contemporary philosophers do not believe in an unseen world at all. And this fact in turn implies that if John were to give his sermon today, it would not be concerns about Jesus's humanity that he would be addressing, since today even most skeptics agree that there was a man who lived in Palestine some two thousand years ago named Jesus of Nazareth.[12] Rather, the scandalous claim today is that God exists and, in Christ, God is with us. Moreover, contemporary accounts of what it is to be a human being often focus on the preeminence of bodily continuity (as opposed to the soul) and, to a lesser degree, on memory, on intellectual, emotional, and psychological capabilities, and on a coherent narrative of self. Also, of course, a focus on the brain, where it is presumed that most of what makes us us is happening. What is interesting about these proposed anthropological criteria is that they presuppose true humanity to be limited and ephemeral—two qualities that seem to be the exact opposite of God. God is perfect in power, perfect in subsistence, and perfect in every other way. Humans are not. So the problem for any contemporary Christology is not that God could not be fully human but that a fully human being could not, by definition, be God.

Admittedly, 1–3 John have little to say to such a view, though we might take a kind of *via negativa* to think theologically with John and fashion a contemporary Christology that can speak to contemporary skepticism. Just as John begins with the visibility, audibility, and tactility of the human Christ, so a contemporary Christology must begin with the divine words and Godlike actions of the divine Christ. And we do not mean pointing to the miraculous, as if pointing to the wedding at Cana will convince the skeptic that Jesus could do magic. Instead, we must point to the continuity between Jesus of Nazareth as depicted in the fourfold Gospel and the nature and character of YHWH in Israel's Scriptures. What the Hebrew Scriptures say of God is manifested in Jesus's liberating actions and his teachings.

And insofar as Jesus is portrayed as bearing emotions, it is worth noticing that YHWH is too. YHWH does not strongly resemble the god of the philosophers, whose perfections are incomprehensibly perfect. YHWH is God, yes, but "God" is not what humans might want God to be. God is neither the bloodthirsty monster so casually dismissed by contemporary skeptics nor the timeless, apathetic Supreme Being one supposes Descartes or Kant or Leibniz had in mind.

Nevertheless, YHWH is certainly not human, possessing a glory that would

12. Not all skeptics have accepted this conclusion. Over the last two hundred years it has been quite fashionable for skeptical thinkers to suppose that "Jesus" was a myth made up from whole cloth. Now, even agnostic and atheist Bible scholars will agree that Jesus lived; the question they have is, "What was he really like?"—since it is assumed that the Gospels are mostly made up. For a recent and popular treatment, see Bart D. Ehrman, *Did Jesus Really Exist? The Historical Argument for Jesus of Nazareth* (New York: HarperOne, 2012).

have killed Moses, had he beheld it. How can YHWH be fully present in the man Jesus of Nazareth? Even if Jesus need not be timeless or apathetic, surely divinity is too much for human bodies! Paul, in Philippians 2, answers this question with the idea of kenosis: the Logos of God "empties Godself" to come as a human being. The notion seems to be that the eternal Second Person temporarily sets aside some of what the Godhead can do in order to fit into a human body.

John has no such language. Instead, John emphasizes Jesus's uncreatedness and his eternal Sonship. Rather than a Christology of self-emptying and loss, John's is a Christology of Sonship, of the mutual revealing of the Father by the Son and of the Son by the Father through the Spirit. Where Pauline Christology reminds us of what the Second Person gave up to take on flesh, Johannine Christology highlights what the eternal Logos reveals about the nature and character of the Father. If there is a sense of what Jesus is not in 1–3 John, it is that, while in union with the Father in the Spirit, the Son is not coterminous with Father or Spirit. Father, Son, and Spirit share a nature but are not identical. To speak of the Son is not always to speak of the Father, though it is difficult to know where one stops and the other-who-is-not-other begins.

To answer the question another way, John's Christology acknowledges that the possibility of Jesus's divinity depends on a triune doctrine of God. If God is not a trinity, then of course Jesus cannot be divine! If, however, what it is to be God is to be a trinity, then perhaps there is space within God's being for incarnation. John will probably agree that the Second Person gives up something of the eternal divine life to come in flesh, but the very fact that the Godhead admits within Godself both infinite differentiation and the overcoming of differentiation makes conceptual space for a Son in union with the Father but not the Father.

With respect to modern atheism and agnosticism, John's Christology posits that the problem skeptics have is their impoverished notion of what God is. John would probably be appalled at any apology defending unqualified monotheism. "God" is not unqualifiedly monotheistic; so long as people suppose God might be, they will find the notion of Jesus's divinity silly—and rightly so. A Johannine apology would instead defend trinitarianism—and admit quite freely that the simple, timeless, apathetic monotheism of the philosophers is a terrible hypothesis. The evidence just does not bear it out. The variety we see in the world, its beautiful and terrible diversity—this speaks of a Creator whose very nature is variegated. Likewise, the patterns and consistencies, the physical laws and purity of mathematics—these speak to the Creator, whose nature is One. Only trinitarianism hypothesizes a God who could be responsible for both. And if such a God exists, it is less bizarre to imagine that that God could be Father and Son, eternally in union in the Spirit.

Novel but Never New: Orthodox Theology in 1–3 John

> "Anyone who runs off ahead and doesn't stay with Christ's teaching doesn't have God."

Since academia prizes fresh discoveries above all else, there is an oxymoronic quality to the idea of "academic theology," or at least that is how John makes it sound. "Having God," it seems, is to be theologically conservative. We do not mean "conservative" in the contemporary Western sense of holding fast to fundamentalist doctrines. Rather, we mean the broad, ideological sense: John cautions against any theological formulations that "get ahead" of Jesus, that "go beyond" what Christ himself taught and his disciples (presumably including John) have transmitted to subsequent Christian generations. The question, then, is what more—if anything—can be said?

At its core, this is a question about the nature of interpretation and meaning, for surely plenty of Christians have spilled plenty of ink over the millennia saying much about God, Christ, and the universe. And to whatever extent they have felt the need to be under John's apostolic authority, they seem to have been able to do so with a clear conscience. After the death of the apostles—and many believe that John was himself the last of them—the apostolic doctrine was passed down in conjunction with Christian literature that was quickly taken to be Scripture, though there was some dispute over which surviving letters and treatises were divinely inspired and which were not. After Nicaea, the Christian story about God and the universe was given a textual lens in the Nicene Creed, and the question about what Christian literature was taken to be Scripture was more or less closed.[13] Since that time, any trinitarian-based account of the universe—that is, any account proceeding from within the way-of-seeing-the-world provided by the creed—is likely orthodox in the Johannine sense of the word. That is, John is concerned about getting God right—and for him this means Father, Son, and Spirit—and recognizing the impact this understanding of God has on one's rendering of the rest of the world. John just wants to make sure that the gospel that the apostles told is the one that shapes everything, and not the other way around.

But John was also probably not aware that he was authoring Scripture when he wrote 2 John, which leaves us with a bit of a conundrum. If 2 John is the Word of God and we expect it to speak, what can or should it say? How can we be sure

13. See Jenson's *Canon and Creed* for the best recent account of the mutually informing relationship between protocreeds and circulating Christian literature before the fourth century.

that we will not err on the side of "getting ahead of Christ's teaching" when we interpret, assess, and preach it?

Over the last several decades, scholarship concerned with theological interpretation of Scripture has wrestled with this problem, although in many places indirectly or inchoately. The reason is that interest in the philosophy of interpretation came primarily because biblical scholars increasingly noticed (1) how little academic theology had to do with, well, the Bible and (2) how little biblical studies had to do with the truth about God and the world. From Augustine to the Reformation, theology had been done with Scripture, and biblical interpretation had informed theological reflection; there was not a substantial differentiation between the disciplines. However, the Enlightenment and the post-Enlightenment academy—beginning in Europe and then in North America—separated the methods and aims of the two, to the point that Bible scholars were expected to re-create the history "behind the text," and theologians nattered on about this or that papal bull or about the approaches of various traditions to paedobaptism, with little feel for the grand arc of God's story as textualized in the Bible. For classically orthodox academics on both sides of the theology-Bible divide, there has been an awakening to the need for Bible and theology to come back together.[14]

Critically, Christian interpretation has benefited from twentieth-century advances in philosophical hermeneutics, that is, the philosophy of the interpretation of texts. While we are happy to remain mostly agnostic with respect to various approaches and interpretive methodologies, we can make some substantive claims about the possibility of the meaning of ancient texts today, or in Christian parlance, the possibility of God the Spirit speaking to us through Scripture in theologically meaningful ways. We can expect to develop fresh theological reflection with and through Scripture while never "getting ahead of Jesus's teaching."

Hans Georg Gadamer's *Truth and Method* takes a phenomenological approach to interpretation that considers the reader's subjectivity, the history of the text and its interpretation, and the limitations of interpretive method. Though quasi-mystical in some places, Gadamer's insights that (1) we bring our own horizons of meaning to texts and develop provisional, subjective horizons for them when we genuinely encounter them and (2) opening ourselves to texts creates

14. For some classics of the genre, see Kevin Vanhoozer, *The Drama of Doctrine: A Canonical-Linguistic Approach* (Louisville: Westminster John Knox, 2005), Joel B. Green, *Seized by Truth: Reading the Bible as Scripture* (Nashville: Abingdon, 2007), and Robert W. Wall, "Reading the Bible from within Our Traditions: The 'Rule of Faith' in Theological Hermeneutics," in *Between Two Horizons: Spanning New Testament Studies and Systematic Theology*, ed. Joel B. Green and Max Turner (Grand Rapids: Eerdmans, 2000), 88–107.

the potential for the merging of these horizons strike a profoundly Christian note. Gadamer deems the process *Horizontverschmelzung* ("fusion of horizons"), the place where the world of the artistic artifact reshapes our world. In many ways, Gadamer gives the language of philosophical account to what Christians have experienced with biblical texts throughout the ages. For what do Christians come to the Scriptures to do if not hear them narrate the world as God speaks it and have that narration encounter and merge with and override and renarrate our own?

Gadamer had little use for this or that method; he believed that textual encounters were a species of artistic encounter as such. Language has a role to play in one's encounter with the Mona Lisa, but not as interpretive method. And to be fair, some "pneumatic interpretations" of biblical texts forgo method in favor of a sort of direct divine speech, but these questionable approaches are notorious for leading to interpretations that depart from a creedal interpretive lens and thus—at their best—lead to inane, banal words of comfort from the interpreter to himself or herself. At their worst, they lead to full-blown heresy.

Somewhat downstream in Gadamer's intellectual heritage, Paul Ricoeur's poststructuralism provides an interpretive schema that respects Gadamer's insight while creating space for various interpretive methods to be deployed.[15] Ricoeur suggests that applying interpretive methodologies to texts initiates a process through which the interpreter develops the text's horizon but that different methodologies can produce different textual horizons. Moreover, the same interpretive method might yield varying horizons, since the inherent lack of precision in language opens the door to texts having multiple—indeed infinite—meanings. Approaching texts this way does not, however, lead to interpretive anarchy, since interpretive methods themselves come with criteria for legitimate readings. Ricoeur uses the analogy of a detective investigating a crime. The text provides the clues; the interpreter arranges these clues to suggest a "world of the text"—something akin to Gadamer's horizon. Each interpretation of the text depicts the world in a particular way, and this way is both similar and different from my own. Christian theological interpretation of Scripture is the process by which the Spirit enables the former to subsume the latter.

For our purposes, the key takeaway is that there is space for orthodox theology that does not "get ahead" of apostolic doctrine. Since the Nicene Creed is itself the definitive lens of viewing the world biblically—which is, again, to say "apostolically"—close attention to the language of Scripture will reliably

15. For a more in-depth explanation of what follows, see Thomas Andrew Bennett, "Paul Ricoeur and the Hypothesis of the Text in Theological Interpretation," *JTI* 5, no. 2 (2011): 211–29.

generate fresh horizons in every age that are creedal and therefore orthodox, yet novel and especially adapted to the contemporary needs of the church. When authored by the Spirit, these horizons constitute the Word of God to the people of God.

God and Creation

A Redeemable Creation

"the sins of the entire cosmos"

John is pessimistic about the state of the world. His terminology is nigh Manichaean, depicting light on the one hand and darkness on the other. God is light; the world is darkness; we are called to exit the darkness and join the light, and never shall the two be mixed or mistaken. This dualism might lead theology to stark pronouncements beyond what is warranted by John's language. For example, theology might posit that the world is utterly and wholly evil, that there is nothing salvageable in it, that it is completely and hopelessly depraved and disordered. Without denying the severity of the sin disorder that plagues the world, the very fact of the incarnation should give us some hope, should temper pronouncements about the world's incorrigibility. Whatever else we might say about this place and human beings, the revelation of the Son who bears the divine life makes it abundantly clear that the created order can actually accommodate the divine being. The one who was from the beginning can "fit"—if we might put it that way—into human flesh and can live in this world. This is not to say that the fit is easy or that human nature does not need to be mightily transformed in order to be adequate to the divine life, but it is to say that things are not so far gone that an encounter with the divine simply annihilates anything sullied by a denatured creation.

Exodus 33:11–23 tells the story of YHWH showing "all goodness" to Moses, the unvarnished measure of God's glory. Even with this offer, however, God cannot allow Moses to see the divine face, for no one can see it and live (33:20). John's claim about the eternal life revealed in the Son indicates that there is a way that human beings can have genuine, face-to-face encounter with the divine life, but that it comes through the Son's mediation. What would have killed Moses is the normal experience of the church; the fullness of divine life and glory *can* tabernacle here. However corrupt the world is, however extant the darkness, redemption remains possible. In a sense, the Son is the conduit through which the divine life is filtered and becomes accessible. But where does that leave John's notion of the world? Is it good, bad, or neutral?

Perhaps John's martial language in 1 John 2:8–11 can help here. That is, it seems as though John's language might be thinking "the world" in the same way that American and British soldiers thought "Europe" during the Second World War. The world is a realm that has been overtaken and held captive by darkness. In many cases, the Stockholm Syndrome has taken over, and the world's denizens—who are captives—prefer their captor(s) to any liberating forces. So much so, in fact, that they will fight on their enemy's behalf, becoming something of the enemy themselves, not unlike, perhaps, a sympathetic, occupied town in Vichy France. The world is therefore both good and bad. It is a realm of darkness that has been pierced by the invasion of the light. Furthermore, that light represents the world's truest nature, the end toward which its present and future are aimed. Though the darkness has obscured the fact, the light of the world (John 8:12) really is the light of the world. Jesus is not an invader on foreign territory so much as the true ruler coming to reclaim his throne. In this figuration we can hold together two facets of traditional Christian theology: that the world is good because it has been fashioned by the Father through the Word, and that the world is corrupt and enslaved, owned by the enemy and caught up in the enemy's systems.

In atonement theology, this is the language of *Christus Victor*, where the life, death, and resurrection of Jesus is likened to a victorious defeat of sin, death, and demonic power that subsequently inaugurates the counterpolity that is the Spirit-empowered church.[16] On this view, the church functions much like a beachhead or a forward observation post, establishing God's liberating, enlightening rule over and against the now-waning powers of darkness. This perspective is not hard to hear in 1 John 2; indeed, we have already seen that the darkness is fading away and the true light is already shining.

There may be eschatological implications here as well. If the world is in fact redeemable, then John might be envisioning its end as refreshed and glorified rather than annihilated and re-created. If so, there might be a connection between John's vision in 1 John 2:8 of the current world order "fading away" and the vision in Revelation 21:1 of the first heaven and earth having "passed away," or left in favor of the new. The Greek terms are not the same, but the metaphor of movement beyond one thing to the next is. The vision in Revelation is of a physical place, a city, with city-features. It is not hard to imagine that John expects there to be a physical world that is "fit" for a fully divine nature that is enfleshed in glorified bodies. This belief, in turn, might help make sense of what John expects, which is that "we will be like him, because we will see him as he really is" (1 John 3:2).

16. I borrow the term "counterpolity" from John Milbank (*Being Reconciled: Ontology and Pardon* [New York: Routledge, 2003], 105).

Time in 1–3 John

"Children, it is the last hour!"

The celebrated second chapter of William Faulkner's *The Sound and the Fury* is a melancholy and uncompromising reflection on the nature of time. Perhaps it is our fleeting nature (see Ps 90), but human beings have an inordinate capacity to obsess—and not usually in a positive way—over time. In Faulkner's tale, Harvard freshman Quentin Compson spends June 2, 1910, tortured by his inability to escape time's ravages before committing suicide by casting himself into the Charles River. Throughout the narrative, Compson broods jealously over those for whom time stands still. His friend Spoade, who never needs to hurry to class. The black man who stands with a mule, "the two of them shabby and motionless and unimpatient."[17] Not "patient," not "content," but "unimpatient," as if time is not only not a concern, but illusory: once it has been known as such, there is the possibility of moving beyond patience and impatience altogether. Before defacing the watch his father has given him by tearing off its hands, he remembers the words that accompanied the gift: "I give it to you not that you may remember time, but that you might forget it now and then for a moment and not spend all your breath trying to conquer it. Because no battle is ever won he said. They are not even fought. The field only reveals to man his own folly and despair, and victory is an illusion of philosophers and fools."[18] Quentin's father recuses himself from trying to conquer time through drunkenness; Quentin affords himself no such luxury. Tortured by the past, the present is endlessly allusive to it, and Quentin can neither function nor look forward.

Compson does not want resurrection—he is not looking for endless life. He imagines his body decomposing so that when Jesus comes back and says, "Rise[,] only the flat-iron [that Compson uses to weight his body to the bottom of the river] would come floating up."[19] He does not yearn for a new beginning. Compson wishes instead—insofar as he wishes for anything at all—for agency, the ability to act with efficacy, and in that to recover something of the eternity of childhood, where time passes but does not seem to matter.

Quentin's bleak vision emerges from an impossible but also ubiquitously human desire, to freeze time in place—somewhere innocent and congenial—and live in stasis, untouched by the sadnesses, losses, failures, and deaths that are, in

17. William Faulkner, *The Sound and the Fury*, corr. ed. (New York: Random House, 1984), 87.

18. Faulkner, *The Sound and the Fury*, 76.

19. Faulkner, *The Sound and the Fury*, 80.

human experience, always right around the corner. Quentin's actions indicate that the solution lies in something like Daoist passivity or in Stoic acceptance and endurance. For John and for his Christian hearers, however, the language of the last hour perhaps suggests a sort of converse to Dylan Thomas's raging against the dying of the light. Who knows how long the last hour might, well, last? We know only that it will, that the light is creeping above the horizon and that this is a call not to passivity but to battle. The martial metaphor is not, however, fully adequate. John says that life in "the last hour" is still *divine, eternal* life. The life known fully in the loving communion of the Godhead is given by faith and in the Spirit to believers now. It might appear that there is a kind of dualism at work: the believer outwardly lives and battles against the receding-yet-far-reaching grasp of antichristic forces but inwardly lives in peaceful, joyous, union with the divine. If we were to assume no space for such a dualism in John's conception of human life in Christ, how could this circle be squared?

To answer this question is to unite Compson's lament, the meaning of the last hour, and one of John's strongest, overriding themes: Christian union in love. The very love of the triune God poured out of the believer onto other believers marks the bridge between ages. The last hour may last quite long, but neither despair nor a longing for stasis enters into a decidedly Christian understanding of time, because the active, transformative love of God activates eschatological life in the midst of a community of human beings—even as they live under relentless antichristic siege.

Nevertheless, experience teaches that such states rarely obtain and never last. It is worth juxtaposing John's vision of the turning of ages and his admonitions to the patroness in 2 John and Gaius in 3 John and their communities. Yes, God's transformative love exists in those communities, but it can be betrayed, lost, and then reignited. The Christian condition is not quite paradox, but it does hold two realities in tension: the night is passing and true dawn is dawning, and yet dawn has not fully arrived. It is as if the sun is peeking over the horizon more and more, but it still manages to stay just peeking over the horizon. There is movement and we are moving, but night still holds fast.

The Unseen World: Spirit and Spirits in 1–3 John

> "Dear friends, don't trust every spirit. Instead, evaluate the spirits to see if they come from God."

In a letter to fellow pulp writer Robert E. Howard, H. P. Lovecraft opines on the spiritual realm:

> All I say is that I think it is damned unlikely that anything like a central cosmic will, a spirit world, or an eternal survival of personality exist. They are the most preposterous and unjustified of all the guesses which can be made about the universe, and I am not enough of a hair-splitter to pretend that I don't regard them as arrant and negligible moonshine. In theory I am an agnostic, but pending the appearance of radical evidence I must be classed, practically and provisionally, as an atheist.[20]

Lovecraft, the master fashioner of monsters and gods, had little time for the notion of a world that lurks behind the veil, to say nothing of believing that such a world could influence our own. Lovecraft is a typical example of empiricist skeptics, that class of agnostics and atheists who, having studied some religious anthropology and been impressed by the remarkable advances of the natural sciences, regard the idea of an angel, demon, or spirit primitive nonsense better left to the Bronze Age from whence it came. There is a certain intellectual hubris to such a view; one wonders what to make of the legions of folk who testify to some experience of the unseen or the miraculous, but the material success of the West appears to be fertile soil out of which it is growing and multiplying.

To be fair, there is an attraction to it. Prayer does not work like modern medicine. There does not appear to be any statistical variation in the outcomes of the sick who receive prayer and the sick who do not.[21] If the unseen world exists, where do we see its effects? As we noted in the exegesis of 1 John, the Johannine vision of the world is rife with different sorts of spirits. How do such spirits operate? Is there a quantifiable, observable aspect to their works? If not, would it not be better to simply ignore them? The questions matter because if John is right, attending to the spirits is a matter of life and death, of being led into the light or being mired in the dark. And one supposes that life in the light and life in the dark manifest themselves in some very different, easily observable ways.

John seems to think that a person's or a community's adherence to truth and avoidance of error is the primary effect of a spirit's influence in the world. The Spirit of Error causes people like Diotrephes in 3 John to cease attending to those who carry the apostolic truth like John and his cohort. The way John talks about them makes it sound as if the spirits are connected to specific people and places,

20. H. P. Lovecraft, "Letter to Robert E. Howard (August 16, 1932)," in *Selected Letters, 1932–1934*, ed. August William Derleth and James Turner (Sauk City, WI: Arkham House, 1976), 57.

21. So H. Benson et al., "Study of the Therapeutic Effects of Intercessory Prayer (STEP) in Cardiac Bypass Patients: A Multicenter Randomized Trial of Uncertainty and Certainty of Receiving Intercessory Prayer," *American Heart Journal* 151, no. 4 (2006): 934–42. The study divided a group of approximately 1,100 heart patients into two groups. One received intercessory prayer, while the other did not. Authors could find no statistical correlation in the outcomes of the two groups.

that those people and places take on certain attributes of the spirits animating them. Similarly, the places animated by the Spirit of Truth have people who confess that, among other things, Jesus came as a human being. Places under the sway of the Spirit of Error have people who, among other things, refuse to hear what John has to say.

In modern parlance, this connection between the spirits and human communities sounds a great deal like the "institutional culture" touted in management books or "prevailing winds" or "what's in the air." It does not sound much like the angelic beings in the Old Testament or Luke's birth narrative, where angelic messengers take on a much more human cast and act as independent agents. For John, the Spirit can even be an abstract "truth," just as God can be love. John's angelology—if we can even call it that—is amorphous and vague in description, even as it is monumentally important in consequence. But in some respects, this angelology means that John's understanding of the unseen world is less mystical and perhaps easier to integrate with contemporary demythologized conceptions of the world.

Since the late nineteenth century, philosophers and scientists have been investigating the phenomenon of "emergence." The basic definition of an emergent property is a property possessed by a whole that is not possessed by any of its constituent parts. A classic example is the convection process named after its discoverer, French physicist Henri Bénard. In Bénard convection, a determinate process of heating from below causes a nondeterministic but highly organized cellular pattern. That is, despite predictable, stable operating conditions, the cells spontaneously self-organize in an unpredictable but highly patterned fashion. That undetermined organization is an emergent property of Bénard cells.

What if human communities and institutions have an analogous emergent potential? Walter Wink suggests we view "spiritual Powers not as separate heavenly or ethereal entities but as *the inner aspect of material or tangible manifestations of power*."[22] It is difficult to pin Wink down on what exactly an "inner aspect" is, but maybe emergence theory can help. Perhaps John's "spirits" are real, invisible, emergent properties that can exert bottom-up and top-down influence in human communities. We use the word "property" to leave open the possibility of the spirit's agency (without committing to it) and use "influence" to retain the agency of the individuals composing a community while recognizing that they are not "fully free," in the libertarian sense of the term. On this definition, it is possible to ascribe to Diotrephes's community the "Spirit of Error." Doing so would mean that this faux church is a place where people tend to believe certain

22. Walter Wink, *Naming the Powers: The Language of Power in the New Testament* (Philadelphia: Fortress Press, 1984), 104, italics in original.

wrong things and act in certain wrong ways. It is difficult to locate exactly where and how this spirit arose, but it is easy to notice that Diotrephes's people mostly deny Jesus's humanity and mostly fail to operate out of love. When people join Diotrephes's community, they tend to become like other members. The Spirit of Error emerges from this community and then influences it.[23]

When John counsels us to "evaluate the spirits" (1 John 4:1), he is asking us to gauge the community in toto. What are we predisposed to be like? What sorts of beliefs define us? What kind of people are forming? Such evaluative questions are extremely difficult to answer because the spirit that influences us is doing so as we self-reflect. It makes sense that identifying and exorcizing these spirits is described by John as "overcoming" or "defeating" them. Any antichristic spirit of a community depends for its survival on deceiving the community as to its own existence. You cannot exorcize the demon of which you are not aware. This need for discernment, in turn, explains why his primary focus is on the Spirit of Truth and the Spirit of Error: when dominated by error, truth is more important than any other spirit. And when living in the light of Truth, the Spirit of Error is easy to identify.

On the Importance of the Physical in 1–3 John

> "I'm hoping to come to you and speak face to face so our joy can be full."

John repeatedly reminds his readers that Jesus was human, that touching, seeing, hearing matter, and that anyone who denies these aspects of Christ and, at the end of 2 John, face-to-face human interaction is missing something essential to joyful spirituality. So pervasive is his focus on flesh that scholars have spun up a historical backstory to 1–3 John to explain it. On their telling, John is counter-

23. It is critical to note that such a view requires that an emergent property be irreducible, that is, not susceptible to deterministic causation. The pattern of Bénard cells is an emergent property because it cannot be explained or predicted by any of its causal conditions. Notice that Bénard cells do not exercise any downward causation, that is, they do not alter the heat or pressure of the environment that produced them. Spirits clearly do. For a clear if complicated paper laying down the groundwork for a robust emergentism, see Jaegwon Kim, "Making Sense of Emergence," *Philosophical Studies* 95 (1999): 3–36. And for a contemporary defense of downward causation in emergent systems, see Mark A. Bedau, "Downward Causation and Autonomy in Weak Emergence," in *Emergence: Contemporary Readings in Philosophy and Science*, ed. Mark A. Bedau and Paul Humphreys (Cambridge: MIT Press, 2008).

ing a form of docetism, a neo-Platonic twisting of the gospel that denies Jesus's humanity; Jesus may have looked human, but he really was not. There could be a number of reasons why the docetists wanted to deny Jesus's humanity. For example, it might have been thought that mixing the divine and human was metaphysically impossible: the invisible eternal forms have no—and could have no—congress with the physical world. Or maybe the problem is theological: Christ is too holy, too transcendent, too otherworldly to be wrapped up in or sullied by the mud and blood of our domain.

Such dualisms spring from an often justified skepticism about the goodness of the universe. Given the obvious sin in humanity and the vicissitudes of human life—to say nothing of the apparent pandemonium of the created order and its violence—there seems to be good reason to say that physicality is at best irremediably broken and at worst fully and deeply evil. And if so, docetism makes sense. God should not want to be a part of the world. God should be trying to rescue people out of it! The ascension of Christ to heaven was not the firstborn resurrected from the dead drawing humanity into the Godhead; it was an escape, an ejection, a final rejection of the fatally flawed.

We have noted consistently that John knows that humanity and the material universe are indeed ruled by a dark empire, but he also knows that God is not finished, that the goal is redemption and glory, victory over the darkness, not eternal retreat. God loves the world, and God does not love evil, which says something very important about materiality. We see below (under "Election and Eschatology," p. 179) that the divine election of Jesus Christ is an eternal election of physical human being. God sees fit from eternity to subsume human flesh into divine life and draw human beings into eternal union with Godself. But such an election implies something else: God's eternal election of the physical, the material. By electing Jesus Christ, God must also elect a physical universe, a physical redemption, and a physical eschaton. In effect, God covenants with the natural world. The same kind of commitment God has to believers God also has to the material nature of creation itself.

God's election of and covenanting with the universe's materiality authorize us to cultivate and care for creation. Yes, God makes this vocation quite explicit in Genesis, handing over care of the world to Adam and Eve, but there is a theological reason behind God giving us this vocation. God has eternally chosen the universe and—through Christ—the universe's *human* redemption. Jesus Christ, firstborn of the dead, begins the glorification not just of humanity but of the natural world itself. This seems to be Paul's belief in Romans 8, where the created order— the rocks and hills and trees and cats and pythons too—aches for God's children to be revealed. We should not be impressed by the glorification of humanity, though that might be quite impressive. No, the creation longs for itself to be fully liberated too, which cannot happen before God's children are revealed. Perhaps this ordering implies that we are going to take part in glorifying all things physical, just as Adam and Eve were invited to take part in creation care. If so, our present work to make the world beautiful and lush and vibrant is preview and practice for our eschatological future.

John knows that there is something special about being "face to face," being physically with the object of one's love. This is just the natural result of God choosing a material world to be the place where God reveals God's glory and goodness and love. God decides that physicality will be the stage on which the play will be acted. So joy cannot be complete without physical presence, because God has elected presence—not spiritual, but physical presence—to be the setting for true spirituality.

One supposes that this preference for the physical has further ethical implications regarding any attempt or desire to be "free from the flesh" or transcend the physical or be raptured away never to return. Yes, the material world is the location of temptation and sin and ugliness and violence, and no, those are not good things, but that does not mean that flesh and physicality themselves are evil, just that they are unredeemed and unglorified. So, for example, self-harm as a means to escape or punish or purge sin is misguided and wrong, damaging something good in a misguided attempt to fix it. So too are lusty visions of leaving the world forever and watching the cleansing fire of God consume it all wrongheaded and crucially missing the goodness, the electedness of all things material. Temptations to denigrate the world and flesh will be with us so long as the ugliness of sin remains. But these are to be resisted, because only when we are in the flesh, truly human, and truly with each other and God is our joy complete.

God's Character

God Beyond, God In: Transcendence and Immanence in 1 John

"what we have seen and heard"

It would be difficult to overemphasize the import of John's claim that the eternal life of the Father has been revealed as a person and to the people of this world as a person. To begin with, John's language forces Christian theology to affirm both that God is *transcendent*, that is, beyond and before the world (and, by extension, humanity), and that God is *immanent*, that is, in the world and, in the incarnation, specifically humanity. Note that John does not explain how it is possible for God to be so, only that it is the case, known viscerally because John and his friends have heard, seen, gazed in awe upon, and handled a life that could be only the eternal life of the Father.

It is probably for the best that John leaves all hows to the side, because the claim throws theology onto the horns. On the one hand, if God is wholly transcendent, then there is confusion about how there can be any interaction between God and the universe. In Christian theology, some versions of the tradition try to square this circle by placing all that God "does" in the world as a part of God's timeless, implacable decree, such that God is not a part of or interacting with the world and human beings so much as God, in God's infinite and unsearchable wisdom, foresees all that will take place and wills various "responses" in advance that unfold and take place at their appointed times.[24] Such an account is certainly possible.

On the other hand, if God is wholly immanent, then God is actually subject to, or perhaps evolving and changing with, the created order.[25] If God is part and parcel of the universe, then God changes as the universe changes, and if the sciences have shown anything at all, it is that this world is wholly in flux. This too is certainly possible, and many branches of Christian theology—especially in the past century—have affirmed it.

But John seems to want to have it both ways. The ambiguity of the whats in conjunction with his echo of Genesis 1:1 and the beginning of the Fourth Gospel indicate that whatever else he thinks of the Father, he knows this God as sovereign Creator, the God of gods, as it were. We will discuss "eternal life" below[26] (2:25; 5:11, 13, 20), but it suffices for now to say that "eternal" (αἰώνιος, *aiōnios*) points to that which is transcendent, beyond the confines of this world. So John pictures the Father as truly beyond and before the world. This is what makes his claims about seeing and hearing and handling the divine life so radical. The God that is wholly transcendent is also wholly immanent; God is not just one or the other, nor can God be one or the other if God truly is manifest in the person of the Son. Philosophically speaking, if God is totally beyond and above and before, then the experience of praying and receiving answers to prayer is something of a fraud, merely the outworking of a wind-up toy that only seems to be interactive.[27] God is not the subject of tensed verbs because God eternally Is,

24. This is a sketch of the classical view often attributed to Boethius in the late fifth and early sixth centuries. Various iterations have developed to account for how a timeless being can have personality and be said to interact with the world. For modern accounts, see, for example, Paul Helm, *Eternal God: A Study of God without Time*, 2nd ed. (Oxford: Oxford University Press, 2011), and Brian Leftow, *Time and Eternity* (Ithaca, NY: Cornell University Press, 1991).

25. Classic defenders of process thought and theology include Alfred North Whitehead and Charles Hartshorne.

26. See "The Love of God and the Death of God," pp. 166–68.

27. See chapter 12 in Richard Swinburne, *The Coherence of Theism*, 2nd ed. (Oxford: Oxford University Press, 1993).

and nothing more can be said. Even God's love seems less intimate when it is all and only willed from eternity rather than generated in real response in real time. In fact, nothing that we know of the world can really be predicated of God; God is utterly and completely alien, perhaps a disinterested watchmaker or perhaps not, but how could human beings decide?

John is also right to maintain the Father's fatherhood, the Father's transcendence and monarchy in the midst of confessing a manifest eternal life in human flesh. For if God is just human, is just a part of this world, then God relinquishes sovereignty and has given up the reins, forfeited the keys to the kingdom. God has ceased to be God in any determinative, meaningful sense.

Instead, John affirms that the Father remains the Father and has sent a unique Son into the world. The Father is transcendent, the Son is immanent and accessible by the Spirit (1 John 4:13), and in the bargain human beings gain access to the Father's life through the Son. The fact that the Father is "up there" and the Son "down here" and yet the two remain in union pushes on the bounds of human comprehension. Perhaps the bond of love uniting the two is, as Augustine claimed, the Holy Spirit, the third hypostasis of the Trinity. The mystery here is difficult to parse. What is demanded of Christian theology is, not an exhaustive explanation of how God can be both beyond the world and in it, but a confession that this is so and a pattern of prayer that testifies as such. Neither should we close off any rational inquiry. As models and metaphors and discoveries offer new and better ways to express the why and how of God's transcendent immanence, we may freely appropriate them, but perhaps not to the exclusion of awe. Never should human knowledge claim to have boxed God in and splayed God out so that God becomes fully known and—perish the thought—banal, for all that is known exhaustively must eventually become so. Rather, the sheer incomprehensibility of a united transcendent Father and immanent Son as one God exclusively and endlessly retains God's capacity for surprise and improbable action and hope. In this we see that even with the revelation of the Son, the God of whom John witnesses remains Israel's God: sovereign yet engaged, over all yet faithfully committed to rescuing and exalting the elect. The manifestation of God's eternal life in the Son in fact helps make sense of the mercurial nature of Israel's God. For the revelation of the Son demonstrates that it is in God's nature to be before the beginning and yet deeply connected to the world, interested in its affairs, and working out a future for human beings. In a sense, the revelation of the Son is an exclamation point, a once-for-all acknowledgment that the kind of God Israel has confessed Yahweh to be is in fact the kind of God that God is: supreme—and supremely with us.

To put it all another way, a trinitarian hermeneutic gives John—and subsequently the church—a way to understand how the one God of Israel can in fact be and do all that Israel has claimed that God is and does. Old Testament theology even organizes its portrait of Israel's God according to God's acts, such that knowing Israel's God simply means reckoning the truth that, for example, God *began*, God *promised*, God *delivered*, and so forth.[28] For God to be able to do all that Israel claims, YHWH must be a transcendent, sovereign ruler, above the mundane affairs of the earthly realm. Yet God is also interested in these affairs, interacts with them, shapes them, and moves them. In light of the incarnation, John gives us a trinitarian hermeneutic that explains how this can be: the Father lives the eternal life of the heavens, the Son reveals and mediates that life in this sphere. The revelation of the Son confirms and illuminates Israel's proclamation of God as being over all and yet as specially located and active among God's people.

It should be no surprise, then, that Johaninne theology in general, and certainly what is here in 1 John, evinces a strong rereckoning of the temple being recapitulated in the life of Jesus and subsequently the church. For where else is the mystery of God's transcendence and immanence more pointed than in the Jerusalem temple, the earthly encampment of the God of the heavenly realms? The confession that the God of the universe would dwell in the temple of a minor, beleaguered (and, by the time of Jesus, thoroughly conquered) nation is a theological scandal all of its own. Nevertheless, this is the choice God made. And then, when the time was right, everything that the temple was meant to be—the meeting point between God's transcendent and immanent rule—is fulfilled in the eternal life-bearing Son, who (and we tread carefully with the term) democratizes God's immanent presence in the world.[29]

Divine Pathos in 1–3 John: God's Joy

"our joy may be made complete"

In a sense, God sent his Son "for us," but in another sense God sent his Son for God. Bringing us into eternal life is something that increases God's joy, despite the costs of incarnation, death, and glory. God delights in sharing God's life; analogously, properly functioning Christian communities do the same. And again, this is not sharing between equals or even between similar persons or beings. The gap between Trinity and humanity is surmountable only in an egregious self-giving

28. So John Goldingay's *Old Testament Theology*, vol. 1, *Israel's Gospel* (Downers Grove, IL: InterVarsity Press, 2003), in which chapter titles are based on particular divine activities.

29. See comment on 1 John 2:7–11 above.

of "what was from the beginning." The analogy holds for us: we are sharing in the divine life when we share union not with those to whom we are already close but with those with whom we are most different. David Bentley Hart writes, "As created being is the analogical expression of the infinite Trinity, it 'corresponds' to its source . . . by way of its own motion of differential excess, as the expressive rhetoric of an infinitely responsive and differentiating God."[30] Hart means that the sheer variety—what he calls "differential excess"—of human persons is itself a reflection of God's eternal self-differentiation, that is, God's own being as three-personed. Because, as we saw in Clement and 1 John 1:1–4, the Father eternally generates the Son in differentiation from himself, it is no surprise that the creation itself demonstrates a bewildering tendency toward variegation. But just as the Father and Son are eternally united in the Spirit, so the eschatological goal of created being in all its diversity is to join in that divine union. Therefore, for those who have seen and heard and touched eternal life in the person of Jesus Christ, it is the most natural desire to mirror eschatological reconciliation within the church. They derive the greatest joy from extending the union-in-difference they have known in Christ to all and sundry. Thus when the hearers of John's sermon believe his announcement, they make his joy complete.

Nothing in this discussion means that God's joy is imperfect or deficient apart from union with us. To think this way is to mistake the nature of the divine perfections—here, specifically, joy. In itself, the joy of God is joy-through-union. Constitutive of this joy is that it is shared in the oneness and threeness of the Godhead. God's joy is complete in the Godhead, and yet God's joy increases when divine union is extended to us. To have joy to the uttermost does not mean that joy cannot become greater; it only means that whatever joy is possible at any moment, God has that. It does suggest, however, that God is not impassible; that is, that God can change. John's language assumes this to be the case: God has more love to give, more joy to share and experience—God is not done expanding and deepening and increasing.

Theological Aesthetics in 1–3 John

"God is light . . ."

Because 1 John is a sermon, themes weave in and out, are repeated and expanded upon. Thus it is too much to say that "God is light" is the thesis or central concern of 1 John, or even that this statement can be wholly abstracted from the

30. David Bentley Hart, *The Beauty of the Infinite: The Aesthetics of Christian Truth* (Grand Rapids: Eerdmans, 2003), 105–6.

announcement of the first chapter of 1 John.[31] Nevertheless, the message that God is light is one way of getting at the profundity of the revelation of God's character and action in and through Jesus Christ.

It is worth emphasizing here that we are encountering a metaphor, for God is not literally light, as pagan or gnostic religion might mistakenly suppose. Metaphors by their very nature are highly associative and semantically slippery. We should not hope to simply replace the word "light" with some less metaphoric descriptor and expect to have captured the meaning once and for all. That said, the Johannine writings are replete with the metaphor of light being the means by which people walk without stumbling. So, for example, Jesus is explicit about this connection in John 11:9–10, where he points out that people walk around during the day because it is easier to avoid stumbling when there is light. Elsewhere, the Gospel is likewise explicit that Jesus is the light of the world (John 1:4–11; 8:12; 9:5; 12:46), that he is himself the light by which all people avoid walking or living in darkness. Therefore the light—whatever we suggest it is—directly reveals a particular kind of life or living that is proper to human beings.

This understanding is, interestingly, very much in keeping with how light is used metaphorically in the Old Testament, especially the wisdom literature and the prophets (e.g., Job 24:13; Pss 36:9; 56:13; Prov 13:9; Isa 51:4; 58:10). Micah 7:8–9 (CEB) is particularly suggestive:

> 8 Do not rejoice over me, my enemy, because when I fall, I will rise; if I sit in
> darkness, the LORD is my light. 9 I must bear the raging of the LORD, for I have sinned against him, until he decides my case and provides justice for me. He will bring me out into the light; I will see by means of his righteousness.

Here the prophet, speaking for a sinful Israel, laments, yet he is convinced that God will not leave the country wayward, mired in lawlessness and its attendant misery. This condition, it seems, is darkness. Not only are the people not acting according to God's principles of justice (*mišpat*) and right-ordering (*tsedaqa*), but failing to do so results in a sordid mess of a society, where household plots against household, the corruption of the powerful exempts them from justice, friends stab one another in the back, and even the household sees internal strife (7:2–6). But God will not let the darkness last indefinitely. At some future time, Yahweh will set things right (*mišpat*) and bring Israel into the light, where it will be able to recognize and live according to God's own ordering of things (*tsedaqa*).

31. Yarbrough (*1–3 John*, 46–51), following and extending the thought of Marianne Meye Thompson (*1–3 John* [Downers Grove, IL: InterVarsity Press, 1992], 40), claims that "in many ways 'God is light' is the thesis of the epistle." But this claim goes too far. If 1 John has a "thesis," it is, as we have seen, stated and restated a number of times in a number of different ways.

Third Isaiah's oracle similarly conjoins God's justice and right-ordering with light:

> [4] Listen to me, my people, and give heed to me, my nation; for a teaching [*torah*] will go out from me, and my justice [*mišpat*] for a light to the peoples. [5] I will bring near my deliverance swiftly, my salvation has gone out and my arms will rule the peoples; the coastlands wait for me, and for my arm they hope. . . . [7] Listen to me, you who know righteousness [*tsedaqa*], you people who have my teaching [*torah*] in your hearts; do not fear the reproach of others, and do not be dismayed when they revile you. (Isa 51:4–5, 7 NRSV)

In this text, interestingly, it is God's *torah*, that is, "teaching," "instruction," or "law," that is sent out to the peoples of the world. Isaiah is here specifically referencing the teachings found in the first five books of the Bible known to Jews and Christians as Torah. The oracle suggests that the proper ordering of the universe is found in God's law, but this right-ordering is now going to be expressed in actual acts of deliverance in which God's just ordering of things is meted out. Thus, knowledge of how the world is meant to be is given flesh, as it were, when God initiates salvific actions. Then, the combination of knowing the world's true structure—as delineated in Torah—and witnessing God's mighty acts of deliverance that put the world as it ought to be constitutes "light."

This "true structure" of the world is, especially in the wisdom literature, known as God's Word (λόγος, *logos*). We can think of God's word as the principle according to which all of creation is laid out, the architecture of the universe. It is therefore no coincidence that in the first chapter of the Fourth Gospel, we find out that the Word is God, true light, the one who gives us the power to become God's children and who became a human being to live with us (John 1:1, 9, 12, 14). Notice that the Word both reveals and empowers, is and does.

Thus, John's announcement that "God is light, and there is no darkness in him" is a declaration of what we might call God's "being-in-act." Light is found to be not only revelatory but right-making or perhaps "purifying," if we could shift the metaphor just a bit. Light, as we have just seen, is both the proper order of the universe and God's right-setting, purifying actions that themselves instantiate that order where it has been disrupted, broken, or sullied. Understanding this truth helps us to make sense of what follows in verses 6–10 and, as we shall see, throughout 1 John as a whole. Specifically, 1 John adamantly refuses to separate one's spiritual status—wherein we have union with God and his children in the Spirit—from one's participation in God's ongoing purification.

To picture "light" in, for example, the mind's eye, necessarily involves an aesthetic component. Shining light does not present itself to us in the abstract, coldly, as, say, logic. And John could very well have presented God's revealing and purifying nature using technical terms—speaking quite literally of distinguishing between good and evil and righting what is disordered—but does not. Instead, he relies on a metaphor that is soaked, as we have seen, with Old Testament associations. This use of the metaphor should be instructive: God is not revealed as light only so that we may distinguish between two categories such as good and evil. In fact, if he were, then we would have to suggest that John—and, consequently, God(!)—has done a rather poor job, since the sermon very rarely delineates specific parameters for what, exactly, is "good" and what, exactly, is "sin." Rather than parsing, as might a philosopher, the particular qualities of right and wrong, good and evil, John announces Light. The implication is as stunning as it is simple: those who saw, heard, handled, and touched the Son of God came away from the experience not with a mental compendium of what human thoughts, inclinations, actions, and circumstances are Godward or worldward, that is, good or evil, but as those who had been united to the Good, the True, and the Beautiful as such. John's announcement that God is light is a claim at once both aesthetic and epistemological. John has perceived and can now reliably preach the God who is from the beginning, who is achingly glorious light. He does not parse the metaphor because to do so would be, as Gregory of Nyssa notes, to lie:

> As our treatise shows, . . . every man who commits his interpretation of the ineffable light into words is really a liar, not because of any hatred of the truth, but because of the weakness of his description. Perceptible beauty as far as it dwells here below in our life . . . is within our power to admire and to describe. . . . But how could a treatise, even if it explored every means of description, bring into view that whose archetype eludes comprehension, being without color or form or size or shape or any such foolishness?[32]

If the announcement that God is light sounds conceptually anemic to us, it is likely because we have mistakenly assumed that the content of the metaphor can be spelled out rationally and, if it were to be so articulated, that we would be able to reckon it by practicing the rules of interpretation according to grammar and syntax. Both postulates, Gregory avers, betray a categorical misapprehension of what "knowing God" entails.

Origen, altogether more optimistic about the vision of God, comments on 1 John 1:5 as follows:

32. *On Virginity*, paragraph 10, quoted in Gesa Elsbeth Thiessen, ed., *Theological Aesthetics: A Reader* (Grand Rapids: Eerdmans, 2004), 24.

> According to John, "God is light." The only-begotten Son, therefore, is the glory of this light, proceeding inseparably from (God) Himself, as brightness does from light, and illuminating the whole of creation. For, agreeably to what we have already explained as to the manner in which He is the Way, and conducts to the Father . . . in the same way ought we to understand also the meaning of His being the brightness: for it is by its splendor that we understand and feel what light itself is. And this splendor, presenting itself gently and softly to the frail and weak eyes of mortals, and gradually training, as it were, and accustoming them to bear the brightness of the light, when it has put away from them every hindrance and obstruction to vision . . . renders them capable of enduring the splendor of the light, being made in this respect also a sort of mediator between men and the light. (*Princ.* 1.2.7)

Origen makes an analogy to the way that light's brightness gradually accustoms our eyes to be able to apprehend the light itself. Origen shares Gregory's assumption that God, the true light, is beautiful beyond description. He explains—in a fashion that Gregory will ultimately endorse[33]—that Christ, and presumably our meditation on him and imitation of his life, functions as a mediator between us and God, slowly rendering our benighted eyes adequate to perceiving God as such. In our contemporary context we might immediately think of the power of practices to shape neural pathways, thereby enabling—and, we might add, ennobling—our eyes to perceive what was invisible to them in their untutored state. John's proclamation that God is light, following on his claim to have seen, heard, handled, and touched the light, drives a wedge between us, his hearers, and himself, the authoritative witness.

It is now appropriate to take note of what might have appeared redundant in the whats of 1 John 1:1. John mentions seeing twice ("what our eyes have seen, what we have gazed upon"). The second term, a participial form of the verb θεάομαι (*theaomai*), often carries a connotation of gazing intently, of being caught up in the awe or wonder of something. It is likely that that is what John conjures here, because the quality of life revealed in the person of the Son is, as we have just seen, beautiful beyond description. The response of John and his friends to this revelation was the proper one: transformative awe, sober and reflective contemplation and consideration. It is almost as if the person of Jesus

33. Gregory writes, "Through his participation in the true light, [the Christian] will himself be in a state of brightness and illumination. . . . I refer to the person who has purified all the powers of his soul from every form of evil, and I dare say that it is clear that the only thing which is beautiful by nature is that which is the cause of all beauty and all goodness" (*On Virginity*, para. 2). Gregory understands holiness as prerequisite to recognizing God, who is beauty and goodness.

is like a multifaceted gem, one whose full glory cannot be grasped apart from careful inspection, as each surface reveals some new beauty. John has seen and experienced Jesus in this way. We his readers/hearers have not. As we shall now see, if John is right about God and, by implication, the world, then we who have not seen, heard, handled, and touched are not in an aesthetic/epistemological position to make any right judgments at all, let alone any about John's proclamation.

". . . and there is no darkness in him."

That is, if God is a pure and purifying light who reveals the true structure of the cosmos and corrects it where it has been perverted, then the very fact that revelation and purification are needed indicates that something is very, very wrong with the world. This conclusion suggests that there is such a thing as darkness and that it is always and everywhere distorted and distorting. If God must reveal the universe's proper architecture, we can only conclude that this ordering is normally obscured. If God must do the work of a doctor and set the world's bones, then they must currently be broken.

But the corollary to this line of thinking is a terrible problem—an aesthetic and epistemological problem—for we must ask how we might be able to tell the light from the dark, or perhaps more subtly: we must wonder whether or not we would recognize the light as light if we were confronted with it. In First Isaiah we read of those who "call evil good and good evil, who put darkness for light and light for darkness, who put bitter for sweet and sweet for bitter" (Isa 5:20). If given enough time, the relentless substitution of evil for good, dark for light, and bitter for sweet corrupts the senses, twists the mind, and leaves us wholly deceived. Those who are thoroughly darkened cannot properly perceive, let alone name, the good as the good. The perverted world order is known as the true world order, and vice versa. That such a possibility even exists is frightening enough and drags us into the vicious circle of Cartesian doubt, in which every shaft of light must be suspected to be—or contain—a shadow.

Augustine faced a similar question about our ability to see God. In his day some were teaching that we would literally see God with our eyes in the body of the resurrection; Augustine thought that we would instead perceive God perfectly with the "mind's eye," that is, with the "inner person" (*interioris hominis*). While the question of the means by which we perceive God is itself interesting, it is Augustine's thinking about our ability to perceive God at all that is germane to the question of darkness in 1 John 1:5. Augustine, commenting on *visio Dei*, writes, "Therefore, we will see [Christ] only inasmuch as we will be like him; for now we do not see him only to the extent that we are unlike him."[34] John asserts that God is light and without darkness, but he goes on to point out that if we are walking in the darkness, that is, if we are part of the world's ordering of things, then we are not united with God. That is, we are not perceiving the light—*even if we think we are*. Some claim not to have any sin; they must be corrected precisely because they believe that what they say is true. And notice that life characterized by "walking in the light" is not coextensive with a life that is "without sin." This qualification makes good sense if we remember to associate light in 1 John with the revealed right-ordering of the world and God's actualization of that right-ordering through the Son in the power of the Spirit. Those who walk in the light trust that the world is the way God has revealed it to be and not how it normally seems. Sinning, for such a person, is reversion to life according to the appearance of the world and not the world as God has revealed it in the life, death, and resurrection of the Son.

But conversely, walking in the light is part and parcel of knowing light to be light in the first place. As Origen and Gregory attested above, it is by meditating on and imitating the Son that his brightness gradually empowers our eyes to know the beautiful, glorious light in all its fullness. The process is circular but not viciously so; it is what many twentieth-century philosophers and theologians would have deemed "dialectical." We must begin the quest for beauty somewhere; what the Christian tradition—and here, specifically, John's preaching—furnishes us with are some trustworthy practices and teachings to help us on the way. From this point forward John's sermon exposes the claims, practices, patterns, and life-forms that do and do not conform to the light. In this way John invites us into practices that will make the light easier to see and warns us against people absorbed in life patterns that will bedim it.

This aesthetic epistemology will strike modern persons as hopelessly retrograde, for one cannot honestly foray into critical inquiry as traditionally conceived without first presupposing that one's deeds, past, or proclivities ought to have no decisive bearing on one's ability to think. With respect to the question of God and God's revelation, the assumption is that dispassionate reflection is color-blind, tradition-blind, and community-blind and should achieve the same results for all practitioners. From an evaluative perspective, modern and—depending on how one uses the word—postmodern persons approach John saying, "We have union with him" while walking in darkness, "We have no sin" while possessing eyes wholly inured to light, and "We have never sinned" while not having the slightest sense of God's right-ordering in the first place. If we are to take John's sermon seriously, therefore, we must first be willing to entertain

34. Augustine, letter 92, paragraph 3.

the related notions that we are separated from him, saturated in sin's disordering, and unable even to detect the symptoms of our condition.

The Love of God and the Death of God

> "This is how God's love for us has been revealed in us: God sent his one and only Son into the world so that we could live because of him."

John has explained that the love of God is best expressed in God's action to send the Son as an atoning sacrifice so that "we could live because of him" (1 John 4:9). This wording is as close as John gets to the language of exchange; it is far less explicit than, for example, Jesus's words in Mark 10:45 about the Son being a "ransom for many." What is notable in John's formulation is that the cross is where the life of God enters into human life and community, with the love involved in the sending of the Son being manifested "in us," that is, in the life of the church.

The divine love initiates, sends, and ultimately results in death. In the labor of the cross, that death issues forth in new life, the birth from above; Jesus endures agony, absorbs death so that we can have the same sort of divine life he has. From a trinitarian perspective, then, the love of God is the ultimate act of self-abnegation, the self-emptying into death that life might abound to others. God's love is finally and ultimately expressed in God's death.

We cannot say these things lightly. If there is a fundamental clash between contemporary constructive theology and classical systematic theism, the reality of God tasting death in Christ is it. The problems are manifold. Classical theism, the so-called God of the philosophers, posits that God is impassible, that is, changeless. God is eternal, that is, above or beyond time and thus unfazed by its vagaries. God cannot be hurt or damaged. All of these attributes of God are threatened by what Moltmann called "the crucified God."

Classical Christianity sidesteps the problem by suggesting that the hypostatic union, the conjoining of the divine and human natures in Jesus Christ, goes only "one way," as it were. On this view, the divine nature of Christ can affect his human nature (and, in the Spirit, ours), but the divine nature remains unaffected—at least in any negative way—by entering the world. Varying theological anthropologies will have different ways of explaining the cross, but on all classical models Jesus's divine nature escapes crucifixion unscathed. The stakes for classical theism are monumental: if the divine nature dies in some real way, then Jesus is not God, because God cannot suffer change, and we are all still dead in our sins.

There are several problems with this view, however. First, it is difficult to square with the Gospel accounts of the cross. While the Gospels are not concerned with the finer points of trinitarianism, they are basically unflinching when it comes to Jesus's death. Matthew and Mark both include Jesus's cry of dereliction—not the sort of material that sounds as if any part of Jesus, divine or otherwise, is avoiding death. Next, the tradition of Jesus's "harrowing of hell," the belief that Jesus descends into hell in between his crucifixion and resurrection, is problematic from a trinitarian perspective: if hell is the place where God is not and Jesus goes there, then Jesus is, by definition, taking the divine nature where it cannot go; the divine nature undergoes true death.[35] While it is difficult to know what to make of Jesus's supposed descent into hell,[36] the fact of the view itself suggests that the tradition has taken seriously the idea that Jesus—divine and human nature both—tasted the full measure of death.[37] Third, from the perspective of trinitarianism, it is hard to know how we can strongly distinguish "what happens to the Son" from "what happens to the Father." Jürgen Moltmann writes, "When the crucified Jesus is called 'the image of the invisible God,' the meaning is that *this* is God, and God is like *this*."[38] Whatever Jesus does is the economic manifestation of who God is in Godself. So if Jesus weeps or heals or frees or gets angry at sin or forgives or loves or dies, then we are seeing God's being revealed in the world. And as Moltmann rightly points out—and John agrees!—the singular event of Jesus's revealing God-in-the-world is his being crucified so that he can function as an atoning sacrifice for us. Death-for-us reveals the inner being of the glorious, almighty Creator God.

Moltmann and other orthodox appropriators of so-called death-of-God theology beg Christian reflection to stay with the cross for a time, to reckon that God's truest act is to pour out Godself into death, absorb death, and overcome death in eternal life. The implications are stunning, forcing theology to notice that God's immanent experience of eternal joy consists of the self-giving of the Father to send

35. Christian art and iconography of the event are extensive. A paradigm example is *The Anastasis*, a mosaic housed at St. Mark's Basilica in Venice, dating from the thirteenth century. Christ is depicted as leading the march of pre-Christian saints out of hell. Available online at https://www.christianiconography.info/Edited%20in%202013/Italy/anastasisStMarks.html. The inscription at the top of the piece begins, "Mors et ero mortis" ("I will be the death of death").

36. The biblical basis of the tradition is 1 Peter 3:18–20, where Jesus "preaches to the spirits in prison." Exegetically, verse 18 indicates that Jesus has been "made alive in the Spirit" before the preaching, suggesting that whatever the author is after, it is something that has happened after the resurrection and not while Jesus's body was lying in the tomb.

37. Hans Urs von Balthasar was one of the first in twentieth-century theology to deeply engage these questions at the ontological level. See his *Mysterium Paschale*, trans. Aiden Nichols (San Francisco: Ignatius Press, 1990; first published in German in 1970), and especially the section "The Being Dead of the Son of God" (168–77), which wrestles with, among other things, the harrowing of hell and biblical texts related to it.

38. Moltmann, *Crucified God*, 295, italics in original.

the Son, the self-emptying of the Son to abandonment, and the all-powerful union of the Spirit that overcomes every distance and every act of gift and loss in life and glory. Yes, saying "God is dead" is not enough. At the very least, God is dead-to-life. But it is still not wrong to say that God is dead. This is an incomplete and incomprehensible truth, but still a truth. If God is love, then God is also dead-to-life, eternally experiencing what is manifested in God's economy as cross-to-resurrection.

Therefore, if we are to agree with John that God is love, if we are to take seriously the New Testament, if we are to take seriously the tradition, and if we are to think as responsible trinitarians—then we must reject classical theism's notion of a timeless, impassible God. Or if we are to retain something of it—as we see in Barth and some others—we must acknowledge the reality of Jesus's life and death as emblematic and revelatory of what and who God is in Godself, apart from creation.

The pastoral fallout from this treatment of love and of God's nature is that when we claim that Christ is Immanuel, "God with us," we can really mean it. We can claim that God shares and walks with us even in extremis, even in death itself. We can know that God has experienced—and redeemed, conquered, overcome!—all that we have experienced and yet did so without sin. God-in-Christ can truly promise us understanding, empathy, and in the end, victory in life.

Moreover, we have a criterion by which to measure love, a heuristic to identify it: self-abnegation to bring life. Especially in the contemporary West, where "love" has been co-opted by cheap, desultory graspings at happiness and endlessly unfulfilled quests for personal fulfillment, we can know deeply and truly that true eternal life, the life of the heavens and the future life of all who believe, is the life of self-emptying that grants, augments, amd deepens life in and for the other.[39]

God Listens: Divine Passibility in 1–3 John

> "Now this is the confidence we have before God: when we ask for something in keeping with his will, he listens to us."

Divine impassibility, the doctrine that God cannot change or be affected, is difficult to reconcile with most biblical texts; it is impossible to reconcile with 1–3 John.

39. Jüngel (*God as the Mystery of the World*, 329) captures a bit of our argument here: "But we have seen that God is love precisely in that he loves his Son in his identity with man, that is, with the scandalously murdered man Jesus. Love here is not directed toward a loveworthy Thou. That is emphasized in the Johannine scriptures with the statement that God loves *the world* in which sin and death dominate" (italics in original).

At every point in these texts, the Father, Son, and Spirit relate with, are engaged with, human beings. Jesus appears to us, and we meet him with confidence or shame. The Spirit anoints us, preparing us for priestly ministry. The Father listens to our prayers and is pleased to grant them when we are in union with him. The very idea that we can share union with God—this is a dynamic relation!

Under the influence of observations like these, some Protestants and evangelicals have tried to advance "open theism," an attempt to develop a systematic theology that accounts for the biblical narratives in which God changes course, responds to events, and hears and responds to prayers.[40] "Open theists," as they are sometimes called, begin with philosophy—specifically, the view that the future is undetermined, that it is open. With such an assumption, we may conclude, for example, that there is no fact right now about the winner of the World Cup in 2038. If we look more closely at the idea of the 2038 World Cup winner, we have to admit that on this view of time, there are presently no facts at all about the 2038 World Cup or its winner. It might be that there is a fact right now about the likelihood of "The United States wins the World Cup in 2038" becoming true. If there is, surely God knows what the odds are, and God knows how those odds fluctuate from moment to moment and from day to day. But God does not know who will win the World Cup in 2038 because there are no facts about the 2038 World Cup yet; its existence and winner are just possibilities. God knows all that can be known, but God does not know what cannot be known. God not knowing the winner of the World Cup in 2038 keeps the future open and protects human freedom.

Open theism is tempting but unnecessary. The Christian tradition has long described the intratriune divine relations as existing in perichoresis, that is, "mutual permeation" or "interprenetration." Clark Pinnock, a leading open theist, remarks, "God is a dynamic event of communion and communication, sometimes envisaged by the church fathers as a 'dance' of trinitarian life; he is not a featureless, isolated and motionless monad."[41] Pinnock is likely not correct that any of the fathers referred to trinitarian life as a "dance,"[42] but he is right to

40. See, for example, Clark H. Pinnock, *Most Moved Mover: A Theology of God's Openness* (Carlisle, UK: Paternoster, 2001), or Gregory A. Boyd, *God of the Possible: A Biblical Introduction to the Open View of God* (Grand Rapids: Baker, 2000).

41. Pinnock, *Most Moved Mover*, 124.

42. Pinnock is probably relying on Catherine Mowry Lacugna's philological treatment of perichoresis in *God for Us: The Trinity and Christian Life* (New York: HarperCollins, 1991), 271–72. Unfortunately, Lacugna never says that any of the fathers used "divine dance" to describe the Trinity; indeed, she notes that "the philological warrant for this is scant." Still, she thinks, "the metaphor is effective," and in this she is right. There has been a lively battle for the meaning of perichoresis, though it is not uncommon now to believe that the standard theological meaning for the Greek fathers was "permeation" or "interpenetration." Without taking sides over the notion of perichoresis indicating "a divine dance," we can at least note that the fathers

describe God's inner life as "a dynamic event of communion and communication" in the tradition. We need not commit to a strong social trinitarianism to see that, as Eberhard Jüngel puts it, God's being is in becoming,[43] God does not exist statically. Even if we were to agree that God's being is in a timeless, eternal moment, that moment is an eternal moment of dynamic interrelationality.

It would appear, then, that contemporary theology that is truly *trinitarian* theology will be strongly inclined to deny divine impassibility. God's own being is a being-in-act; there is nothing static about God. Now, we can imagine a thoroughgoing trinitarianism that admits of impassibility, but it is passing strange. How could the Godhead, eternally mutually interpenetrating, sharing in endless love, also be changeless? In some sense it would be possible for God to exist this way and only this way and for this to be deemed "changelessness," but on all normal definitions, movement and dynamism necessarily involve change.[44]

Election and Eschatology

Transformation: Soteriology and Purgatory in 1–3 John

> "When he appears, we will be like him, because we will see him as he really is."

established the inner being of the Godhead as "interpenetrative" or "mutually permeating" and that these are active, relational terms. However trendy it has become to describe the Trinity as a divine dance and however philologically unfair it might be, to suggest that the inner life of the Godhead is anything other than dynamic, mutual, and deeply unitive is misleading.

43. Eberhard Jüngel, *God's Being Is in Becoming: The Trinitarian Being of God in the Theology of Karl Barth*, trans. John Webster (Grand Rapids: Eerdmans, 2001). Jüngel explains Barth's understanding of God's inner being as follows: "The being of God was conceived of in the unity of the three modes of being differentiated from each other. God's being is thus *self-related* being. As being it is relationally structured. But this relational order of God's being does not structure God's being as an impersonal structure over against this being; rather, the modes of God's being which are differentiated from each other are related to each other in such a way that each mode of God's being *becomes* what it *is* only *with* the two other modes of being" (77, italics in original). Barth describes the divine Persons as "three modes of being." Jüngel means that what it is to be "God" is to be the self-relations of the three Persons becoming with each other. Barth is by no means describing God's triunity as a divine dance, but he is acknowledging its dynamism.

44. For a rousing counterargument, see David Bentley Hart, "No Shadow of Turning: On Divine Impassibility," in *The Hidden and the Manifest: Essays in Theology and Metaphysics* (Grand Rapids: Eerdmans, 2017), 45–69. Hart thinks it "unlikely that such approaches to Trinitarian theology can withstand very close philosophical scrutiny" (51). We are inclined to agree but wonder the extent to which this is much of a mark against them. Nevertheless, Hart's polemic is indispensable and worth careful consideration.

John's relentless emphasis on transformation—on crossing over from darkness to light, falsehood to truth, and so forth—reaches its zenith in the eschatological proclamation of 1 John 3:2 that seeing Jesus "as he really is" will make believers "like him." As per our comment on that section, John seems to believe that the act of perceptive apprehension of the fullness of Christ brings about a change to those of us who are already a part of God's family. There seems to be a continuum: some members of the family will already almost fully resemble Christ, while others, to varying degrees, will not. The promise of Jesus's eschatological arrival is that those who are already "pure" (1 John 3:3) will have very little in the way of transformation left to do. It would be like washing a white dress that just has one or two little streaks on it: a dab here or there, and it is good as new. But conjoined to the promise is the threat: what if a member of the family is something of a black sheep? What of the wayward rebel? What of the white dress that has been soiled again and again, smudged, stained, and torn?

We are passing here beyond the known into the speculative, but it is worth considering the possibility that 1 John 3:2–3 opens the door to a Protestant doctrine of purgatory.[45] John's sermon clearly expects but remains vague about the nature of Jesus's second coming. In the Johannine corpus, Revelation is not much better, given its apocalyptic cast. Certainly John expects a cataclysmic confrontation between good and evil, with glory and honor for the faithful, but it would be foolhardy to try to map a chronology of the prophetic future. The apocalyptic genre just does not admit of that kind of interpretation.

What we have, however, is a straightforward recognition by John that Jesus's coming is going to transform members of the family into the perfect image of God. Concomitant to this expectation is that on which it is predicated: believers will not be "like him" before he comes and they see him as he is. We may derive from this comment that some will face less of a transformation than others, and we may also infer that the transformative process will be less than pleasant, since John notes that all who hope for the arrival "purify themselves just as he is pure" (1 John 3:3).

To summarize: (1) in the eschatological reality believers will be conformed to Christ; (2) the process will be easy for some, hard for others, maybe for most.

45. Ironically, 1 John 3:2 has been pressed into service to make the opposite case. For those deeply influenced by eschatological timelines, Jesus's arrival might be a single event that admits of one moment of transformation. This understanding is problematic for several reasons. First, it would be to conflate Pauline accounts of the parousia with Johannine accounts. While I do not think Paul and John are incommensurable, they are also clearly different, and those differences and tensions should be acknowledged and accepted. Second, there is nothing in the text in 1 John that suggests immediacy. If anything, notions of immediate transformation have their origins in Middle Platonism or Gnosticism. John is neither a Platonist nor a gnostic. To see the objection noted, see Walls, *Purgatory*, 124n5.

Forgive the stating of the obvious, but this just is the inner core of the doctrine of purgatory. It is stripped of mythos and the accretions of doctrine supplied throughout the history of dogma in the Roman Catholic Church, but the kernel remains intact. In a provocative final chapter, Jerry L. Walls mines the work of C. S. Lewis—especially *The Great Divorce*, *Letters to Malcolm*, and *A Grief Observed*—for an ecumenical doctrine of purgatory.[46] Lewis's overall stance might best be summed up in his account of his prayers for his deceased wife. She was "not a perfected saint"; there were yet "tears to be dried" and "stains to be scoured."[47] Lewis could be honest enough about his wife (to say nothing of himself!) to recognize that her transformation was not done when she died; Joy has work yet to finish. For himself, Lewis rejected the idea of settling on a literal, dogmatic conceptualization of what purgatory will look like, but he accepted it in the abstract as a matter of course. How could people like us be at all comfortable in heaven? If we take God's righteousness, holiness, and glory at all seriously, then we are compelled to admit that John is right: Jesus's arrival will be, for all but the saintliest of us, bittersweet. The relief and release of final victory will necessarily be tempered by the realization of just how far short all of us fell.

The mechanics must, of course, remain occluded. But we may make some theological suggestions. First, eschatological time is not time as we know it. As outlined in the section "Time in 1–3 John," the sermon and the letters smear the moment of the passing of darkness to dawn across—so far—some two thousand years. We are perpetually living in the moment when the light begins its total victory over the dark. Moreover, we experience this moment in fits and starts, always moving forward and yet sometimes moving back. Already John has rejected the notion that time functions in anything like the straightforward manner of the tick, tick, ticking of the clock to which we have become accustomed. He would have been unperturbed by current scientific speculation about the physical and elastic nature of space-time. Thus, to suggest that transformation happens "in a moment" when we come face-to-face with Christ is to suggest nothing at all in terms of subjective experience. Christ brings eternity with him when he comes; there is no reason to think that our transition to the true, unvarnished eternal life will *feel* instantaneous. It might feel like, well, like another several thousand years—or like no time at all. Neither would be surprising.

Moreover, nothing here impinges on our status as redeemed, born-from-above, divine-DNA-carrying members of God's family. Our entrance into the family came through the labor of the cross; nothing can or could change who we are. So there is no need to suppose that whatever purgation we will face comes from some defi-

46. Walls, *Purgatory*, 153–74.

47. C. S. Lewis, *A Grief Observed* (San Francisco: HarperSanFrancisco, 2001), 42.

ciency in the gift of the cross or the work of Christ. Our status remains as it has been from the moment of entrance into the family. What must be "scoured away" are the vestiges of life-before-the-family, the antichristic scars and habits we bring with us into eternal life, the bits of us just unfit for heaven. Perhaps it is educational: a final reordering of our loves to be in conformity with the agapic love fully known in the giving of the Son by the Father. Perhaps it is psychological: a grinding down of the drive to self through which the sin of pride manifests in its myriad forms. However it happens, we should expect it to address the antitrinity of the world's antichristic bent that John highlights in 1 John 2:16: the things the body craves, the things the eyes long to see, and the overconfidence in what we have. From a contemporary neuroscientific perspective, we would expect to see the neural ruts and grooves produced by years of giving in to the body's cravings to be reset and redirected and reimprinted in the glorious flesh of the resurrection. Maybe that transformation happens in a moment, but I suspect it will feel like a very long time.

It is helpful here to consider the implications of relativistic theories of space-time. One of Einstein's revolutionary theories was that there was no absolute time, no universal now.[48] On Einstein's view, rather, time is related physically to space and is truly affected by physical forces like gravity and acceleration. One of the major vindications of Einstein's view has been the observation of "time dilation." Scientists have developed various experiments to see whether two atomic clocks at different elevations will keep the same time. They do not. Time goes faster for clocks at elevation, where the gravitational force of the earth is lower. Likewise, if one clock remains stationary and its twin accelerates to high speeds, the stationary clock "ticks slower"; that is, time passes more slowly sans acceleration. It is important to remember, however, that the personal perception of time does not change. So, an astronaut accompanying a faster clock in orbit around the earth does not experience time's passage any differently than the rocket flight crew on the surface of the earth, even though, relative to the rocket crew, the astronaut is aging faster.

These observations have led to science fiction stories about aging and interstellar travel.[49] In these stories, persons traveling at near light speed experience

48. For those concerned, we need not sign on to or reject any philosophical view of time. For a while, many supposed that general and special relativity made the "A-theory" of time, in which times have real, independent locations on an absolute timeline, untenable. But the science, as they say, is not settled. In his essay "Presentism and the Space-Time Manifold" (in *The Oxford Handbook of Philosophy of Time*, ed. Craig Callender [Clarendon: Oxford, 2011], 163–245), Dean Zimmerman offers a defense of A-theory time that specifically takes general and special relativity into account, ultimately suggesting that an outside observer like God could provide an objective and universal present, a "truthmaker," as it were.

49. Classic examples are Arthur C. Clarke, *Childhood's End* (New York: Del Rey, 1953), and Orson Scott Card, *Speaker for the Dead* (New York: Tor, 1986).

very little passage of time. When they arrive at destinations, however, years, even centuries, have passed during their transit. Of course this is science fiction, but given what we know about the physics of time, the possibility for something like this in our own universe does seem live. And if it is possible in the here and now, it is surely possible in a glorified, refreshed eschaton. What this all means is that we have some physical bases for believing in a subjective experience of purgatory that is quite long-lasting, even though it happens—from God's perspective (and perhaps the perspective of others)—instantaneously. Thus, any objection to an ecumenical approach to purgatory based on exegesis of 1 John 3:2 will fail to carry the day.

Eternal Security and Purgatory in 1–3 John

> "Those born from God don't practice sin, because they have God's DNA in them. They can't sin because they are God-born."

Our apocalyptic interpretation of 1 John 3:4–10 may suggest a version of the Free-Will Baptist "once saved, always saved" doctrine. The reasoning would go like this: in 1 John 3:4–10 "sin" is really "sin-to-death," a categorical rejection of the light of Christ and an ultimate, antichristic orientation. The New Testament authors write in these apocalyptic, totalizing ways in various places. So, for example, there is the "unforgivable sin," that is, "blasphemy against the Holy Spirit" in Mark 3:28–30 and its Synoptic siblings Matthew 12:30–32 and Luke 12:8–10.

Early Protestant theologians such as Calvin and Arminius associated the blasphemy of the Spirit with a determined, persistent refusal to acknowledge the witness of the Holy Spirit that Jesus is the Christ.[50] In Protestant, evangelical terms this step is tantamount to rejecting the gospel once it has been clearly articulated. Calvin is especially vociferous on this point, noting that the Matthean and Lukan versions of the pericope include forgiveness of those who speak against the Son of Man but not for those who reject the Spirit. Calvin reasons that speaking against the Son of Man would be rejecting Christ out of ignorance: a person without knowledge of who Jesus is might think it ridiculous that he was said to

50. So, Calvin, *Institutes*, 3.3.22, and Jacob Arminius, "A Letter on the Sin against the Holy Spirit." John Wesley demurs on exegetical grounds, suggesting that the blasphemy of the Holy Spirit is attributing to the devil the works of Christ (Wesley, "A Call to Backsliders [Sermon 86]," 9) and draws no universal example from it. Wesley's concern appears to be pastoral, to prevent despairing self-examination.

be raised from the dead. Calvin even suggests that Paul self-identifies as one of these in 1 Timothy 1:13. But this is not the case when the Spirit—who guides us into all truth—is involved. Here, Calvin thinks, is a situation in which the Holy Spirit has clarified the gospel and witnessed to the truth of Christ, and still the unbeliever persists in rejecting Christ and rebelling against God.

Notice that this position is almost identical to what we have suggested John's "rebellion" and "sin" are in 1 John 3:4–10—persistent rejection of the light and preference for the dark. Moreover, notice how closely the pneumatology tracks: John wants his people to be good at discerning the spirits, at being able to recognize the Spirit of Truth and deny the Spirit of Error (e.g., 1 John 4:1–6), just as Calvin reads Jesus in Matthew and Luke focusing on rejecting the Spirit more than he does on those who reject him.

Arminius agrees with Calvin on what the blasphemy of the Holy Spirit is, but he reads Hebrews 6:4–6 as a warning that believers too can commit the unforgivable sin. The key to his exegesis is the textual link in 6:4 that mentions those who have "shared in the Holy Spirit." Arminius supposes that some Christians who have received the Holy Spirit's witness concerning Christ will go back on their belief and consign themselves to dogged resistance, insisting on excommunicating themselves from the church.

If our exegesis is correct, however, John disagrees. 1 John 3:9 straightforwardly claims that the God-born cannot sin-to-death. As members of the family, they are as incapable of denying the Spirit as they are of changing their DNA. You are either God-born or you are not. But this black-and-white approach plainly contradicts our experience—and very likely the experiences that caused Arminius to read Hebrews 6 as he did—because all believers know somebody who has "fallen away," or in Wesley's lingo, become a "backslider." The reasons and individual circumstances vary from case to case, but there are some very committed atheists and agnostics, such as Friedrich Nietzsche and Bart Ehrman, who grew up as devout Christian believers and seminarians. Are they really still members of the family? How can John be right that Christians cannot sin-to-death?

There appear to be a few possibilities. First, they may have been convincing frauds, never truly members of the family at all. John seems to castigate groups like this in 1 John 2:19, where those who left were never truly family to begin with. It is interesting to note that in the following verse, John highlights the fact that those who hear and agree with him have an "anointing from the Holy Spirit," indicating that those who left never really did. Similarly, John's opponent Diotrephes in 3 John 9–10 sounds like someone who started out looking like family but ultimately showed his true colors as a self-seeker. And it is very likely that convincing frauds, hungry wolves, and antichristic invaders are on the prowl, trying to disrupt those who are in the light. But such people do not seem to be the kind of person Arminius is worried about. Rather, they are ones who walked in the light for years and years—obviously committed, serious believers who trusted the Spirit's testimony and received spiritual gifts. What about these sorts? Are we really to believe that they were hoodwinking the church all along? The very idea strains credulity.

A second possibility. If John is right and the God-born cannot rebel, with rebellion here being the ultimate rejection of the Spirit's testimony about Christ, then perhaps the only internally consistent answer to Arminius is that our continued membership in the divine family is *not something over which we have any control*. On this view, one's DNA is determined by God and not by us; once we have crossed over into the light, it is the Light that holds us and not the other way around. In this case, ones who once believed, who now are trying as hard as they can to rebel, are just unsuccessful; the true light will not let them go. Whatever Nietzsche thinks he is doing, and no matter how loudly he proclaims it, rebellion is no more his choice than the blood running through his veins. It is up to God and God alone. But this position borders on paradox: how could one of the God-born—who bears the family resemblance to the Father and Son—end life a fanatic syphilitic, collapsing to the ground clutching the neck of a flogged horse before degenerating into a mindless, pneumonia-ridden shell of a man?[51]

Such reasoning veers unnervingly close to historically blackballed regions of Protestant theology. "Once God-born, always God-born" could quite easily be transformed into the antinomian Puritanism of John Cotton and Anne Hutchinson,[52] the "cheap grace" decried by Dietrich Bonhoeffer,[53] or more recently, the "free grace" espoused by independent evangelical baptists such as Charles Ry-

51. Nietzsche's tragic life and ignominious end are brought to life in Sue Prideaux's popular biography *I Am Dynamite!* (New York: Tim Duggan, 2018).

52. See David D. Hall, ed., *The Antinomian Controversy: 1636–1638: A Documentary History*, 2nd ed. (Durham, NC: Duke University Press, 1990), for the definitive collection of primary documents. "Antinomianism" is a radical view in which Christians are bound by no ethical laws and instead should be governed by promptings of the Spirit. Anne Hutchinson fully subscribed to this view and relied on a sort of Spirit-led mysticism. Søren Kierkegaard's famous "teleological suspension of the ethical" (*Fear and Trembling*, trans. Alistair Hannay [London: Penguin, 1985], 83–95) supposes that God's command to Abraham to sacrifice his son is a biblical example of this. On most rational accounts of ethics, filicide is unconscionable, but when God's goal ("telos") demands it, normal rules do not apply. Taken to its extreme, the Christian could be seen to be existing in this state permanently.

53. The first chapter of Bonhoeffer's *The Cost of Discipleship* (trans. R. H. Fuller [London: SCM Press, 1959]) begins, "Cheap grace is the deadly enemy of our Church." Bonhoeffer's target is a telling of Christianity that excludes responsibility, sin, sacrifice, and the way of the cross in favor of a limp, anemic focus on God's gracious love and forgiveness. It is an intellectual assent to the overabundance of God's grace that the Christian need not—sometimes should not—appear any different from the world.

rie and Zane Hodges and opposed by John MacArthur and John Piper.[54] The concern is as follows: if a Christian can remain God-born despite any and all outward actions to the contrary, then the life of heaven is cheap and easy to obtain. It is therefore best to live as one pleases and depend on "fire insurance" to enter eternal life. Making salvation completely independent of action appears to completely undermine the goal of gospel transformation.

The possibilities warrant further consideration. First, any such view would be wholly rejected by John. Remember, John thinks of eternal life as the union we experience with the Father and Son here and now. Of course it extends into the eschaton at Jesus's arrival, but it is first and foremost a present reality. And those God-born determined to be black sheep are no more enjoying divine union than a runaway prodigal son is enjoying the comforts of his father's house. One suspects that part of the problem is a sense of injustice, as if living in the thrall of the world, ruled as it is by wayward spirits, is better than living in divine union. If it is, then yes, it is patently unfair for God to allow black sheep to remain family. But if living under the world's domination, enslaved to sin, is a kind of living hell, then perhaps some of God's justice is being preserved in accordance with God's divine mercy. Moreover, if we are willing to entertain the notion of purgatory—to say nothing of the rewards promised to faithful servants—then perhaps those God-born content to live as if the darkness is not fading have some unpleasant and eternally shaming, painful shocks waiting for them at the arrival. Second, it seems to me that such concerns are brought about by wrongly reducing the scope of "salvation" to a question about who goes to heaven and who goes to hell. But even a cursory study of the New Testament shows that biblical soteriology is concerned with much more than who is going up and who is going down. There is rescue from sin now, from the power of sin-to-death, from the clutches of the world, from demonic forces, from physical disease, shame, fear, and so forth. Total soteriology—the sort that John preaches—is about bringing as much of the triune, divine life of the Godhead into union with human beings and human communities as possible. In some ways, John sees the current world order to be a sort of demonic hellscape and the coming of the unoriginated Son as an invasion from heaven. Flitting about in academic speculation about who must do or believe what to "get in" just misses the point.

54. Probably the two seminal texts in the controversy are John MacArthur's *The Gospel according to Jesus*, rev. ed. (Grand Rapids: Zondervan, 1988) and Zane Hodges's *Absolutely Free! A Reply to Lordship Salvation* (Grand Rapids: Zondervan, 1989). MacArthur targets "easy believism" and suggests that true Christianity involves submission to Jesus's lordship. His detractors call his view "lordship salvation" and paint it as a kind of modern Pelagianism in which salvation from hell depends on works. For his part, MacArthur pushes back, suggesting instead that salvation is by grace, but that true Christians will be known by their fruits.

It is no coincidence that these debates are peculiar to Protestant sects and often pit Reformed and Wesleyan traditions at odds with derivations of Baptist/Anabaptist thought. One suspects that Roman Catholic theology does not need to worry over these concerns because Catholicism has a highly developed eschatology that has reckoned both with Scripture and experience. If the afterlife pictured by Dante is closer to the truth than the bodiless bliss imagined by populist Protestant Christendom, then one need not worry that some denizens of heaven do not really deserve to be there and that others, who suffered on earth, are getting a bad deal. Instead, those who reject union now can expect painful purgation and a certain heavenly lowliness. Those who remain in union now can expect joyful consummation, vindication, and eternal glory.

From the perspective of biblical theology, 1 John 3:4–10's soteriology causes a tension with the perspective in Hebrews 6:4–6, one that may be unresolvable this side of the eschaton. Such a tension resting within the New Testament canon suggests a simple pastoral response in the case of backsliders: we do not know. We know that God is gracious and just, and that conviction is going to have to be enough. We know that backsliders were members of the family at one time and that they drifted away and that it is up to God to rule on their relationship with the rest of us. That said, if Protestant theology develops a robust biblical account of purgatory, then perhaps the tension can be laid to rest and, furthermore, a major step can be taken toward a conciliatory ecumenism between the Protestant and Roman Catholic churches.

Eternity and Election: The Economy of Election in 1–3 John

> "The Elder, to a chosen lady and her children"

At the beginning of 2 John, the elder refers to the patroness as "chosen" or "elect." To be chosen or elect is more than just an honorific and, given the Reformed tradition's emphasis on divine election, theologically fraught. John uses the word only here in 2 John, though it does appear also in Revelation 17:14. The question that has plagued Protestant theology is not one that John answers, however. With respect to the patroness, does John's calling her "chosen" imply that the Godhead, from eternity, elected her to believe in Jesus and lead a church and be saved from hell? Fortunately or unfortunately—depending on one's perspective—John is silent here, primarily because his language never involves an atemporal eternal perspective. He is, rather, narrating the lived experience of the church at the dawning of the age to come. Thus, "chosen" is more like the battlefield commission of a sergeant as an officer because a new lieutenant is needed now and this man has what it takes. As the darkness passes and the light expands, God chooses different individuals to fulfill different roles. The patroness has the resources and wisdom to house the church, so God elects her to that role. This is not to say that a Reformed reading is wrong, only that it is not demanded by John's language. It is altogether possible that in the eternal election of the church in Christ, the Godhead foreknew and selected this woman to this church. But if so, it is demanded by philosophy, not the text.

On this topic, John is fully in keeping with God's pattern of electing certain leaders and individuals all throughout Israel's history. The Septuagint typically uses ἐκλεκτός (*eklektos*, "chosen," "elect") to describe "choice" or "elite" warriors or persons (e.g., Judg 20:15; 1 Sam 24:2). In the wisdom and prophetic literature, however, it often denotes those with whom God has covenanted. So Psalm 88:4 (89:3 Vul.) uses the plural to refer to all of Israel, God's "chosen ones" whom God "took an oath to David" to keep. Here God chooses a people rather than this or that person. The same logic undergirds the suffering servant—that is, Israel—in Isaiah 42:1, ὁ ἐκλεκτός μου (*ho eklektos mou*, "my chosen one"). In both of these cases God selects a community of people, Israel, to accomplish God's purposes; in so doing, God enters into a reciprocal relationship in which God commits to faithfully love and preserve and bless the community.

Furthermore, this selection and covenanting is an expression of God's eternal being. As Karl Barth recognized, God eternally elects Jesus Christ to save the world.[55] This conclusion is profoundly mysterious but worth reflection. God's eternal self-determination is, in part, Son-as-human-redeemer-of-humanity. We can imagine a god eternally decreeing some other being and act—an eternal oneness, a Leibnizian monad-god perhaps—but that is not the content of God's eternal being-in-act. Rather, in electing triunity and Son-as-savior, God's first (if we can put it that way) being-in-act logically results in the conjuration of a universe in which there is a humanity whose purpose and perfect expression are summed up in a member of the Godhead. By saying that God and the universe will be this way and not some other, the triune God covenants with all of humanity in and through the eternal election of its savior, who himself shares in the divine life. Electing Christ therefore sets the shape of all elections in God's economy: there will be a redemptive purpose fulfilled by this community or

55. Barth, *CD* II/2. Barth's philosophical-theological concern is not ours. Barth is trying to preserve a biblical notion of election while departing from some of the more controversial versions of Calvinist double predestination. We are more concerned with a proper reckoning of God's economic election of, here, the patroness, as an economic expression of the eternal divine being-in-act by which we may better know God, election, and ethics.

that person. The very dynamic of salvation is built into the world from beyond it. One of the key insights that this reworking of classical Calvinist views of election brings is that election is about participating in someone else's salvation, not oneself being saved.

The patroness thus joins a long line of persons and communities that have been elected by God to participate in the salvation of other people. God chooses Moses not for Moses's sake but for Israel's (and therefore God's own) sake. God chooses John not for John's sake but for the patroness's sake, and the patroness not for her sake but for the sake of "her children," that is, the church she leads and supports. In all of this, God's electing leads to covenanting, which leads to the righteous glorification of the electing and covenanting God. As with every divine act, the act itself contributes to the perfection of God's being.

We may say, then, that every Christian is elected and therefore called. Since our election is not "for us," it entails our discerning whom we have been called to serve and how. Election theologically demands vocation. Once a believing woman finds herself in the church, she has concomitantly found herself called to participate in some way in God's salvation of others. There simply cannot be a Christian without a calling. If there were, it would mean that someone had been elected by God in an election that is unchristic or, following John's language, antichristic. And as we have seen throughout John's preaching above, God does not do anything that is not in perfect keeping with the nature and character of the Son, precisely because the Son is the human economic disclosure of the nature and character of God. Just as the Father is for the Son and the Son is for the Father and God is for us in the Spirit, so are we for whomever we have been called to bless. The patroness's election entailed her calling to serve and preserve a community of believers in Asia Minor; ours might be markedly different or similar, according to God's purposes.

In contemporary ecclesiology, no one would object to a woman supporting a church financially or housing it in her home or purchasing a building in which to gather. The pressing question in the twenty-first-century church is the extent to which women can or ought to participate in pastoral ministry. 2 John helps point the way in this regard because it assumes the patroness's spiritual headship over the community. Critically, verse 5 begins with an entreaty to the patroness alone, indicating that it is her responsibility to see that the "command from the beginning," that the people of all the churches "love each other," gets communicated and executed. Yes, the command is communal, but John begs the patroness—not the plural we or you—to see it done.[56]

56. See "Gender and Leadership" on pp. 196–98 for more reflection here.

Being Rewarded: Eschatology and Divine and Human Economics in 1–3 John

> "Check yourselves so that you don't lose what we've worked for but instead receive your full reward."

While it would be too much to say that John expects a tiered heaven à la Dante, he does seem to think that there are differing levels of reward to be had in the heavenly kingdom. This expectation makes for a strange fit with his relentless emphasis on trinitarianism. That is, how could one person's experience of the divine eternal life be qualitatively different from someone else's? It would seem that we either are or are not "like him," and if a Christian is "like him," how could he or she have a reward that is fuller or less full than someone else who is "like him"? It is a circle that needs squaring, however, because the Johannine corpus consistently suggests a divine economy that rewards believers eternally for faithfulness in this life. Jesus uses μισθός (*misthos*, "reward," "payment," "wages") in John 4:36 to describe being "paid" in the eternal age for accomplishing God's work here and now. The term appears twice in Revelation (11:18; 22:12), in both cases indicating varying degrees of reward. In 11:18 rewards are distributed to all who fear God's name, both "small and great." In 22:12 the usage is more specific, promising payment to everyone "according to their work." In Revelation 2–3 specific rewards are promised to churches and Christians who overcome very specific spiritual battles. We might be forgiven for imagining a smorgasbord of various commendations and prizes or an array of ribbons and medals merited by heroic conduct in battle; the language, while metaphoric, is not far off.

Several considerations may help point the way forward. First, the election of Jesus Christ as a *human being* has consequences for the Godhead and for us, namely, that whatever else the eschaton is, it is a physical place with human beings, with whom the Father, via the Son through the Spirit, interacts. It is not just like earth—the Fourth Gospel paints a portrait of the glorified Christ that is not exactly "normal humanity"—but it also is not some wholly unknowable dimension, with no contact points to the physicality with which we are familiar. Life in the kingdom, then, is recognizably life, even if it is not "life as we know it."[57] N. T. Wright has argued that something similar lurks in Pauline eschatology,

57. My sense is that this summary helps explains John's vision of the "new heavens and the new earth" at the end of Revelation. There is an odd confluence of the normal and the fantastic; there is a city, but it is outlandishly adorned. There is a tree, but its fruit is overabundant and

proffering an empty chalice as a metaphor for the current order.[58] This chalice is the natural world waiting to be filled with the wine of God's glory. Wright takes this image to reflect the theological substance of Romans 8 and 1 Corinthians 15 (he mentions Rev 21–22 as well but unfortunately does not elaborate). The eschatological vision of John and Paul seems to be not the subsuming of a glorified created order into the Godhead but rather an emptying out of divine glory in its absolute fullness into creation. Claiming Jesus as firstborn from the dead is Paul's shorthand for what our eschatological future entails. All things will experience the en-Spiriting of the risen Lord. If this is indeed the case—and we must admit that it nicely ameliorates Johannine preoccupation with divine union and the notion of an eschaton that is still physical and human—then we might be able to make sense of eschatological rewards.

To begin with, John's language forces us to confront an uncomfortable truth for those acclimated to global capitalism: rewards are not earned or distributed individually. John cautions the patroness and her children not against losing what *they* have worked for but instead against losing what *we* have worked for. The pronouns are ambiguous. John could be referring to himself and other members of his congregation, or he could be referring to himself and the patroness and her congregation. It is even possible that he is referring to the entire Christian family. Since the grammar does not push in any one direction, we cannot say for sure, but however we read it, John's work is bound up with the patroness's reward. That is, the divine economy does not distribute "wages" in the ordinary sense. John's thinking in this regard echoes the odd economy of Jesus's parable of the laborers in Matthew 20:1–16. There, all receive the same wage, regardless of how long they work in the master's vineyard. Jesus's parable cautions his righteous Jewish followers not to expect that sinners and gentiles will somehow be second-class citizens in the kingdom of God. Here, John suggests that our participation in God's will is not individualistic; it is bound up with the faithfulness of others. At the very least, the lives and commitments of those within our sphere of influence affect our rewards.

Next, the divine economy differs from market economies in its definition of success. "Not being deceived" appears to be what will qualify the patroness and her church for reward. It implies that John's "work" with the patroness's church was establishing its foundation on the doctrine that Jesus came as true humanity. All the church must do is hold fast to this starting point and "not go beyond it."

---

variegated and capable of doing things no fruit has done since the forbidden fruit in Eden. The vision asks us to imagine a physical world but one glorified beyond anything we have known.

58. N. T. Wright, *History and Eschatology: Jesus and the Promise of Eschatology* (Waco, TX: Baylor University Press, 2019), see especially chapter 8.

Doctrinal stasis is surely a strange metric by which to gauge success, but that is what John commends. Global markets thrive on dynamism and growth; John seems to think that the kingdom is better served by changelessness and the shrinkage that accompanies the unwillingness to innovate. This attitude further implies John's certainty about God's ultimate victory, the conviction that even when the church endures loss, the end is still not in doubt. The goal is not to heap up converts as much as it is to nourish the spiritual health and maintain the family relations holding among those who already believe.

Note that John would rather the church be small than entertain new guests who might corrupt it. He goes so far as to recommend acting inhospitably(!) to those bearing winds of unsavory doctrine. The notion that less is more is a bizarre one in the twenty-first-century West, where inclusion is the first priority and where big tents are preferred to small. But the present world order has witnessed firsthand corporatist capitalism lift millions from poverty, innovating, creating, and erasing differences across cultures. It is, the neoliberal fetishists might argue, exceedingly difficult to argue with success. But our "success" has been accompanied by the collapse of community traditions, by environmental devastation, and by increasingly atomistic individuals coaxed into lives of radical alienation, so we might surmise that something is amiss. John's eschatologically informed insight would probably be that the Western economy is tragically malformed, that the economy of heavenly rewards has divine and human union as its goal and motivates accordingly. Western economies offer a different game with a different prize. What John can or should say to the diversity of human communities in our pluralistic age is hard to say, but the word for Christ's church is obvious: "success" is not measured in congregational sizes or expanding budgets or increased cultural influence; it is measured in faithfulness. And not the faithfulness of this or that person or even this or that church but the faithfulness of the church as such. If we are a divine family, we rise and fall together. We must be jealous for classical orthodoxy and unashamed of it.

Still, the question of what, exactly, heavenly rewards are remains vague. Revelation 2–3 is more specific but no less enigmatic, offering, variously, "authority over the nations," "crowns," "the morning star," "a new name," "white robes," and more. If these promises have something in common, it is glorification, that is, God's honor and light. And this common thread returns us to our first insight. Since the age to come is best understood as a physical, human world fully infused with God's glory by the Spirit through the redemption and life of the Son, it might be best to understand rewards as varying measures of the fullness of glory with which we shine, as it were. Reverting to Wright's chalice metaphor, Christian communities are themselves like chalices waiting to be filled with the splendor of the divine life. When the eschaton arrives with the Lord, perhaps the chalices are filled to varying degrees, and moreover, perhaps we share in multiple chalices according to the multiplicity of relations and communities to which we have been called.

We do not wish to speculate too far, but it might be that the Gospel portraits of the risen Christ provide a road map here. Clearly, the risen Christ does not belong to the current order. He appears and vanishes, bears mortal wounds that do not kill, is sometimes unrecognizable; the resurrected Jesus does not "fit" here because our world is not sufficiently glorified. Presumably, Jesus fits perfectly in the age to come because it is the full and unadulterated economic manifestation of the intratriune divine life. It is perfectly willed by the Father, created through the Son, and enlivened in the Spirit in ways that our present universe can only shadow obliquely. The eschatological kingdom, then, is the physical, human world that is appropriate to the lordship of the glorified Christ. And just as the resurrected Lord did not perfectly fit, was strangely maladapted to this unglorified nature, perhaps our eternal fit in the eschaton will be determined by the extent to which we participate in our divinely appointed vocations now. Perhaps in the next age the martyrs will shine like the sun, while privileged Christian academics will perform the role of the pale moon by comparison. Glorious, yes, but still bedimmed. And perhaps the martyrs will travel within the divine presence as naturally as we now stroll through the park, while comfortable, anodyne, middle-class Christians will need to work to arrive there in the same way that taking in the view from the top of Fuji now entails a cost.

Scripture

Apostolic Authority and Truth

"so that you might have union with us"

The second-century apologist and theologian Irenaeus wrote a good deal about the dynamic of trust, authority, and the truth. In his own context, Irenaeus was engaged in a "battle for the Bible," as it were. Gnostic opponents were, in Irenaeus's view, infamous for patching together this or that scrap of Scripture without consideration of "proper order or sequence." The problem was acute for those who did not know what to believe or whom to trust: how could they know whether the Scriptures were being manipulated or faithfully transmitted? Irenaeus likened the problem to a mosaic of a king whose pieces had been reworked into the image of a dog or a fox. Which version of the mosaic—king or fox—was right?

Irenaeus answers the question much as John does, by appealing to the union holding between Christ and the would-be authority. This union has many facets. For example, it must feature the cross of Christ as a hermeneutical key: "But when [the Bible] is read by the Christians, it is a treasure, hid indeed in a field, *but brought to light by the cross of Christ and explained*, both enriching the understanding of people, and showing forth the wisdom of God."[59] To understand the truth about the Bible—and for John, the universe—one must reckon it according to the nature and character of the one who was "from the beginning." His perfection, his beauty, is reflected across the cosmos and reaches its zenith in his willing self-offering as an atonement sacrifice for the whole world (1 John 2:1–2). True light will operate according to that measure. Anyone with authority will be forthright about the nature and character of a Christ who came as a human being (1 John 4:2) to set the whole world to rights.

Another facet of the union holding between Christ and the would-be authority is what the church has long called "apostolic succession." Irenaeus goes into detail showing his connection to real apostles (John possibly among them!) who really knew Jesus. Their testimony is sure because it was received firsthand and in agreement. Irenaeus points out that the various gnostic sects have confused and contradictory points of view about God and the universe. Not so with the true church. Every church founded on the apostles' doctrine tells the same basic story about the same King. There are conflicts and differences to be sure, but the life, death, and resurrection of Christ is constant. Their union with each other demonstrates the union they have with the divine itself. Wherever we see such unity, we should be compelled; wherever we see division and strife, we should be suspicious. This distinction, of course, is precisely the same thing John claims. It is not happenstance that he begins 1 John with the plural "We." *We* have seen and touched and heard and now announce to *you*. Because John stands in the apostolic community, sharing union with God and others, his authority is derived from the Father.

A final facet: the conduct and character of the would-be authority. Irenaeus stakes a great deal on the character of any supposed church leader. "Sound speech and blameless conduct" are the marks of those who maintain true union with the apostles and with Christ.[60] It is worth noting that nothing John has said will carry any authority whatsoever if it is not evident that this leader loves, walks in the light, and so forth. John's claim at the beginning of the sermon to share union with the Father and the Son must be evident in this leader's sharing of their love and light. If it is not, then this would-be leader breaks union with

59. Irenaeus, *Against Heresies* 4.26.1.

60. Irenaeus, *Against Heresies* 4.26.4.

the apostles and exposes himself as the very of fraud against which he warns his hearers. Determining what is true and who is trustworthy appears to be based on the confluence of these evidences.

Theological Epistemology: Community and Discernment

"Don't trust every spirit. Instead, evaluate the spirits."

George Lindbeck's classic text *The Nature of Doctrine* appropriates some of the hermeneutical insights of Ludwig Wittgenstein to suggest that the truth claims of a community, their "doctrines," function in part as a language game.[61] When a person begins to play chess, the rules and their match-time consequences are obscure. Before encountering chess, the sentence "knight takes pawn" is probably incomprehensible. By playing the game and studying it, chess players gradually acclimate to the rules and become well-versed in the "world of chess," as it were. Lindbeck applies this insight to Christian communities, suggesting that Christians have a peculiar "Christian world," a way of making sense of the universe that is incomprehensible to those outside of the faith. Embracing suffering, for example, might strike a non-Christian as bizarre, even unhealthy.

1 John assumes something similar, though the text also assumes that the "Christian world" or "Christian language game" is the result of spiritual realities, namely, the influence of the Spirit of Truth and the Spirit of Deception (1 John 4:1–6). People animated by the Spirit of Truth and those animated by the Spirit of Deception literally talk past each other and live in, for all intents and purposes, different worlds. Thus the very nature of 1 John as an evangelistic sermon is paradoxical. If John is right and those in thrall to the Spirit of Deception literally cannot understand anyone but themselves, then the sort of evangelism Jesus espouses in Matthew 28 ought to be impossible; there is no point preaching John's sermon to anyone but the choir.

John is, of course, right to an extent. For many who have been wholly subsumed by the Spirit of Deception, the incarnation and life of the Son just is and always will be absurd at best and incomprehensible at worst. Moreover, the lives Christians live will be, from the perspective of those rooted in the world, pitiable and in many cases dangerous to one's mental and emotional health. But John's

61. George A. Lindbeck, *The Nature of Doctrine*, 25th ann. ed. (Louisville: Westminster John Knox, 2009).

preaching also veers somewhat into the apocalyptic: in the eschaton, perhaps, the sheep and goats will be clearly demarcated and suffer no transfers from one group to the other. In the present day, however, conversion very clearly happens. John's preaching would not constantly be calling for self-identification and response if this possibility did not exist.

Lindbeck's theology is helpful here. Some who hear John's preaching, though they are rooted in the world, may be enticed by the Spirit of Truth to play a new game, as it were. The process—what Christians once called "conversion"—is lifelong, because the Christian telling of the universe and life lived in light of it is intricate, exhaustive, and consequential. What, then, are we to make of 1 John's rhetoric?

Perhaps 1 John provides a theology of preaching: preaching apocalyptically demands a constant string of small (and sometimes large) conversions. A Johannine sermon, to put it crudely, is one that invites hearers to identify themselves within the Christian telling of whatever subject the sermon happens to be addressing, and it demands a response predicated on that identification. In effect, Johannine preaching follows a fourfold format:

1. This is Christ.
2. Are you in Christ?
3. Those in Christ live this way.
4. Are you living this way?

In the rhetoric "this way" refers to the doctrinal matter at hand. It could range anywhere from the humanity of the eternal Son (as it does in 1 John) to God's relationship to money. The sermon establishes the orthodoxy of the subject in point 1 and then invites hearers to affirm it in point 2. The third point establishes the relationship between doctrine and life, assuming, it should be noted, that the Christian telling of the universe always entails an ethic; and the final point invites hearers to self-examination, confession, repentance, and renewal.

Returning to the Wittgensteinian analogy, every sermon is like a game of chess. By participating regularly, hearers become more and more knowledgeable, appreciative, and competent in Christian life and doctrine. From the perspective of ecclesiology, 1 John might suggest that sermons and homilies are an ecclesial practice aimed at conversion—something many Baptists and Wesleyans would no doubt be happy to hear—and that they function in the community as a way of introducing and reintroducing the Christian language game to those who still have origins in the world and who are still under the sway of the Spirit of Deception.

What a Canon! The Theological Import of 2–3 John

"to my dear friend Gaius, whom I love in the Spirit"

If a committee of interested theologians were placed behind John Rawls's veil of ignorance[62] and asked to provide an outline for the best possible religious text, it is hard to imagine that they would settle on anything like the Bible. The Bible is almost impossibly odd. Iron Age law codes, poetry, collected sayings, stories, retellings of those stories, visions, literal Jeremiads, and of all things, the mail of early groups of Jesus followers. We have shown that 1 John is best understood as a sermon, but 2 and 3 John are just letters—letters about some internecine struggles that seem to have little to do with anything or anybody but those concerned, now all long dead. Their inclusion in the Christian canon raises two questions: (1) How did anyone decide that they were the Word of God? and (2) What does it mean to live under their authority as Scripture?

The earliest unambiguous citation of 2 or 3 John as Scripture[63] is found in Irenaeus's *Against Heresies* 1.16.3, where he writes, "John, disciple of the Lord, pronounced judgment against them, that we shouldn't be willing to greet them, since, he says, 'anyone who greets them partners in their evil work.'" Note a few things. First, Irenaeus believes he is quoting John, who knew and followed Jesus. He trusts in John's apostolic authority to make pronouncements that have divine imprimatur. Second, he makes no distinction between the gnostic heretics he is refuting in the later part of the second century and whomever John is warning

62. Originally published in 1971 and revised in 1999, Rawls's *A Theory of Justice* (Cambridge: Harvard University Press) lays out a case for establishing liberal orders. The "veil of ignorance" is a thought experiment in which we are asked to imagine what kind of society we would want to live in if we did not know who we are or what our role in the society would be. Rawls thought that the right response would be a society ordered to maximally benefit those at the bottom. That way, no matter who you ended up being, you would have it at least pretty good. This, in turn, implies that democracy, guided capitalism, the impartial rule of law, and generous social welfare initiatives are features of the best kind of society. It probably needs not be said, but the idea has been battered by a number of major objections, not the least of which is that the veil of ignorance is itself impossible—as embodied humans we are not really capable of a truly disembodied, God's-eye view and Rawls's preferred social vision says as much about Rawls as anything else.

63. Polycarp (ca. 130 CE) might be referencing 2 John 7 in his *Epistle to the Philippians* 7:1. The problem is that 2 John 7 and 1 John 4:3 are very similar, and Polycarp's diction mirrors neither exactly. It is reasonable to conclude that Polycarp is aware of 2 John, but the evidence is not enough to claim an unambiguous quotation. See John Painter, *1, 2, and 3 John* (Collegeville, MN: Liturgical Press, 2002), 41, for a more extensive consideration.

the patroness about two or three generations earlier. Despite the likelihood that Irenaeus's interlocutors have no ideological connection to John's opponents, Irenaeus still assumes that John is speaking directly to his context.

This early work probably helps answer the first question. Irenaeus believes John wrote 2 John (and maybe 3 John). John has apostolic authority. The same Spirit that animated John now animates Irenaeus, and so John's words continue to carry spiritual immediacy. In the post-Enlightenment—and therefore post-critical—West, many do not share Irenaeus's assumptions. Many posit various identities for "the elder" that are not John. Many invent stories about the Ephesian churches of which John and the elder and the patroness and Gaius were a part and posit divisions and theological strife for which we have no noncanonical evidence. Does it matter? If "the elder" is not John the apostle and did not actually know Jesus, is Irenaeus's use of the letter spurious? We will circle back to these concerns in a moment.

The second question, the question of how 2 and 3 John can function as Scripture today, is more fraught. Irenaeus may be right or wrong that John the apostle wrote 2 John (and possibly 3 John), and ancient history being what it is, there is really no way to know. But since we know that Irenaeus believes John wrote 2 John, it tells us something about the text of 2 John, namely, that Irenaeus reads it as in keeping with *regula fidei*, the "rule of faith." Robert Jenson sums up this concept as follows: "We are to trust the presence of truth in the community because it is confirmed in the Gospels and apostolic letters; and we are to trust these documents because they come from those whose witness forms the community. Canon confirms creed, and creed confirms canon."[64] The "rule of faith" is the way of seeing the universe that comes from the apostles' teaching and, ultimately, from Jesus himself. It is crystallized in the protocreeds and subsequently in the catholic creed at Nicaea. And the writings of the apostles are known to be writings of the apostles because they properly express this apostolic world-rendering, the "apostolic horizon," to borrow Gadamer's terminology. And we know that that is the apostolic horizon because the community traces its roots to the apostles, knows what they said, and lives and embodies those teachings. Because Irenaeus is part of true church, he knows what the apostles taught. When Irenaeus reads 2 John, he recognizes it as a letter written from the apostolic horizon.

For 2 John to be Scripture, then, is for it to witness to us now how Jesus's apostles saw the universe and lived in it. The text is a signpost for a world-rendering in keeping with Jesus's own and an example of what to do and how to do it, given that the world is in fact this way and not some other. Whatever John says to the patroness or to Gaius in these short missives is a distillation of what it means

64. Jenson, *Canon and Creed*, 34.

to be an apostle of Christ in the world as Christ understood it, and reading it in this manner gives us a way of being under 2 and 3 John's authority, even though we are basically reading the mail of some long dead people.

We may now circle back to those earlier concerns. That Irenaeus sees 2 John as "Johannine," as exactly the sort of thing that John the apostle would and in fact did say, indicates that it functionally does not matter who wrote 2 John. Whoever did, wrote from within the rule of faith and truly transmitted the apostolic horizon. Irenaeus and the other members of his community recognized that feature, and so we may too. Canon confirms creed, and creed confirms canon.

We might note that this way of encountering 2 and 3 John has benefits for encountering all of Scripture's odd bits. The Bible as a whole witnesses to a reality (or maybe realities) that must confront and supersede our own. Poetry, prophecy, narratives, wisdom, gospels, visions, and, yes, other people's mail all paint fresh, divine horizons that have always nourished and will continue to nourish the church in the redemptive love of Christ and the power and truth of the Spirit.

The Church

The Spirit of Anointing: Church as Spirit-Temple in 1–3 John

> "The anointing you received from him remains with you, and you do not need anyone to teach you."

In a comment on 1 John 2:27, we noted that Johannine language of "anointing" is tied to the Spirit. Spirit-talk is rife in 1–3 John, though it is difficult to know exactly how to characterize it all. A functional pneumatology, built on John's notion of the church as a fulfilled temple, might help to clarify who John thinks the Spirit is and what the Spirit does. Key to this understanding is the Gospel reference to those who will "worship in Spirit and truth" (John 4:24). That pericope is noteworthy because it specifically references the temple. The woman who had five husbands is a Samaritan, unfit for temple worship in Jerusalem and convinced that the proper worship of her ancestors is located in Samaria (4:20). She supposes that Jesus's Judaism and her Samaritan worship are incompatible; this is a temple problem. Is right worship located in the Jerusalem temple or elsewhere? Jesus's response to the conundrum is future-oriented and a matter of Spirit: "A time is coming, and is now here," he says, "when the true worshipers will worship the Father in Spirit and truth" (4:23). Theologically, then, worship-in-the-Spirit fulfills one of the primary ends of Jerusalem temple worship, the gathering of the nations to worship of true God, YHWH, creator of heaven and earth. Where once the vision was of the nations coming to Jerusalem, the advent of the Spirit means that the nations can worship God anywhere. Wherever the Spirit is—and the Spirit is ubiquitous—true worship can take place. One need not go to the Jerusalem temple or any temple at all, so long as one's worship is in the Spirit.

What the Gospel leaves open, and what the sermon in 1 John clarifies, is how this worship-in-the-Spirit is possible. As noted in the exegetical section, the Spirit anoints all believers as priests. Just as the Spirit expands the location of proper worship, so also does the Spirit expand those who can properly minister from the Aaronic family of priests to any and all who believe. Contextualizing the Spirit's ecclesial economic function this way explains why the Spirit teaches, gives gifts, leads into truth, and more. The Spirit establishes a spiritual temple composed of believer-priests coministering with Jesus, the high priest and atoning sacrifice for all. The church-in-the-Spirit therefore accomplishes everything the Jerusalem temple was meant to accomplish but did not: well-being with God through the atoning sacrifice of Christ, worship that is true, in keeping with God's desires and what God deserves, and a priesthood that is fully empowered to sustain the enterprise.

On this view, John's pneumatic ecclesiology is strangely bereft of sacramental overtones. In one way this feature accords with the lack of an account of the institution of the Eucharist in John's Gospel. And yet, John's Gospel features bread, wine—even the famous "I am the bread of life" statement. Surely John's ecclesiology has some sacramental grounding. The answer, of course, is that for John, ecclesiology is first grounded in the Spirit, and any ministration—whether prayer, singing, Eucharist, baptism, and so forth—must be sourced in the Holy One. The Spirit comes first. The Spirit is what makes sacraments sacraments and not rituals. Consider John 6:48–63. Jesus claims that to have life, one must eat his flesh and drink his blood—as sacramental a claim as there could be! Those who "eat this bread will live forever" (6:58). The talk of bread, wine, flesh, and blood confounds the disciples, so Jesus expands on his words: "It is the Spirit that gives life," he says in 6:63; his words are "Spirit and life." No bread is Bread unless it is eaten in the Spirit. No wine is Wine unless quaffed in the Spirit. The Spirit is the foundation of the church, its ministers, its sacraments, its power, its worship.

This is not to say that Christ is not the foundation of the church.[65] For surely the Spirit is the Spirit of Christ sent by the Father through the Son.[66] The Pauline

65. Compare the Johannine church-as-Spirit-temple to, for example, Moltmann's "worship as Messianic feast" (*The Church in the Power of the Spirit: A Contribution to Messianic Ecclesiology* [Minneapolis: Fortress, 1993], 261–74). Moltmann's ecclesiology is thoroughgoingly Christocentric, even as he tries to make space for a robust pneumatology.

66. Without delving deeply into the *filioque* controversy, in which the Eastern Orthodox

"body of Christ" and the Johannine "Spirit-temple" are certainly different ecclesiologies, but they are not therefore incommensurable ecclesiologies. In defense of the Johannine vision, it is arguably more trinitarian, because the Spirit that descends as a dove at Jesus's baptism, the Spirit that fully empowers and guides the Son, manifests the Son's power and guidance in the church. Just as Jesus is the fulfillment of the temple in his life in John's Gospel,[67] so is the church the fulfilled Spirit-temple once he has been glorified. There is therefore little need to mention bread, wine, or baptism in 1–3 John; all worship—sacramental or otherwise—is grounded in the Spirit.

Ecclesiology in 1–3 John: The Family of God

> "Those born from God don't practice sin, because they have God's DNA in them."

John relentlessly uses familial language to describe Christians. Children, young people, brothers and sisters, and more. Who or what is the church, if the church is primarily understood as the family of God? To put the question this way is, of course, to push against classical understandings of what makes the church the church. Various answers have included the baptized (spiritually or physically or both), those who believe something (say, a creed or a truth about Jesus), and those who participate in the sacraments. The problem with these definitions is not that they do not accurately characterize communities of faith but that they place the definition of membership on particular acts, attitudes, or beliefs. We should note that John surely implicates certain beliefs and acts as signifying whether one is in the light or the dark, but John's primary understanding of the church is as a family, and family membership cannot be reduced to doing this or believing that.

To take the family metaphor seriously is to ask what makes one one's parents' child? The answer to this question is just not simple. The question cannot be an-

Church rejects the idea that the Spirit is sent by the Father "and the Son," I have elected to formulate the sending of the Spirit as "from the Father, *through* the Son" to be conciliatory and to accurately describe the Spirit's eternal and economic procession. This rendering is indebted to Maximus the Confessor.

67. Hoskins's *Jesus as the Fulfillment of the Temple in the Gospel of John* shows, among other things, the connections between Jesus's "I am" statements and the various festivals where he makes them. There is little doubt that John envisages Jesus as the eschatological fulfillment of God's temple purposes.

swered biologically, for this would exclude the adopted from being their parents' children. Nor can it be answered legally, for surely one does not need the laws of a society to be in a family. It cannot even be sufficiently answered with regards to one's own associative or disassociating choice, for surely we can imagine—as Jesus did—a father claiming a son as son even after the child has gone prodigal. The boundaries by which one is defined as a member of a family or not a member are strangely permeable and impermeable, sometimes unbreakable and other times shattered without remainder. And even in cases of total, unabated estrangement, a biological child still carries a father's or mother's DNA.

John is aware of these complexities, of course. Notice that in 1 John 2:11 one "hates a brother or sister" rather than one "hates a *former* brother or sister." It is telling that John himself struggles with classificatory schemes, offering markers and signs without ultimately coming down and saying, "That is it: this person is family, that person is not, and here is why." The situation appears to be fluid. John has—as has every Christian community—known dear brothers and sisters who have abandoned the church and the faith for other things. Yet the words of Jesus in John 10:28 would seem to push against this possibility. Jesus risks death to claim, "I give them eternal life; they will never die, and no one will tear them from my grasp."

The question of ecclesiology is therefore bound up with the question of soteriology, for presumably the members of the family of God are those who have union with God and live the eternal divine life, and those who are not in the family do not. This issue has vexed Christian theology from the beginning for the reasons already mentioned: it does not seem possible for us to truly say, "This person is in the family of God, and that one is not." If we think of family networks along the lines of a continuum, then the problem becomes clearer. For example, a family matriarch, a woman who holds an extended family together, might occupy an extreme end: she's clearly a member of the clan. Her devoted children would be not much further from that end. But what of her dear, lifelong friends? Are they family? From a biblical perspective, we would have to say yes, as the ancient household included close, loyal associates.[68] But surely they would be further down the continuum, closer to the middle. And perhaps the middle might be occupied by an in-law who divorces the matriarch's daughter but re-

68. The historical evidence indicates that it was common for extended families to live together. Some have contested this conclusion, but multiple anecdotes from the ancient Mediterranean—to say nothing of the communal nature of Pauline household codes—indicate that early Christians held a wide view of the composition of the household. For a contemporary review of the evidence, see Sabine R. Huebner, "Household Composition in the Ancient Mediterranean—What Do We Really Know?," in *A Companion to Families in the Greek and Roman World*, ed. Beryl Rawson (West Sussex: Blackwell, 2011), 73–91.

mains present for family gatherings for the sake of the children and, over time, develops a working rapport with his ex. There can be no doubt that things get messy quickly and that there simply might be no way for us to speak definitively on any number of cases—especially those that feature a prodigal who swears off the whole bunch and is never seen again.

Contemporary philosophers call it the problem of vagueness. Derived from the ancient "problem of the many"[69] and the famous Ship of Theseus example,[70] knowing who is family and who is not is a lot like trying to tell whether Daniel is bald or whether there are enough grains of sand in that pile for it to truly be a "heap."[71] Following Elizabeth Barnes's telling, consider the problem of trying to determine whether a man, Daniel, who has some hair but not very much, is bald or not bald. We may assume that the truth of the statement "Daniel is bald" is difficult to ascertain for three possible reasons: (1) representational or semantic vagueness, (2) epistemic vagueness, or (3) ontic vagueness. As for the first reason, it could be that the word "bald" does not admit of precisification. There may be an inherent vagueness to the language we use, in which case we are not able to characterize aspects of the world accurately or precisely. In this case, it might be that the word "bald" cannot be adequately specified to determine whether Daniel is or is not bald. The second reason is one of human ignorance. It might be that there really is an actual number of hairs that must be on the head for Daniel to be "not bald" but that it is impossible for human beings to ascertain this number accurately. In this case it is a problem with our ability to know and navigate the world that renders the question difficult to answer. The third possibility, however—ontic vagueness—is the most tantalizing. Perhaps the universe is just not settled, with Daniel's baldness or not baldness being simply indeterminate.

Barnes tries to clarify this indeterminateness. Suppose that we can get a determination of baldness, that is, an adequate account of precisification—say, 846 hairs. Anyone with 846 hairs is not bald, and anyone with 845 or less is bald. This statement would seem to remove the problem of semantic vagueness. However, suppose that 845 hairs are firmly secured to Daniel's scalp and that one hair is "teetering on the brink, about to be dropped,"[72] making it practically impossible to say exactly how many hairs Daniel has. Such a case would be an example of ontic vagueness, an indeterminate state of affairs in which Daniel is neither bald nor not bald.

Perhaps the family of God is in a similar way indeterminate. The statement

69. Peter Unger, "The Problem of the Many," *Midwest Studies in Philosophy* 5 (1980): 411–67.

70. https://en.wikipedia.org/wiki/Ship_of_Theseus.

71. Elizabeth Barnes, "Ontic Vagueness: A Guide for the Perplexed," *Noûs* 44, no. 4 (2010): 601–27.

72. Barnes, "Ontic Vagueness," 605.

"you are a member of the family" might clearly obtain in many cases, clearly not obtain in many others, but might also be simply and irreducibly indeterminate in many as well. There may just not be a fact that would let us know whether Daniel is in the family of God, just as there may be no conclusive fact about his baldness. Presumably at some point, like when the 846th hair definitively disentangles from the scalp, Daniel will settle into "bald" or "not bald," though it is not clear exactly how or when this state of affairs will come to pass. It might be that one's familial status in the family of God is indeterminate even unto—perhaps beyond?—death.

In some ways such a view helps to make sense of the stark language John employs. While useful as heuristics, light and dark and love and hate do not easily map onto our actual experience of people. There are saints and antichrists, to be sure, but there are also kind and peaceable but nevertheless wayward friends and loved ones. There are aspects of the light and the dark in us all, and where the lines are not entirely clear, the possibility that there just might not be a fact of the matter relieves us of the responsibility of trying to determine it. We might best relegate that responsibility—indeed, even the decision—to God.

Alternatively, it could be that there is no ontic vagueness, but there might be epistemic vagueness, meaning that we just cannot tell whether this or that prodigal meets the relevant criteria. The question is inescapably impossible to answer because human comprehension is not adequate to the task of deciphering it. In either case, membership in the family—or, in the parlance of evangelical lay theology, whether one is "saved"—is not properly a province of human inquiry.

This conclusion would, in turn, mean that any reading of 1–3 John focused on the determining soteriological status is fundamentally a *misreading*.[73] The sermon and the letters do not give us criteria by which to know who is in and who is out; we have just gone to some length to show that trying to find such a criterion is impossible. John's sermon is really something more like a speech act intended to invite hearers to identify, internally at least, as one or the other. To

73. Of course this claim pushes against the scholarly consensus. Yarbrough (*1–3 John*, 296–97), for whom it is "a major concern," and Kruse (*The Letters of John*, 27), who writes, "the author provided other criteria which, if applied by the readers to themselves, would show that they are in the right; they are the ones who know God, who have fellowship with him, and who have eternal life," are representative. The widespread adoption of this sort of reading appears to be linked to a speculative history behind the text. If John is writing in response to a secessionist movement or movements or if John is writing to Ephesian Christians in order to assure them that they are in the right, then this sort of reading makes sense: If you do or believe *x*, *y*, and *z*, then you have eternal life. The text then functions as a spiritual test of sorts. It is some of the burden of this commentary to offer a better, more compelling reading, one that does not hinge on a historical mirror-reading that is necessarily speculative and therefore unconfirmable.

put this more forcefully, John is not writing to convince or assure this or that group that they are family. Instead, he is writing in such a way that a hearer will listen to the words and be forced to self-identify: "Yes, I am a member of the group John describes" or "This is definitely *not* my family" or "I want to be a part of this family" or "I worry that I am drifting away from this family." The point is not to discern whether these self-identifications are correct but to elicit them and so compel a response.

Suppose we are sitting in a warm room in your home and you are right next to the air conditioner controls. If I say, "Boy, it sure is hot in here!" I may be making a comment on the temperature, but it is more likely that I am pushing you to consider lowering the thermostat.[74] The situation, our relationship, and the rules of discourse create multiple possibilities for what my comment on the temperature really means or is meant to do. While we cannot reconstruct the historical context in which John was writing, we do not need to do so to hear the language for what it is.

John says that anyone who hates a brother or sister is in the dark. If John has spiritual authority, then any community hearing that statement must ask itself, "Are we in the dark?" or "Do we hate any group of fellow believers?"

Such a reading listens to John more for *formation* rather than *information*. The information is present, of course, but it is instrumentalized, pressing hearers to respond, self-examine, pray, repent, and be reconciled. John does not give a checklist of actions, beliefs, and attitudes that demonstrate family membership; he asks everyone to decide the family of which they are a part.[75]

Gender and Leadership: The Role of Women in 1–3 John

> "But now, friend, I'm begging you . . . that we love each other."

Biblical studies in the twenty-first century have contributed a panoply of gender-related inquiries into Johannine literature.[76] With few exceptions, however, most of the literature has been restricted to the Fourth Gospel, for obvious reasons.

74. The account offered here draws on the speech-act theories of J. L. Austin (*How to Do Things with Words*, 2nd ed. [Clarendon: Oxford, 1975]) and John Searle (*Speech Acts: An Essay in the Philosophy of Language* [Cambridge: Cambridge University Press, 1969]).

75. See also comments in the first section of the commentary on 1 John 3:9 and 5:13.

76. For an expansive retrospective, see Colleen M. Conway, "Gender and the Fourth Gospel," in *The Oxford Handbook of Johannine Studies*, ed. Judith M. Lieu and Martinus C. de Boer (Oxford: Oxford University Press, 2018), chapter 14.

1–3 John do not feature much in the way of pointed consideration of women or narratives in which they are depicted, and academic inquiries into John's Apocalypse are pressed by other concerns. Scholars generally agree, however, that the Fourth Gospel is at least historically subversive in its depiction of the masculine, feminine, and potentially queer.[77] John depicts the women around Jesus as catalysts of his ministry and signs and trustworthy witnesses of the resurrection. Jesus himself retains the authority of the Son of the Father but surrounds himself with women who ultimately prove themselves more loyal than the disciples. Ultimately, Jesus mothers the church through the labor of the cross, giving spiritual birth to true sons and daughters.

Whatever else we might say, the Fourth Gospel evinces nothing of the apparent misogyny of the Pauline corpus. So it should not be a surprise that the church the elder addresses in 2 John is led by a woman. The language is too vague to know anything of the patroness's role in worship, but it is clear enough on some important issues. John recognizes that the patroness is responsible for the spiritual health of the church, referring to the congregation as "her children." This wording mirrors John's own self-understanding in 1 John, where he repeatedly addresses his hearers as progeny. We noted above that this language indicates that John sees himself as continuing the spiritual parenthood first exercised by Father and Son through the Spirit.

Theologically, John sees all human beings—not only men!—as partakers or sharers in this aspect of the divine economy. Just as the immanent Trinity's eternal self-relation is expressed economically in the Father's fatherhood of the Son, so is that aspect of triune self-relation given over to human beings in the church by the Spirit. John fathers Christians as the Father fathers the Son and as the patroness mothers them. Presumably, this is a vocation available to anyone who shares in union with God.

Moreover, John entreats the κυρία (*kyria*, "lady," "mistress," "friend") to ensure that the Christians continue to love each other—John included. Here John addresses the power dynamic in a fashion like Jesus in the Fourth Gospel: he has authority but does not wield it. Instead, he asks the patroness—even going so far as to qualify the "ask" not as a command he writes but as one handed down to them both from the Unoriginated One (2 John 5). This too is a manifestation of the eternal divine life: whereas the Father has authority and power, he glorifies the Son in the Spirit, and, although the Son is from the beginning, he submits by the Spirit to the Father's will, glorifying him. The patroness's acquiescence to John's request beautifully reembodies the dynamic holding between Father and Son, made possible and enlivened by the Holy Spirit.

77. Conway, "Gender and the Fourth Gospel."

John's treatment of the patroness suggests an ecclesial approach to gender that is different from, or at least radically recontextualizes, the traditional egalitarian-complementarian-patriarchal debates animated almost entirely by Pauline texts. The Fourth Gospel and 2 John set the Christian ideal for gendered humanity sharing life together in the church by the Spirit. To call it egalitarian or any of the traditional labels would be gross anachronism: John envisions something of the mutual indwelling of the Godhead, a mutual indwelling that upsets traditional notions of power. Because in the end, power is really what is at issue. Who should or should not wield it? John's interaction with the patroness suggests that the right answer is "no one." Spiritual parenthood is not about having and exercising power, any more than the Father's fatherhood is about lording fatherhood over the Son. It is, rather, about mutual glorification, shared union, and self-giving love. And because it is so wholly counter to anything we know in the world, such mutualities absolutely must be empowered by the Spirit. Only the divine livelihood of God can—and does—manifest relations of this sort. Should the church embrace and embody John's vision, one wonders whether it would not constitute yet another sign to the increasingly fractious, failing empire of the darkness that its days are numbered and that the light is now shining.

Intolerance and the Power of Speech in 1–3 John

"for anyone who greets them partners in their evil work"

As noted above, 2 John is shocking in its radical qualification of Christian hospitality. But John's hyperbole is powerfully instructive to churches that, like the patroness's, exist in a pluralistic empire. Early Christian writers often warn churches against providing hospitality for wolves. Ignatius of Antioch, likely a disciple of John himself, calls dangerous teachers "wild animals" (θηρίον, *thērion*, "beast," "savage animal") "in human form" and likewise recommends avoiding any meeting with them.[78] The likening to an animal helps to justify offering not even the common courtesy of a polite greeting—after all, one does not need to greet a wild dog—and John's teaching is probably responsible for Ignatius's own opinions.

Ignatius does recommend praying for deceivers but is pessimistic about it doing any good. This attitude suggests that John's recommendation is an extreme and counterintuitive expression not of hate but love. The proper Christian response to deception and evil is not, it would seem, niceness. It is instead benign

78. Ignatius, *Epistle to the Smyrnaeans* 4:1.

intolerance, a refusal to associate with or countenance the deceiver unless that one repents and submits to apostolic doctrine.

One of the oddities of God's triunity is that while God exists eternally in perichoretic union, creation that is truly created and not merely an extension of Godself demands things and beings that are not (yet) united to the divine life. In some way, God must "make space" for creation. Moltmann once suggested borrowing Issac Luria's kabbalistic concept of "zimzum," or the "contraction" or "withdrawing" of God.[79] Logically prior to the creative act, on this view the Godhead must allow a self-negation so that there can be nothingness, that is, somewhere where there is an absence of the one who is all in all. Given that we have already posited an eternal self-abnegation within the Godhead in the Father's eternally sending the Son and the Son's eternal return to the Father in the Spirit, it does seem right that the first act of the divine economy would be an act of self-abnegation—especially if the final eschatological act of God's economy is consummation, en-glorifying all that is created in the Spirit to union with the Father through the Son.

John's teaching about the church's response to would-be corruptors thus draws its shape from God's noncreative act: the church withdraws, contracts, retreats. This response is self-abnegating love, a giving of space and freedom that hopes for and maybe even anticipates eventual union. The church practices nonviolent patience for evil, allowing and expecting to be pilloried and lied about—much what God has long experienced while trying to rescue humanity and the world it mars.

This response is nonviolent and noncoercive, yes, but it is also not very nice. It is intolerant and stubborn and will draw the ire of those still under imperial sway. Studied silence, the refusal to sit down at the table and negotiate—these tactics are especially contrarian in contemporary Western social orders. The church's task in the present day is to discern when and against whom to deploy intolerance and exclusion, because doing so will inevitably invite unwanted attention and probably persecution. If we take John as the model, note whom and what he advises the church to exclude. First, it is deceivers, not the innocently curious. These are wolves, allied with the darkness and trying to destroy the church. These are not potential converts; they are certain corruptors. They are, moreover, in search of influence and power. Their attraction to the people of God emanates not from a realization that they need rescue from a bent generation but from a desire to control. Second, what they purvey is not a differing opinion on whether we should baptize children. No, they are denying Jesus's very humanity, which is to say that they are denying that true humanity can be united to true

79. Jürgen Moltmann, *God in Creation* (Minneapolis: Fortress Press, 1993), 87.

divinity. They are perverting the very message of salvation itself. Theirs is heresy, not a quibble over uncertain things. Third, and perhaps most important, they are coreligionists. Theirs is a different religion, but they are still in the business of making statements about the nature of God and the universe. The danger is that they sell dangerous theology, not that they have differing views on economic policy or how to properly educate the young.

Taken together, John's sketch of someone the church should not tolerate and actively exclude is a power-hungry, deluded theologian, of all people. In our present age, of course, we must remember that it is not just Christians, Muslims, and Buddhists who advocate a theological vision of the world: atheists and agnostics can be just as dogmatic as the most vociferous sectarian. So whatever color of sheep's wool the wolf has donned, if it is trying to get into the church to take over and change it, the shepherds must act. No open doors, no financial help, not even a greeting.

True Church and Excommunication in 2–3 John

"He . . . tosses them out of the church!"

One of the ironies of setting 2 and 3 John next to each other in the canon is that John's message to the patroness is the obverse of his message to Gaius. John tells the patroness not to be hospitable to, associate with, or even greet certain charlatans. In 3 John he excoriates Diotrephes for not being hospitable to, associating with, or even greeting John and his friends. Diotrephes seems to be following John's advice perfectly, with the exception that the target of his excommunication is, well, John.

One wonders whether there is a lesson to be learned here beyond the importance of orthodoxy. Give Diotrephes the benefit of the doubt for a moment. Maybe he believes he is right and that John is the charlatan. Maybe he is genuinely appalled that John is spreading false rumors about, say, the humanity of Jesus and demanding strict conformity to this metaphysical atrocity. According to the logic of John's appeal to the patroness, Diotrephes is doing the right thing! The only reason Diotrephes is to be condemned, it seems, is that he happens to be wrong. John did know Jesus, and Jesus was a human being. Should Diotrephes really be condemned?

Careful readers will note that the first criticism John has of Diotrephes is not that he does not know the truth, not that he does not help missionaries, and not even that he does not accept John's authority. It is that he "craves leadership."

The more standard translation is "likes to put himself first" or, in the old King James, "loveth to have the preeminence among them." John's meaning is that he wants to be in charge, but our translation does admittedly lose some of the cut of the Greek. Diotrephes is all about Diotrephes. Diotrephes thinks Diotrephes should be on top because Diotrephes recognizes just how great Diotrephes is.

Thus, it is not just that John knew Jesus and is therefore more trustworthy. That is not the whole of his complaint to Gaius. Instead, the substance of the complaint comes from a major personality defect, a part of Diotrephes's character that remains wholly owned by the darkness. And in this case the demonic corruption of the darkness is having deleterious effects on the whole congregation. Diotrephes's narcissism is destroying the church. This calamity accords well with John's bedrock conviction that truth and actions are deeply intertwined. Those who know the truth will walk in the light, and those who walk in the light will recognize the truth. Gaius can be sure that Diotrephes is wrong about God because he is wrong about himself.

One of the drawbacks to the rise of globalized mass media and communication is that it has radically amplified the enemy's ability to prey on human pride. Developing a brand, gathering a following, being the center, the shining figure all starving eyes long to see—this pattern has become ubiquitous in Western culture and, sadly, in the church. The cult of personality has always been a temptation, and self-preening wolves have always been attracted to the pulpit's limelight, but the impact of digital communication has exacerbated these temptations exponentially. The irony, of course, is that the people who draw the most eyes do so because they are very good! Some are quite adept at "preaching the Bible" and "communicating the truth." They do not appear to be hucksters; their doctrine appears sound.

On John's view, though, it most decidedly is not. If, like Diotrephes, some Christian man has been captured by the darkness, seeks himself, and craves leadership, his doctrine is false—even if it is true. That is, the criterion of truth for John is not right thinking; it is right thinking *embodied in right loving*. And right loving is agapic; it is the absolute opposite of self-seeking, of desiring to be first.

We must therefore be neither swayed nor dismayed by the power of the market that buoys these feral creatures, especially in nondenominational Christianity. What sells, sells; even when called out for highly disordered loves, the talented preacher, pastor, influencer, or singer can move on, start another "ministry," and spread the enemy's corruption anew. The fact of worldly success for narcissists implies that a true church might often be small and unattractive as the evil empire judges such things. And it also implies that it is better to excommunicate a charismatic, self-interested Diotrephes and run the risk of remaining small and ugly than to let the boil fester, regardless of how many seats are filled and buildings built. Because those seats and those buildings are monuments, not to the encroaching light that heralds the Son's everlasting dominion, but as sad relics of a dying age, the last gasp of a spent, exhausted, damned antichrist.

Ethics

Ethics in 1–3 John: In Him

> "The one who says, 'I am still in him,' ought to walk just as he walked."

In 1 John "in him" occurs fourteen times. As we have noted above, the referent is ambiguous, sometimes seeming to indicate God and other times indicating Christ. As metaphor, the meaning is likewise a bit obscure. There are many things we can think of metaphorically "being in"—such as love or a cloud of confusion—but note that these are abstracts; persons are not usually included. Robert Yarbrough suggests that being "in him" is "to be in the positive domain marked out by the pistic, ethical, and agapic trajectories sketched [in verse 2:1]."[80] Yarbrough appears to mean by "pistic, ethical, and agapic" a state of believing rightly, acting rightly, and loving rightly. And Yarbrough appears to take the location part of the metaphor as literally as possible, such that there is some abstract faithful-ethical-loving space that we can inhabit, and when we are correctly doing these things, we can claim to be "in him." One wonders whether such a view is not properly circumscribed, however, by John's aesthetic bent. That is, Yarbrough's view of being "in him" could quite easily be reduced to the observance of some set of rules or even attitudes that do not appear to be present in John's sermon. It is probably not a coincidence that 1 John does not feature either recitations or subversions of, say, Greco-Roman household codes (as does Paul) or revivified accounts of commands in the Torah (as featured in, e.g., the Sermon

80. Yarbrough, *1–3 John*, 87. It is worth noting that our departure from Yarbrough here is likely the interpretive fallout of rejecting historical speculation about the circumstances (or even existence) of an identifiable "Johannine community" as the basis of meaning in 1 John. That is, if we follow the broad consensus that 1 John is addressed to a group of Christians that have survived recent schism with some protognostic group, then it makes sense to graft in certain content to "being in him" that just does not exist in John's actual language. By giving the text interpretive priority—rather than imagined historical circumstances—1 John speaks as a sermon to all rather than an obscure letter to some.

on the Mount in Matthew). To do so would be to give unnecessary concretization to what is ultimately better understood as an aesthetic mode of being, what John has already deemed "walking in the light."

What John has emphatically not provided is a list of specific faithful-ethical-loving do's and don'ts that cover the daily life of those to whom he preaches. God's vectored love reaches its goal when the Christian sees the world ordered according to God's ordering and lives in light of that. Such a life is no doubt characterized by certain "pistic, ethical, and agapic" virtues and attitudes, but these qualities are symptoms rather than causes. It might even be that John's construal of Christian life is actually quite free and freeing. There are some touchstone practices such as confession and being in loving communion with other believers, but being "in him" is not a category subject to a high degree of regulation. What it is to be in him will, moreover, change according to person, place, and circumstance, broadly construed.

It has already been suggested that John's sermon outlines some contours for faithful temple worship where Christians themselves constitute the temple. In a more classical parlance, John is concerned with ecclesiology, that is, the doctrine of the church. Rather than developing a strict classificatory scheme for the behaviors and practices that delineate between "true church" and "false church," John has instead offered a set of metaphors, the first of which is being "in him."

The church of the first century was inter- or transcultural, featuring a number of various groups from different backgrounds. The Christians of Ephesus were different from the Christians of Rome or Jerusalem; the church itself prized membership from Jews, gentiles, barbarians, Scythians, slaves, free-persons, men, women, and so forth. The situation on the ground was likely quite similar to current global contexts, in which the gospel lands in every place and among every kind of person. With such a dizzying diversity of thought and culture, one wonders whether there is some sort of baseline commonality, a litmus test of sorts for defining Christian ecclesiology. Yarbrough's view of John's "in him" seems to indicate that there is. There is a matrix of "pistic-ethical-agapic" mores into which we should aim to live. We have already seen, however, that John's actual language and themes—indeed, his utter refusal to engage in specificity, such that Yarbrough must conjure it from whole cloth—pushes against such a view. Interestingly, Lesslie Newbigin, a missionary theologian, gives a much more compelling ecclesiological account. He suggests that the life of Christ—what John shorthands as being "in him"—will be as follows:

> It will not be by the universal application of an unchanging pattern of personal and social behavior as laid down in the faith and practice of Islam. It

> will not be in a series of abstract moral and political principles. It will be in the life of a community which remembers, rehearses, and lives by the story which the Bible tells and of which the central focus is the story told in the New Testament. This remembering and rehearsing will be through the continual reading of and reflection on the Bible and the continual repetition of the sacraments. . . . It will maintain its link with, its continuity with the body of men to whom Jesus said, "As the Father sent me, so I send you," through a ministry in which the personal call of Jesus, "Follow me," is continued through the generations, not in abstract moral or political principles but in the actual encounters in which men and women who have themselves been called, call others to follow.[81]

Though Newbigin writes about conducting mission in a globalist, pluralist context, it is difficult not to hear echoes of John's own language. Behavior and culture changes, but it does not exclude Christians from being "in him." Newbigin's emphasis on the telling and retelling of Jesus's story should bring to mind the cosmic whats of the beginning of the sermon, as well as John's naming Christ an "atonement sacrifice" in 2:1–2. Crucial too is John's self-commendation of one who truly touched, heard, and handled the one who was from the beginning. Newbigin calls this factor maintaining a link or continuity with the apostles. John has implicated believers' co-priesthood with Christ in temple ministrations; Newbigin calls for carrying out the Christian tradition of baptism and communion. John calls believers to live in union with one another; Newbigin recommends "actual encounters" between those who have been called that lead to a call to others. From a philosophical perspective, Newbigin recognizes, or perhaps rerecognizes, what John and other early Christians intuited: walking in the light is always an embodied, enculturated act. Precisely for this reason the walking metaphor is appropriate—it suggests journeying, the very act of moving from here to there. Being in the light, as it were, is not a fixed position. It is a fool's errand to try to retain the "true kernel" or the "unchanging core" of Christian faith and ethics because every attempt to categorize the "pistic-ethical-agapic" essentials of being "in him" will be rooted in a particular cultural context by particular individuals with particular histories.

81. Lesslie Newbigin, *The Gospel in a Pluralist Society* (Grand Rapids: Eerdmans, 1989), 147–48.

Open and Closed Doors: Christian Hospitality in 1–3 John

> "Don't invite anyone who comes to you and doesn't bring this teaching into your home."

Hospitality is a hallmark of Christian ethics. In the Synoptic Gospels, Jesus places a serious premium on being open-handed, inviting, and welcoming. Invitations to the marginalized imitate the gracious invite of God to all of us; Christine Pohl suggests, "offering hospitality to strangers is central to the gospel and the Christian moral tradition."[82] John might not agree. In 2 and 3 John hospitality is reserved for members of the family. The reason, it seems, is that John has come to understand that unreserved hospitality can be dangerous to the health of the church. Since there are wolves that seek to infiltrate and harm the flock, John counsels the church to reject "deceivers," those who have not stayed "with Christ's teaching." He worries that outsiders will derail the right belief and right action of orthodox churches. This concern implies that the kinds of people the church should refuse hospitality to are those who want to shape the church rather than let the church shape them.

It might be that what John envisions is for strangers to come to the church as spiritual (and possibly material) supplicants, people who recognize—or at least suspect—that they are not in the light and need to be transformed by those who are. The person who enters the church humbly, who leaves open the possibility that the church has something he or she needs: this is the kind of stranger one should welcome in and offer succor. But those who wish to come in and have a say, as it were, this is the kind of person of whom we should be wary. Just as we are called to discern the spirits that animate others, so must we evaluate those who say they need our help. John acts the shepherd here, warding off the wolves for the sake of the sheep. In so doing, he must counsel the sheep to be ready to reject those who presume to know the light best, who think they have a better plan for the family than he does.

In any case, John's teaching about hospitality sits in some tension with Jesus's teaching to "give to anyone who asks" in the Synoptics. It might be that Jesus's command expresses the spirit of the church's relationship to material things: we should be open-handed and ready to give, secure in the knowledge that God will provide what we need. John's command considers the lived experience of

82. Christine D. Pohl, "Hospitality," in *Dictionary of Scripture and Ethics*, ed. Joel B. Green (Grand Rapids: Baker, 2011), 378–81.

communities of faith: wherever the Spirit of God moves, parasites and disrupters will be attracted like moths to a flame. Without losing its spirit of generosity and welcome, the church must be on guard, always prepared to shut the door on a wolf to protect those who are most vulnerable.

Money in 1–3 John

"They don't take any help from nonbelievers."

In 3 John the elder commends Gaius for his community's hospitality and financial help for traveling Christians. These are probably missionaries or itinerants of some sort; few Christians will be unfamiliar with visitors to the congregation who raise support for various works of the gospel. John's attitude toward money is emblematic of the New Testament in general. Money is a means to an end, something that belongs to God and is shared out as needed, ensuring that God's desires for the church and the world become reality.

When John tells Gaius that these visitors receive no support from nonbelievers, he is making a powerful theological statement. The assumption is that God will meet their needs, full stop. They see no need to involve the world; after all, the world is God's, so whatever they need, God will give them. While basic, this conviction remains a cornerstone of Christian faith even to the present day, and for good reason.

John knows that money buys influence. He knows that having money and giving it out generate a client-patron relationship. This dynamic may have been even more true in the ancient world than it is today. To ensure freedom from the world's corruption, John's missionary friends commit themselves to receiving patronage only from those they trust, those who share union with John and with the Son. This approach keeps money and resources in the family, where, ideally, they will be shared out without strings attached.

But we must admit that such an ideal is almost impossible to realize at all, much less sustain in the actual tangle of human relationships within which we find ourselves. The story of the early church in Acts suggests that this complication has always been the case. The church begins with true communion in chapter 2, but by chapters 5 and 6 money and resources have become points of contention, hostility, and deception. In 3 John 8 John the elder explains the rationale behind the ideal. We should "be hospitable to such people, so we can be coworkers for the truth." While not capitalized in the translation here, we have argued that "truth" is basically a cipher for "Spirit" in 2 and 3 John. The dative rendered "for the truth" captures the relationship between John, Gaius, and all other Christians and the Spirit, namely, that the Spirit is the boss.[83] There is a power dynamic at work here, and it is decidedly lopsided. All of humanity is or ought to be expressing self-giving love as service to the redeeming, glorifying, empowering Spirit. Of course God is not so gauche as to put it this way. God's station and power are revealed in self-emptying love, which is precisely the point. The Spirit exercises authority by enlivening and empowering John and Gaius, not by lording that power over them. The Son lavishes forgiveness over them; the Father richly provides everything they need. If the Spirit is "the Boss," it is quite clear how the Spirit wants us to do our jobs, as it were: generously, graciously, totally open-handed. The intratrinitarian dynamic of eternal glorification is made manifest in the Spirit's gifts. The Father glorifies the Son in the Spirit, and the Son's en-Spirited obedience glorifies the Father. Father and Son send out glorification in the Spirit to each other and do so without reserve or constraint. To be a "coworker for the Spirit," then, is to participate in the Spirit's power to give and gift to whoever has need.

The only hope for the church to embody this ideal is to remain "in him," constantly aware of God's own outrageous, egregious generosity and zealous to share union with the divine nature in this regard. Where there is union, there will be plenty, and no one need beg of nonbelievers.

Power and Authority in 1–3 John

> "Diotrephes—who craves leadership—isn't acknowledging our authority."

John knows who God is and what love is. Agapic love—the very substance of God's inner life—is self-giving and self-emptying. It produces divine union and

83. Wallace (*Greek Grammar beyond the Basics* [Grand Rapids: Zondervan, 1996], 159–60) cites this verse as an example of a dative of association, suggesting that the antecedent term "coworkers" (συνεργοὶ, *synergoi*) implies "association with the truth." Though grammatically possible, this interpretation is not right for theological reasons. Even without supposing that "the truth" is "the Spirit," "the truth" is still something that, in the Johannine literature, is over and above believers. It is variously Jesus, the Spirit, walked in, known, belonged to, and so forth. Truth is not a coworker with John and Gaius; John and Gaius are called to walk in or serve the truth. Once we recognize that "truth" means "Spirit," the right reading of the dative becomes even more obvious. There is a sense in which, yes, John and Gaius are "in association with the Spirit," but it is the same sense in which the laborer is in association with the foreman.

life in those it engages. John also understands that he has been tasked with embodying this love, preaching it, and ensuring that it flourishes in the church. As a result, he is gentle, affectionate with his people. He persuades and encourages; his commands are neither harsh nor even his own: they come from the Father and the Son; John is just the messenger.

John's power and authority imitate the power and authority of the Father. Just as the Father gives up the Son to make all who believe children in the family, so does John send missionaries into the world to bring more and more into union. Just as the Father holds nothing back to ensure that all will have an atoning sacrifice and priestly life with Christ, so does John wish to lavishly furnish every member of the family who needs it.

"Servant leadership" might be a Christian cliché, but reading 1–3 John shows us why that is as it should be: power and authority are things John has but does not use as the world would. John acts this way because he has been convinced that God, the ultimate possessor of power, authority, majesty, and glory, has decided that the ultimate expression of them is the humiliated, self-giving love of the cross. God—the one who swallowed up Pharaoh and his armies in the waters of the Reed Sea, who gave over the Canaanites to slaughter at the hands of Israel—has laid down the sword and taken up the cross. Perhaps this is a temporary ethic. Maybe Jesus will come back with sword in hand and blood up to the horse's bridle. But for now, God has demonstrated a new kind of power, the power of the labor of the cross to give birth to divine children who possess eternal life and can live in union with the Father and the Son in the *power* of the Spirit.

J. R. R. Tolkien's *Lord of the Rings* trilogy offers a contemporary critique of coercive power.[84] The power of command and violence is bound up with the one ring, the ring of Sauron. With this ring anything is possible; the world can be bent to one's will. The one ring offers the specter of complete domination. What Tolkien reveals, however, is that possessing this ring inevitably leads to evil. Even with the best of intentions, the power of domination twists its wielder, and what began as a desire for good degenerates into endless hate and violence. There are other sorts of power, though. The elfin rings offer creativity, wisdom, and peace, along with the power to preserve and protect. The temptation is to wield the ring of domination and through it to try to generate those other sorts of power. Tolkien's narrative suggests that such a course of action is folly. Rather, the only hope is to destroy the one ring and put an end to the power of domination once for all.

84. I owe this reading to Wendy Farley (*Tragic Vision and Divine Compassion: A Contemporary Theodicy* [Louisville: Westminster John Knox, 1990], 85–94).

Wendy Farley suggests that the story of Frodo's quest to destroy the ring parallels Jesus's road to the cross. Jesus absorbs into himself the worst that the powers of domination can dish out—torture, crucifixion, and death. Jesus does not use the power he undoubtedly has to annihilate his opponents and institute his kingdom on earth. Likewise, Frodo's mission is not to wield the ring and lead the armies of Middle Earth against Sauron. His mission is to get rid of this power once and for all. In resurrection, Jesus puts the powers of violence and command on notice. He has rejected and overcome them. He has endorsed the fruits of the Spirit, accessible only in the Spirit's power. And thus John's exercise of power and authority is an imitation of Christ. Rather than using his place in the church as an opportunity for dominance, John uses it as an opportunity to love in words and actions, an opportunity to give himself for his people. He lets go of self-aggrandizement and humbles himself so that he can build up life in his spiritual children.

Diotrephes, however, reveals his own misunderstanding of the cross in his lust for the old sort of power. He "craves leadership." He wants the eyes on him. He wishes to influence others, not be influenced. He wants to rule, not be ruled. And so he deploys lies to slander John and others who knew the unoriginated Son in life. He withholds his goods and resources from those who listen to John. He expels any of his own people who go against his wishes. His is a Sauronic power, the power of the old regime, the power of the darkness and the devil who spawned it.

John's critique of power echoes the power narratives of the Old Testament.[85] In Israel's Scriptures we see what happens to those who go the way of Diotrephes. The leaders of Israel, from Moses to the judges to the kings, show time and again that those who accustom themselves to power and authority are usually not "servants of God." Rarely if ever do they end well. Instead, they atrophy, they become corrupted, and they eventually decide to serve their own interests instead of God's, usually at the expense of the people they were first called to shepherd. In some respects, the prophetic literature is a sustained criticism of Israel's elites. They lead the people astray or they ignore the needs of the poor or they refuse to obey or enforce God's instructions.

John, Jesus, and the Old Testament narratives agree: power is dangerous, perhaps even evil. It might be a necessary evil that exists now and will disappear in the eschaton. Or maybe it can be redeemed; perhaps the powers of creation and preservation will remain, and humanity will be stripped of the power of domination "when we see him as he is." However God sorts the end, we should take John's example to heart and be very wary of leaders in the church. One suspects

85. So Goldingay's theological interpretation of leadership in *Israel's Gospel*, 541–49.

that the church has many more Diotrepheses than Johns and that many, maybe most Johns become Diotrepheses before they finish. It is a perennial problem. The church needs leaders, but with leadership comes power, and with power comes its corrupting influence. John no doubt agreed with James that teachers could expect a stricter judgment (Jas 3:1).

Bibliography

Adinoff, Bryon, and Eliott A. Stein, eds. *Neuroimaging in Addiction*. Chichester: Wiley-Blackwell, 2011.

Anselm of Canterbury. *Proslogion*. Pages 82–104 in *Anselm: The Major Works*. Edited by Brian Davies. Translated by M. J. Charlesworth. Clarendon: Oxford University Press, 1998.

Arminius, Jacob. "A Letter on the Sin against the Holy Spirit." Pages 511–38 in *The Works of Jacob Arminius*. Translated by James Nichols. Vol. 2. Buffalo, NY: Derby, Orton & Mulligan, 1853.

Augustine of Hippo. "Letter 92." In PL 33.

Austin. J. L. *How to Do Things with Words*. 2nd ed. Clarendon: Oxford University Press, 1975.

von Balthasar, Hans Urs. "The Being Dead of the Son of God." Pages 168–77 in *Mysterium Paschale*. Translated by Aiden Nichols. San Francisco: Ignatius Press, 1990.

Barnes, Elizabeth. "Ontic Vagueness: A Guide for the Perplexed." *Noûs* 44, no. 4 (2010): 601–27.

Barth, Karl. *Church Dogmatics*. 4 vols. New York: T&T Clark, 2009.

Bauckham, Richard. "The Divinity of Jesus in the Letter to the Hebrews." Pages 233–53 in *Jesus and the God of Israel: God Crucified and Other Studies on the New Testament's Christology of Divine Identity*. Grand Rapids: Eerdmans, 2008.

———. *Jesus and the Eyewitness: The Gospels as Eyewitness Testimony*. 2nd ed. Grand Rapids: Eerdmans, 2017.

Bedau, Mark A. "Downward Causation and Autonomy in Weak Emergence." Pages 155–88 in *Emergence: Contemporary Readings in Philosophy and Science*. Edited by Mark A. Bedau and Paul Humphreys. Cambridge: MIT Press, 2008.

Bede the Venerable. *Homiliarum evangelii libri ii*. In PL 94.

Bennett, Thomas Andrew. "Jesus and the Believer as Co-priests: The Temple Cult and Paraklētos in 1 John." Paper presented at the Annual Meeting of the SBL. San Antonio, TX, 21 November 2016.

———. *Labor of God: The Agony of the Cross as the Birth of the Church*. Waco, TX: Baylor University Press, 2017.

———. "Paul Ricoeur and the Hypothesis of the Text in Theological Interpretation." *JTI* 5, no. 2 (2011): 211–29.

Benson, H., et al. "Study of the Therapeutic Effects of Intercessory Prayer (STEP) in Cardiac Bypass Patients: A Multicenter Randomized Trial of Uncertainty and Certainty of Receiving Intercessory Prayer." *American Heart Journal* 151, no. 4 (2006): 934–42.

Boersma, Hans. *Violence, Hospitality, and the Cross: Reappropriating the Atonement Tradition*. Grand Rapids: Baker Academic, 2004.

Bonhoeffer, Dietrich. *The Cost of Discipleship*. Translated by R. H. Fuller. London: SCM Press, 1959.

Boyd, Gregory A. *God of the Possible: A Biblical Introduction to the Open View of God*. Grand Rapids: Baker, 2000.

Brickle, Jeffrey E. *Aural Design and Coherence in the Prologue of First John*. New York: Bloomsbury T&T Clark, 2012.

Brown, Raymond E. *The Epistles of John*. New York: Doubleday, 1982.

Bultmann, Rudolf. *The Johannine Epistles*. Philadelphia: Fortress Press, 1973.

Calvin, John. *Institutes of the Christian Religion*. Edited by John T. McNeill. Translated by Ford Lewis Battles. 2 vols. Westminster: John Knox, 1960.

Card, Orson Scott. *Speaker for the Dead*. New York: Tor, 1986.

Clarke, Arthur C. *Childhood's End*. New York: Del Rey, 1953.

Clement of Alexandria. *Stromata*. In PG 8–9.

Coloe, Mary L. *God Dwells with Us: Temple Symbolism in the Fourth Gospel*. Collegeville, MN: Glazier, 2001.

Conway, Colleen M. "Gender and the Fourth Gospel." Chapter 14 in *The Oxford Handbook of Johannine Studies*. Edited by Judith M. Lieu and Martinus C. de Boer. Oxford: Oxford University Press, 2018.

Cudworth, Ralph. *The Life of Christ the Pith and Kernel of All Religion: A Sermon Preached before the Honorable House of Commons, at Westminster, March 31, 1647*. Westminster: BiblioBazaar, 2010.

Dodd, C. H. *Johannine Epistles*. New York: Harper & Brothers, 1946.

Ehrman, Bart D. *Did Jesus Really Exist? The Historical Argument for Jesus of Nazareth*. New York: HarperOne, 2012.

Ekhitari, Hamed, and Martin Paulus. *Neuroscience for Addiction Medicine: From Prevention to Rehabilitation—Constructs and Drugs*. Amsterdam: Elsevier, 2016.

Farley, Wendy. *Tragic Vision and Divine Compassion: A Contemporary Theodicy*. Louisville: Westminster John Knox, 1990.

Faulkner, William. *The Sound and the Fury*. Rev. ed. New York: Random House, 1984.

Goldingay, John. *Old Testament Theology*. Vol. 1: *Israel's Gospel*. Downers Grove, IL: InterVarsity Press, 2003.

Gorman, Michael J. *Cruciformity: Paul's Narrative Spirituality of the Cross*. Grand Rapids: Eerdmans, 2001.

Green, Joel B. *Seized by Truth: Reading the Bible as Scripture*. Nashville: Abingdon, 2007.

Gregory of Nyssa. *On Virginity*. Chapter 1.7 in *Theological Aesthetics: A Reader*. Edited by Gesa Elsbeth Thiessen. Grand Rapids: Eerdmans, 2004.

Hall, David D., ed. *The Antinomian Controversy, 1636–1638: A Documentary History*. 2nd ed. Durham, NC: Duke University Press, 1990.

Hart, David Bentley. *The Beauty of the Infinite: The Aesthetics of Christian Truth*. Grand Rapids: Eerdmans, 2003.

———. "No Shadow of Turning: On Divine Impassibility." Pages 45–69 in *The Hidden and the Manifest: Essays in Theology and Metaphysics*. Grand Rapids: Eerdmans, 2017.

Hauerwas, Stanley, and William H. Willimon. *Resident Aliens: Life in the Christian Colony*. 25th ann. ed. Nashville: Abingdon, 2014.

Helm, Paul. *Eternal God: A Study of God without Time*. 2nd ed. Oxford: Oxford University Press, 2011.

Hilary of Arles. "Introductory Commentary on 2 John." In PL Supplementum vol. 3. Edited by A. Hamman. Paris: Garnier Frères, 1990.

Hodges, Zane. *Absolutely Free! A Reply to Lordship Salvation*. Grand Rapids: Zondervan, 1989.

Hoskins, Paul M. *Jesus as the Fulfillment of the Temple in the Gospel of John*. Eugene, OR: Wipf & Stock, 2007.

Huebner, Sabine R. "Household Composition in the Ancient Mediterranean—What Do We Really Know?" Pages 73–91 in *A Companion to Families in the Greek and Roman World*. Edited by Beryl Rawson. Chichester: Wiley-Blackwell, 2011.

Hurtado, Larry. *Lord Jesus Christ: Devotion to Jesus in Earliest Christianity*. Grand Rapids: Eerdmans, 2003.

Ignatius of Antioch. *Epistle to the Smyrnaeans*. In PG 5.

Irenaeus. *Against Heresies*. Greek and Latin Texts hosted by TextExcavation online at http://www.textexcavation.com/irenaeusah1.html.

Jenson, Robert W. *Canon and Creed*. Louisville: Westminster John Knox, 2010.

Jobes, Karen H. *1, 2, and 3 John*. Grand Rapids: Zondervan, 2014.

Jüngel, Eberhard. *God as the Mystery of the World: On the Foundation of the Theology of the Crucified One in the Dispute between Theism and Atheism*. Translated by Darrell J. Guder. Grand Rapids: Eerdmans, 1983.

———. *God's Being Is in Becoming: The Trinitarian Being of God in the Theology of Karl Barth*. Translated by John Webster. Grand Rapids: Eerdmans, 2001.

Kaiser, Denis. "Peter Abelard's Theology of Atonement: A Multifaceted Approach and Reevaluation." *JATS* 26 (2015): 3–28.

Kerr, Alan R. *The Temple of Jesus' Body: The Temple Theme in the Gospel of John*. London: Sheffield, 2002.

Kierkegaard, Søren. *Fear and Trembling*. Translated by Alistair Hannay. London: Penguin, 1985.

Kim, Jaegwon. "Making Sense of Emergence." *Philosophical Studies* 95 (1999): 3–36.

Kim, Jintae. "The Concept of Atonement in 1 John: A Redevelopment of the Second Temple Concept of Atonement." PhD diss., Westminster Theological Seminary, 2003.

Köstenberger, Andreas J. *The Missions of Jesus and the Disciples according to the Fourth Gospel*. Grand Rapids: Eerdmans, 1998.

Kruse, Colin G. *The Letters of John*. Grand Rapids: Eerdmans, 2000.

LaCugna, Catherine Mowry. *God for Us: The Trinity and Christian Life*. New York: HarperCollins, 1991.

Larsen, Iver. "The Phrase ἐν τούτῳ in 1 John." *Notes on Translation* 4 (1990): 27–34.

Leftow, Brian. *Time and Eternity*. Ithaca, NY: Cornell University Press, 1991.

Lewis, C. S. *A Grief Observed*. San Francisco: HarperSanFrancisco, 2001.

Lieu, Judith M. *1, 2, and 3 John: A Commentary*. Louisville: Westminster John Knox, 2008.

Lindbeck, George A. *The Nature of Doctrine*. 25th ann. ed. Louisville: Westminster John Knox, 2009.

Loubser, A. "Reconciling Rhetorical Criticism with Its Oral Roots." *Neot* 35 (2001): 95–110.

Lovecraft. H. P. "Letter to Robert E. Howard (August 16, 1932)." In *Selected Letters, 1932–1934*. Edited by August William Derleth and James Turner. Sauk City, WI: Arkham House, 1976.

MacArthur, John. *The Gospel according to Jesus*. Rev. ed. Grand Rapids: Zondervan, 1988.

Marshall, I Howard. *The Epistles of John*. Grand Rapids: Eerdmans, 1978.

McClendon, James W., Jr. *Systematic Theology*. Vol. 1: *Ethics*. Rev. ed. Nashville: Abingdon Press, 2002.

Metzger, Bruce. *A Textual Commentary on the Greek New Testament*. 2nd ed. Stuttgart: German Bible Society, 1994.

Michaels, J. Ramsey. *The Gospel of John*. Grand Rapids: Eerdmans, 2010.

Middleton, J. Richard. *The Liberating Image: The* Imago Dei *in Genesis 1*. Grand Rapids: Brazos, 2005.

Milbank, John. *Being Reconciled: Ontology and Pardon*. New York: Routledge, 2003.

Milgrom, Jacob. *Leviticus 1–16*. New York: Doubleday, 1991.

Moltmann, Jürgen. *The Church in the Power of the Spirit: A Contribution to Messianic Ecclesiology*. Translated by Margaret Kohl. Minneapolis: Fortress Press, 1993.

———. *The Crucified God: The Cross of Christ as the Foundation and Criticism of Christian Theology*. Translated by R. A. Wilson and John Bowden. 40th ann. ed. Minneapolis: Fortress Press, 1993.

———. *God in Creation: A New Theology of Creation and the Spirit of God*. Translated by Margaret Kohl. Minneapolis: Fortress Press, 1993.

Moule, C. F. D. *An Idiom-Book of New Testament Greek*. 2nd ed. Cambridge: Cambridge University Press, 1994.

Mounce, Robert H. *The Book of Revelation*. Rev. ed. NICNT. Grand Rapids: Eerdmans, 1998.

Newbigin, Lesslie. *The Gospel in a Pluralist Society*. Grand Rapids: Eerdmans, 1989.

Origen. *On First Principles*. In PG 11.

Painter, John. *1, 2, and 3 John*. Collegeville, MN: Liturgical Press, 2002.

Pinnock, Clark H. *Most Moved Mover: A Theology of God's Openness*. Carlisle: Paternoster, 2001.

Pohl, Christine D. "Hospitality." Pages 378–81 in *Dictionary of Scripture and Ethics*. Edited by Joel B. Green. Grand Rapids: Baker, 2011.

Prideaux, Sue. *I Am Dynamite! A Life of Nietzsche*. New York: Tim Duggan, 2018.

Rawls, John. *A Theory of Justice*. Rev. ed. Cambridge: Harvard University Press, 1999.

Schnackenburg, Rudolf. *Johannine Epistles: Introduction and Commentary*. Translated by Reginald and Ilse Fuller. New York: Crossroads, 1992.

Searle, John. *Speech Acts: An Essay in the Philosophy of Language*. Cambridge: Cambridge University Press, 1969.

Smalley, Stephen S. *1, 2, and 3 John*. Rev. ed. Grand Rapids: Zondervan, 2008.

Spatafora, Andrea. *From the "Temple of God" to God as the Temple: A Biblical Theological Study of the Temple in the Book of Revelation*. Rome: Editrice Pontificia Università Gregoriana, 1997.

Strecker, Georg. *The Johannine Letters*. Translated by Linda M. Maloney. Minneapolis: Augsburg Fortress, 1996.

Swinburne, Richard. *The Coherence of Theism*. 2nd ed. Oxford: Oxford University Press, 1993.

Thompson, Marianne Meye. *John: A Commentary*. Louisville: Westminster John Knox, 2015.

Unger, Peter "The Problem of the Many." *Midwest Studies in Philosophy* 5 (1980): 411–67.

Vanhoozer, Kevin. *The Drama of Doctrine: A Canonical-Linguistic Approach*. Louisville: Westminster John Knox, 2005.

Wall, Robert W. "Reading the Bible from within Our Traditions: The 'Rule of Faith' in

Theological Hermeneutics." Pages 88–107 in *Between Two Horizons: Spanning New Testament Studies and Systematic Theology*. Edited by Joel B. Green and Max Turner. Grand Rapids: Eerdmans, 2000.

Wall, Robert W., with Richard Steele. *1 and 2 Timothy and Titus*. THNTC. Grand Rapids: Eerdmans, 2012.

Wallace, Daniel B. *Greek Grammar beyond the Basics*. Grand Rapids: Zondervan, 1996.

Walls, Jerry. *Purgatory: The Logic of Total Transformation*. Oxford: Oxford University Press, 2011.

Watson, Duane F. "Amplification Techniques in 1 John: The Interaction of Rhetorical Style and Invention." *JSNT* 51 (1993): 99–123.

Wesley, John. "A Call to Backsliders (Sermon 86)." Available online from the Wesleyan Holiness Digital Library at https://www.whdl.org/call-backsliders-sermon-86.

Westcott, Brooke Foss. *The Epistles of St. John: The Greek Text with Notes and Essays*. Cambridge: Macmillan, 1886.

Wink, Walter. *Naming the Powers: The Language of Power in the New Testament*. Philadelphia: Fortress Press, 1984.

Wright, N. T. *History and Eschatology: Jesus and the Promise of Eschatology*. Waco, TX: Baylor University Press, 2019.

Yarbrough, Robert W. *1–3 John*. Grand Rapids: Baker, 2008.

Zimmerman, Dean. "Presentism and the Space-Time Manifold." Pages 163–245 in the *Oxford Handbook of Philosophy of Time*. Edited by Craig Callender. Clarendon: Oxford University Press, 2011.

Index of Authors

Abelard, Peter, 140
Anselm of Canterbury, 42–43
Arminius, Jacob, 174–76
Augustine of Hippo, 16, 43, 145, 157, 164–65

Barnes, Elizabeth, 194
Barth, Karl, 133, 168, 179
Bauckham, Richard, 9, 138
Bede, 27
Brown, Raymond E., 5

Calvin, John, 174–75, 180
Cassiodorus, 15
Clement of Alexandria, 15, 109, 129–30

Dionysius of Alexandria, 5

Farley, Wendy, 209
Faulkner, William, 149–50

Gadamer, Hans-Georg, 145–46, 189
Gregory of Nyssa, 162–65

Hilary of Arles, 112, 119

Ignatius of Antioch, 198
Irenaeus, 108, 130, 184–85, 188–90

Jenson, Robert, 189
Jüngel, Eberhard, 78, 170

Lewis, C. S., 172
Lindbeck, George, 186–87
Lovecraft, H. P., 150–51
Luria, Issac, 199

Middleton, Richard J., 130
Moltmann, Jürgen, 166–67, 199

Newbigin, Lesslie, 203–4
Nietzsche, Friedrich, 20, 105, 175–76

Origen, 162–65

Papias, 5, 8
Philo of Alexandria, 65, 137
Plato, 56, 105, 141
Pohl, Christine, 205
Polycarp, 5, 188
Polycrates, 8

Rawls, John, 188
Ricoeur, Paul, 146

Thompson, Marianne Meye, 26, 61
Tolkien, J. R. R., 208

Walls, Jerry L., 58, 172
Wesley, John, 62, 131, 174–78, 187
Wink, Walter, 152
Wittgenstein, Ludwig, 186–87
Wright, N. T., 181–83

Yarbrough, Robert, 39, 202–3

Index of Subjects

Aaron, 21, 50–51, 139
aesthetics, 27–28, 129, 159, 161–65, 202–3
Antichrist, antichristic, 47–48, 59–65, 71–72, 85, 114–18, 150–53, 173–75
antinomianism, 19, 176

baptism, 77, 82, 95–99, 139, 191–92, 199, 204
beauty, 20, 30–34, 46, 57, 80, 129, 162–65, 185

Cain (and Abel), 36–37, 64–66, 130
canon, 11–12, 76, 119, 178, 188–90, 200
capitalism, 116, 182–83, 188
Christus Victor, 148
cosmos, 22, 30–32, 37–39, 42, 47, 60–61, 129, 137–40, 141, 147, 164, 185
crucifixion, 78, 85, 94–96, 110, 118, 133, 166–67, 209

devil-born, 7, 63–68, 107
docetism, 7, 40, 96, 154
dualism, 46, 63, 96, 126, 131, 141, 147, 150

ecclesiology, 1–3, 180, 187, 191, 193, 203
economy (divine), 116, 133, 168, 179, 181–83, 197–99
emergence, 152–53
empire, 10, 47–49, 100, 154, 198–201
eyewitness accounts, 8–9

generosity, 120–21, 206, 207
glory, 7, 17, 72, 115, 135, 147, 163–68, 171–72, 182–83
gnosticism, 184–85, 188
God: born of, 7, 55–58, 61–68, 75–73, 86–91, 96–101, 105–8, 174–77; DNA of, 16, 55, 58, 69, 76, 88, 118, 123, 174

hermeneutics, 145, 157–58, 185–86
historical criticism, 1
Holy Spirit, 47, 50–53, 70–73, 111–12, 119, 157, 174–75
hospitality, 116–18, 120–22, 127, 198, 205, 206
hypostatic union, 141, 157, 166

identity, 96–99, 123
immanence, 96, 155–58, 167, 197
impassibility (divine), 159, 166–70
interpenetration, 133, 141, 169–70

John the Baptizer, 60, 97–99, 123

kenosis, 131, 143

labor of God, 29, 69, 95–96, 197, 208

Marcionism, 40
messiah, 7–9, 15, 51–52, 59, 70–73, 87–90, 108, 138–40
mission, 26–27, 34, 60–61, 78, 90, 106, 122, 130, 204, 209
Moses, 51, 92, 125, 143, 147, 180

Nicodemus, 6, 77

open theism, 169

perichoresis, 17, 132, 169
presence: God's, 131, 137, 155, 158, 184; physical or spiritual, 84, 95, 118, 120, 155

rhetoric (Greco-Roman), 10, 13–14, 38, 52, 76, 125–26, 187

sacrifice, 18, 21–24, 60, 84, 90, 111; of atonement, 57, 61, 75–78, 87, 90, 95, 134–38, 139, 166–67, 185, 191, 204–8
sacrificial cult (of Israel), 19–22, 136
Second Person (of the Trinity), 15, 44, 65, 72, 83, 131–32, 143
soul (physical and immaterial), 46, 119, 131, 141–42
Spirit of Deception, 72–74, 105, 116, 186–87
Spirit of Truth, 71–74, 113, 124, 152–53, 175, 186–87

Thomas, 16, 140
transcendence, 96, 155–58
trinity, trinitarianism, 15–17, 25, 44, 65, 72, 83, 112, 128–34, 143–44, 157–59, 166–70

Index of Scripture and Other Ancient Writings

Old Testament

Genesis
1:1 15, 156
22:2 76
22:12 76
22:16 76

Exodus
12:3–8 60
18:18 92
33:11–23 147
33:20 147

Leviticus
5:6 103
9:3–13 60
15:1–13 21
16:8–10 60
16:15–19 20

Numbers
11:14 92
25:1 36
31:16 36

Deuteronomy
19:15 98

Judges
20:15 179

1 Samuel
24:2 179

Job
24:13 160

Psalms
20:2 78
34:8 18
36:9 160
56:13 160
88:4 179
136 112
144:6–7 78

Proverbs
6:25 45
17:24 46
25:25 19

Isaiah
51:4–7 160
53:7 60
58:10 160

Jeremiah
7:25 78

Ezekiel
43:10–11 86

Hosea
6:6 24

Micah
7:2–9 160

Deuterocanonical Books

Wisdom
5:8 46
6:22 15
7:5 15
17:7 46

2 Maccabees
4:38 86
15:4 46
15:6 46

1 Esdras
4:47 122

4 Maccabees
1:26 46
2:15 46

Pseudepigrapha

Testament of Dan
5:4 58
6:6 58

Ancient Jewish Writers

Philo

Life of Moses
2:127 137
2:134 137

Sacrifices
1:2–3 65

New Testament

Matthew
5:21–22 66
6:22 57
7:15 104
11:30 91
20:1–16 182
22:37–40 70
23:4 91
23:16 79
24:3 54
24:12 59
25:1–13 55–56
25:14–30 55–56
25:46 86

Mark
12:30–31 70, 107
12:44 46
13:7 48
13:32–33 48

Luke
2:12 106
7:12 76
8:1–3 110
8:42 76
9:38 76
10:27 70

John
1:1 161
1:4–11 160
1:6 123
1:9 161
1:12 161
1:13 95–96
1:14 106, 161
1:18 106
1:26–33 95
1:41 89
2:12 29
3:5 95, 105
3:16 66, 77, 100, 106
3:16–17 82, 123
3:17 77
3:20 28, 36
3:26 96
3:34 123
4:7–15 95
4:20 190
4:23 190
4:23–24 21
4:24 190
5:7 95
5:16 96
5:23 26
5:24 103
5:25–26 140
5:26 100
5:31–40 98
5:36 97
5:37–47 97
5:43 123
6:28–30 121
6:40 100
6:45 123
6:48–63 191
6:53–56 95, 100
6:58 191
6:63 191
6:66 26
6:69 83
7:3–10 29
7:7 36
7:16–17 116
7:38–39 95
8:12 34–35, 100, 148, 160
8:13 96
8:29 26
8:34 59
8:42 6, 76
8:44 6, 62, 65
9:5 160
10:12 104
10:19–24 96
10:25 123
10:27–29 26, 106
10:30 97
11:4 103
11:22 123
11:52 98
12:13 123
12:28 123
12:46 160
12:49 31
13:5–10 95
14:15 6
14:16–17 53
14:17 73
14:23–24 25, 132
14:26 53, 81
15:11 120
15:18–25 36

15:26 53, 97
15:26–27 97
16:8–10 61
16:13 53
16:20–22 120
16:27 123
16:33 94
17:1–3 26
17:5 61
17:15 106
17:20–24 17
17:23 98
19:26–27 96, 110
19:34 95
20:17 96
20:24–29 15
20:28 140
20:31 9, 101, 140
21:15–19 26–27
21:22–23 54
21:24 9

Acts

2:17 48
15:3 122
16:14–15 110
20:29 104

Romans

8 182
8:3 77
15:24 122

1 Corinthians

1:1 109
3 115
3:9 123
15 182
15:23–24 55

2 Corinthians

12:14 79

Galatians

4:4–5 78

Philippians

2 143

2 Thessalonians

2:2 59
2:3 48
2:8–12 59

2 Timothy

3:1 48

Philemon

19 122

Hebrews

6:4–6 175, 178
10:22 21

James

5:3 48
5:7–8 55

2 Peter

3:3 48
3:3–10 55

1 John

1:1 9, 15, 30, 32, 80, 161, 163
1:1–4 11, 13–14, 32–33, 44, 52, 57, 64, 83, 120, 159
1:3 77, 130
1:4 13, 118
1:5 162
1:6 6
1:6–7 77
1:6–10 45
1:7 95
1:8–9 60–63, 102
1:9 82, 104
1:9–10 42
1:10 59
2:1 4, 13, 29, 35, 38–39, 53, 59, 61, 110, 136–39, 185, 202, 204
2:1–2 20, 57, 136–37, 139, 185, 204
2:2 22, 43, 61, 78
2:3 68
2:3–6 91, 132
2:4 33, 108
2:5 68, 79–80, 108
2:6 27, 60, 85
2:7 38, 64
2:7–8 48
2:8 48, 54, 148
2:8–12 7, 59, 148
2:10–11 42
2:11 35, 193
2:12 4, 29, 38–39, 48, 110, 139
2:13–14 64, 94, 106
2:14 4, 39, 110
2:15 76
2:15–17 7, 44, 91
2:16 173
2:17 48
2:18 39, 58, 85, 110
2:18–23 111
2:19 7, 175
2:20 70, 138
2:22 7, 108
2:22–24 7, 42
2:23 82–83
2:23–25 57
2:24 64, 77
2:25 156
2:27 53, 55, 190
2:28 39, 55, 101, 110
2:29 55–56, 61
3:1 39

3:2 33, 39, 69, 80, 148, 171, 174
3:3 55, 85, 171
3:4 105
3:4–10 103, 175, 178
3:5 61, 85
3:6 60, 77
3:7 39, 85
3:8 64–65, 106
3:8–10 7, 68, 105
3:9 17, 55, 63, 77, 175
3:9–10 64
3:10 6, 39, 73
3:12–13 28
3:13 35
3:14 103–4
3:15 35, 62
3:16 66, 68, 85
3:18 6, 39, 66, 68
3:19–24 31
3:21–22 101
3:22 101
3:23 25, 89–90
4:1–6 175, 186
4:2 7, 40, 82–83, 185
4:2–3 7
4:4 39, 92, 94
4:6 115
4:7 105
4:7–15 33, 72, 79, 83, 95
4:9 33, 43, 77, 106, 166
4:10 77
4:11–16 83
4:13 157
4:14 43, 77
4:15 7, 82
4:17 25, 43
4:20 35, 89, 190
4:20–21 90–91
4:21 90
4:21–5:1 89
5:1 7, 88–89
5:2 39, 110
5:3 91
5:6 108, 127
5:11 156
5:12–13 7
5:13 4, 9, 13, 101, 156
5:14–16 70, 101
5:19 44
5:20 7, 156
5:21 39

2 John

1–3 112
4 6
5 197
13 109

3 John

1 77
3 6
6 111
8 206
9–10 111

Jude

18 48

Revelation

1:5 95
2–3 71, 73, 94, 106, 111, 116, 181, 183
2:1 110
2:7 111
2:10 41, 73, 103
2:11 111
2:12–16 36
2:17 111
2:29 111
3:6 111
3:13 111
3:22 111
5:9 95
7:14 95
7:17 95
8:10–11 95
11:18 181
12:11 94–95
13:1 48
16:5–7 61
16:13 71
17:14 178
19:2 61
19:7–8 110
19:11 61
19:11–21 41
19:19 48
21–22 182
21:1 148
21:6 95
22:1 95
22:7 54
22:12 181
22:17 95

Early Christian Writings

Anselm of Canterbury

Proslogion

1.1 42

Augustine of Hippo

Letter 92

3 163–64

Bede

Homiliae

2:6 27

Clement of Alexandria

Stromata
8–9 129

Gregory of Nyssa

De Virginitate
X 162

Irenaeus of Lyons

Adversus Haereses
1.16.3 188

Origen

De Principiis
1.2.7 163